Developing a Model of Islamic Psychology and Psychotherapy

At a time when there is increasing need to offer psychotherapeutic approaches that accommodate clients' religious and spiritual beliefs, and acknowledge the potential for healing and growth offered by religious frameworks, this book explores psychology from an Islamic paradigm and demonstrates how Islamic understandings of human nature, the self, and the soul can inform an Islamic psychotherapy.

Drawing on a qualitative, grounded theory analysis of interviews with Islamic scholars and clinicians, this unique volume distils complex religious concepts to reconcile Islamic theology with contemporary notions of psychology. Chapters offer nuanced explanations of relevant Islamic tradition and theological sources, consider how this relates to Western notions of psychotherapy and common misconceptions, and draw uniquely on first-hand data to develop a new theory of Islamic psychology. This, in turn, informs an innovative and empirically driven model of practice that translates Islamic understandings of human psychology into a clinical framework for Islamic psychotherapy.

An outstanding scholarly contribution to the modern and emerging discipline of Islamic psychology, this book makes a pioneering contribution to the integration of the Islamic sciences and clinical mental health practice. It will be a key resource for scholars, researchers, and practicing clinicians with an interest in Islamic psychology and Muslim mental health, as well as religion, spirituality and psychology more broadly.

Abdallah Rothman is Professor of Islamic Psychology and Principal at Cambridge Muslim College, UK and Executive Director of the International Association of Islamic Psychology, US.

Routledge Research in Psychology

This series offers an international forum for original and innovative research being conducted across the field of psychology. Titles in the series are empirically or theoretically informed and explore a range of dynamic and timely issues and emerging topics. The series is aimed at upper-level and post-graduate students, researchers, and research students, as well as academics and scholars.

Recent titles in the series include:

A Scientific Assessment of the Validity of Mystical Experiences
Understanding Altered Psychological and Neurophysiological States
Andrew C. Papanicolaou

The Relevance of Alan Watts in Contemporary Culture
Understanding Contributions and Controversies
Edited by Peter J. Columbus

Eastern European Perspectives on Emotional Intelligence
Current developments and research
Edited by Lada Kaliská and John Pellitteri

The Psychological Basis of Moral Judgments
Philosophical and Empirical Approaches to Moral Relativism
John J. Park

Developing a Model of Islamic Psychology and Psychotherapy
Islamic Theology and Contemporary Understandings of Psychology
Abdallah Rothman

Human Interaction with the Divine, the Sacred, and the Deceased
Psychological, Scientific, and Theological Perspectives
Edited by Thomas G. Plante and Gary E. Schwartz

For a complete list of titles in this series, please visit: https://www.routledge.com/Routledge-Research-in-Psychology/book-series/RRIP

Developing a Model of Islamic Psychology and Psychotherapy

Islamic Theology and Contemporary Understandings of Psychology

Abdallah Rothman

Routledge
Taylor & Francis Group

NEW YORK AND LONDON

First published 2022
by Routledge
605 Third Avenue, New York, NY 10158

and by Routledge
2 Park Square, Milton Park, Abingdon, Oxon, OX14 4RN

Routledge is an imprint of the Taylor & Francis Group, an informa business

Library of Congress Cataloging-in-Publication Data
A catalog record for this title has been requested

ISBN: 978-0-367-61150-7 (hbk)
ISBN: 978-0-367-61152-1 (pbk)
ISBN: 978-1-003-10437-7 (ebk)

Typeset in Baskerville
by MPS Limited, Dehradun

MIX
Paper from
responsible sources
FSC
www.fsc.org   FSC™ C013985

Printed in the United Kingdom
by Henry Ling Limited

To Fatima, Wafaa, and Sharif

I wish for you to seek and find the truth of your heart. I hope that my work can both benefit and inspire you in your own journeys of healing and toward wholeness.

You are the biggest blessings in my and your mother's life and I pray you always know the treasure that you have inside you.

Abstract

At a time when there is increasing focus on the need to adapt approaches to psychotherapy to accommodate the cultural and religious/spiritual orientations of clients, this book explores psychology from an Islamic paradigm and shows how foundational assumptions about human nature can inform an Islamic psychotherapy.

Historically, the task of reconciling theology and belief in God with contemporary notions of psychology has been difficult. This book engages with that task by presenting the foundations of a comprehensive framework for psychology from an Islamic perspective and, from this, for an Islamic psychotherapy using a constructivist grounded theory approach to the development of new theory. This is accomplished through a systematic qualitative, data-grounded analysis of concepts of 'the person' or 'soul' within the Islamic tradition that are relevant to an Islamic paradigm of psychology, which was carried out by the author in a rigorous research study with two phases spanning over the course of four years, from 2015 to 2019. Through the analysis of input from the scholars and practitioners in relevant fields who were participants in the research study, the book explores how these concepts can be applied in clinical work. From this, a model of a uniquely Islamic approach to psychotherapy is developed, starting from and grounded in the Islamic tradition (rather than being a secular model with Islam 'added in'). This model offers a fascinating and engaging view of human nature and development from an Islamic perspective and presents a practical framework for Islamically-integrated psychotherapy.

Contents

Figures

Tables

Author's Note

This book is my humble attempt to offer a contribution to the Islam and Psychology movement, specifically with the intention of providing a stepping stone toward the establishment of an indigenous Islamic psychology and psychotherapy. What follows is not an exhaustive study nor is it a definitive discourse on the topic. Rather, it is my own personal attempt and approach at driving the conversation forward in order to bridge what I perceived as a gap in the research at the time of writing this.

Considering the vastness of the topic of the soul and the convergence of Islamic theology and contemporary psychology, it is perhaps overly ambitious or even audacious to attempt to construct theory within such a milieu. Such a large undertaking can be stifled by fears of doing it wrong or not rightfully representing the richness and reverence of and for the Islamic tradition. However, as Winston Churchill said, "perfection is the enemy of progress". One must start somewhere.

The way I have approached this, and the elements that I have chosen to include or neglected due to my own ignorance, are a result of my imperfect and finite perspective. This work is representative of an iterative and emergent process of unfolding which has inevitably evolved and changed since the production of this book. My own ideas and perceptions are constantly growing and changing, as is the developing field of Islamic psychology, as is humanity itself.

In order to develop new ideas and indeed new ways of thinking, we must be willing to take risks. I realize that I, as a psychologist and not an Islamic Studies scholar, have taken a risk in delving into this material. Much of the content in this book is drawing on primary sources written in languages other than English. For the most part I do not directly reference those primary sources, as I am not a scholar of Islamic theology. However, I felt there was an urgent need to bridge the gap between psychology and practitioners of psychotherapy like myself and theology and scholars who have a command of sacred knowledge. I hope this work serves as an impetus for further cooperation and partnerships between Islamic scholars and mental health practitioners.

Acknowledgements

I could not have accomplished this work if it had not been for the foundational ground work that was laid before me by the father of Islamic Psychology and my mentor Dr. Malik Badri. I was blessed to have his guidance and support from the very beginning of my journey in both Islam and psychology, all the way through to advising me on this research. I pray that I and this new generation of Islamic psychologists honour his legacy.

I am grateful beyond measure to my PhD supervisor Professor Adrian Coyle. I was lucky to be one of his last doctoral students before retirement and benefitted immensely from all those years he had to perfect the craft. His guidance was invaluable in that he had the perfect combination of skills and experience in psychology and religion and qualitative research methods.

I am blessed to have a supportive family whose encouragement and faith in me fuels my achievements. To my parents for both instilling in me the value of education and encouraging me to find my own path. To my wife for not only encouraging me to pursue my research but actually committing and following through by picking up my slack, single parenting during my late nights writing and long journeys presenting and teaching, and never once making me feel guilty for taking the time away from our family. And to my kids for being patient and understanding when I only half listened to them while sitting at my computer working on my research at home. You all mean the world to me and I thank God for you and for everything.

Foreword

Theologians of the Abrahamic religions have in the course of their long histories derived from their scriptures a wide range of nuanced theories about the human soul and the sources and remedies of its dysfunctions. Taking as their starting-point the scriptural idea that the human creature is in some mysterious sense made in God's image, and that this 'image' pertains to consciousness and the capacity for morally meaningful choice, they have also reflected on the idea of a 'fall' from an authentic, primordial mode of being in which body, mind and spirit were believed to have flourished in complete harmony.

They have also tended to agree on the sheer difficulty of defining the nature of consciousness, by which humanity is traditionally said to 'image' God, so that the enigma of mind seems to reflect the enigma of God Himself, with His will, power and judgement. Self-knowledge is understood to be key not only to improving the mind's capacity to make free and responsible choices, but also to discerning the divine light in the soul, indicated, again mysteriously, by God's 'breathing of His spirit into Adam' (15:29). What is today called mental health has thus been for the monotheisms a matter of absolutely central religious concern, since we are 'created to worship God' (51:56) and thus to know Him, and disorders in our inward equilibrium do not only generate sinful behaviour but obstruct our capacity to approach God, to be inspired by His qualities, and ultimately, for the mystical traditions, to perceive Him: the very purpose of our creation.

Although faith in God tends to support positive mental health outcomes, modern Muslim societies have not been spared the strains and disorders experienced by Western cultures as the result of the rapid and stressful flux of modern life, which have so often exacerbated existing and perennial human afflictions of the mind and the spirit. The extent to which human creatures can remain in equilibrium when modernity takes them ever further from the natural hunter-gatherer environment for which they were originally adapted, and which was their normal experience for tens of thousands of years, is difficult to guess. Biomedical science has made enormous strides in understanding the body and its disorders, but our comprehension of the mind and its needs has lagged far behind, and many modern pharmaceutical or behavioural remedies seem based more on empirical evidence of effectiveness than on any comprehensive understanding of the mind and the brain.

In the Islamic world, which has struggled with the legacy of a colonialism which brushed aside premodern wisdom in favour of an increasingly absolute materialism, many elites have rejected or simply forgotten their indigenous understanding of their inner lives, and have set their trust in the shifting theories and intellectual fashions of Western psychology. By no means all Western approaches are without value. However they are typically grounded in an experimental base derived from work among Western populations, and, as later commentators complained when considering the dreams reported by Freud's middle-class patients in 19th century Vienna, cultures tend to generate very distinctive inner lives. Mental health practitioners thus need to be profoundly sensitive to cultural context. They should also be aware that Western clinical approaches can be contradictory and tentative, rooted in philosophical and neurological debates which struggle to define consciousness, and to establish canons for distinguishing ordered from disordered forms of behaviour. This remains the most provisional and contested of the sciences.

The broadening of this troubled discipline's episteme to include non-Western strategies of understanding and healing the self is only just beginning among clinicians and theorists with a modern training. The dialogue has not been easy, as Dr Rothman notes, and it is unlikely to become much easier. However it is evident that materialist approaches are being experienced not only as clinically arguable but as culturally hegemonic, often inherently disdainful of non-Western wisdom. In the Muslim case, which is derived ultimately from a scriptural canon which shows intense interest in the human consciousness and conscience, and whose interpretation evolved over more than a thousand years in dialogue with Hellenistic, Indian and Persian therapeutic texts and traditions, modern practitioners are faced with a formidably rich heritage, not all of which may prove applicable or valid, but which nonetheless offers the possibility of nourishing this struggling but vital science with an alternative perspective, rooted in a consideration of the entire human being, and grounded in the experience that there is a transcendent basis for human awareness.

To bring these two traditions into a sensible dialogue, as Abdallah Rothman does in this book, requires equal erudition in two complex and very different worlds. With his knowledge of Islamic as well as contemporary Western theories and therapies, backed up by years of experience in treating Muslim patients, Rothman is unusually qualified to present an approach that is more than a simple comparison or a polemic on behalf of one view, but a reasoned interpretation, rooted in Muslim theological insights, of the travails of the human subject, 'made in God's image', but able to fall in so many traumatic ways. The project is exciting conceptually but is also notably humane, recalling at all times the underlying purpose of scriptural religion, which is to be "a healing to what is in the hearts" (10:57).

Abdal Hakim Murad
Dean, Cambridge Muslim College

1 Beyond Islamization: Re-envisioning Western Psychotherapy within an Indigenous Psychological Paradigm

Aims of the Book

This book is about the construction of a new theory for an emerging field and sets out to provide a clear framework for the further development of new clinical approaches. This is done by distilling complex religious concepts and presenting them as an Islamic model of the soul that can then provide the foundation for an Islamic psychology and the development of a model of Islamic psychotherapy. It unveils the depths of the Islamic tradition of *'ilm an nafs* (the science of the soul) in a way that is clear and understandable for a contemporary audience. Whereas this area of study has previously been shrouded in mystery and misconception due to the esoteric nature of the soul and religious doctrine, the systematic approach to the development of theory takes abstract concepts and translates them into relatable, practical frameworks for understanding what Islam says about human psychology.

The objectives of the book are to a) set the context for the field of Islamic psychology and the need for a new paradigm from an Islamic perspective, b) construct a theory of human psychology that is grounded in the knowledge of the soul from the Islamic tradition (Qur'an, Prophetic tradition, and exegesis), and c) develop a clinical approach to practical applications of that theory in psychotherapy.

There have been several publications that have attempted to provide insight into the convergence of Islam and psychology, but none have attempted to construct a legitimate theory in any systematic way. Given the interdisciplinary nature of this endeavour, it is essential to have the input of religious scholars to provide authoritative knowledge of theology with religious integrity. Other publications have been written from the sole perspective of psychologists and have largely been based in conjecture. What this book does differently is twofold: it builds a theory of psychology upon the direct input and knowledge of relevant religious scholars, and it approaches the task using an established methodology that is explicitly concerned with the construction of new empirically-grounded theory.

As the explicit aim of the research was to develop a data-grounded model of Islamic psychotherapy based upon the Islamic model of the soul, a qualitative, grounded theory approach was adopted for the collection and analysis of data. This approach enables new theoretical insights to be developed directly from a systematic interrogation of data and is particularly useful in areas where existing theory is incomplete, inappropriate, or entirely absent. An unusual feature of the book, informed by the methodology, is the inclusion of first-person reflections by the author. Each chapter is accompanied by a personal reflection from the author-researcher. These reflections provide a window into the author's unfolding stance, experience and process as a researcher during the course of the study that sits at the heart of the book. The reflections provide an engaging change of tone and voice, breaking up the more de-tached narrative style adopted in the rest of the work. More importantly, in keeping with the grounded theory research tradition that informs the em-pirical work, and its focus on reflexivity, they remind the reader that a real, complex person undertook the research and that the research process was characterized by uncertainty, change, and breakthrough. The reflections help keep readers engaged by positioning them alongside the researcher *in situ* and disrupting any illusion of the researcher as a detached authority for whom empirical work was effortlessly smooth.

Unlike previous publications on this topic, this book takes an innovative approach to the application of qualitative research to bridge the gap between theory and practice. It offers a theory that is grounded in the Islamic tradition and theological resources and in systematic qualitative research, thus offering Islamic and empirical grounding and integrity. This book fulfils a great need in the field and will bridge a gap not only in the literature but in the inter-national development of an important and growing field. Currently, there is a surge of interest and attention on mental health with Muslim populations and the question of how to incorporate Islam into clinical approaches with this population. While there are overwhelmingly large numbers of both potential service users in need and eager providers wanting to help, there is very little in the way of guidance and direction in how to approach this field. This book offers an attempt to address a problem that has existed for the 40 years of development since this field has emerged.

Overview

Presently Muslims throughout the world face significant challenges and crises that give rise to a multitude of mental health concerns. From suffering trauma amidst war-torn countries such as Syria and Palestine to managing the re-percussions of Islamophobia in the West, there is an increasing need for mental health services for Muslim populations (Marie, Hannigan, & Jones, 2016). Many Muslims do not seek psychotherapeutic services due to views that psychotherapists do not engage with religious values in an informed and open way (Amri & Bemak, 2012; Killawi, Daneshpour, Elmi, Dadras & Hamid, 2014; Mayers, Leavey, Vallianatou, & Barker, 2007). It would appear that there is a need for an approach to psychotherapy that values Muslims' religious orientations and draws from Islamic sources to inform therapeutic approaches to treatment.

Contextualizing the Topic

In looking into the conceptualization of the person from an Islamic cosmological framework, it becomes clear that many of the fundamental notions of the nature of humankind, the purpose and meaning of existence, and the developmental trajectory of a person's psychology are distinctively different from those of the Western paradigm (Badri, 2008). Thus, rather than simply "Islamizing" psychology and modifying popularly accepted concepts from Western approaches to make more sense from an Islamic viewpoint, there would seem to be a substantial argument for the necessity of a unique paradigm that is rooted in the theology, philosophy, ethics, and guidance that exists within and is unique to Islam. Indeed, given the number of detailed accounts of psychological concepts from Muslim scholars of old (Haque, 2004), there is no need to arbitrarily adapt Islamic values and understandings to fit within a framework of psychology (the study of the psyche). Thus what is perhaps more accurately indicated in the current field of mental health as it relates to Muslim service users or those wishing to operate under the auspices of Islamic guidance is an articulated framework for understanding Islamic psychology principles from within the unique paradigm of the human condition that they present.

The history and practice of psychology in the West is certainly diverse and varied. It is unrealistic and perhaps unfair to paint that diversity of thought and approaches with one broad brush with the label "Western psychology". At the same time there is a precedent for understanding that there is a dominant paradigm of psychology in Western academia and within the professional field, as it has developed primarily in Europe and the United States since the 19th century (Leahey, 2012). It has been recognized that there is a dominant discourse within psychology which has been termed 'the psy-complex' (Rose, 1998). This refers to the set of professions dealing with the psyche – psychology, psychiatry, psychoanalysis, psychotherapy, etc. – and the role these 'psy' professions play in regulating social structure, thought, notions of self and the powerful, medicalized, institutionalized way of understanding and practising psychology (Rose, 1998). For the purposes of this discourse, it is worth underlining that the psy-complex is avowedly secular in its nature and commitments, although the hegemonic psychological discourse has Christian heritage and underpinnings (Richards, 2009). With any dominant discourse there are always critical, counterdiscourses that seek to challenge it, usually developed by those who are positioned on the margins of the dominant discourse (Parker, 2018). However, there remains a reality to the hegemonic position of this psy-complex and its outworkings in the field of contemporary psychology. Thus, within this book, the term "Western psychology" refers to that hegemonic paradigm/discourse.

Given the fact that this discourse is dominant in the field of contemporary psychology and that this book is focused on working from within that professional field and adapting it to fit an Islamic paradigm, some terminology and concepts from the dominant paradigm will be used in speaking from within this larger professional frame. The reason for this is twofold. Firstly, that language is embedded in and gives shape to contemporary thought within and outside psychology and is therefore familiar and recognizable. This is an important consideration in a book that seeks to produce knowledge that can speak clearly to groups of practitioners, even though the criticisms of that hegemonic discourse must be borne in mind. The book is not unusual in making this decision. Indeed, Craven and Coyle (2007) found that, for the same reason, the counselling psychologists whom they studied engaged in 'dilemmatic dances' between medical/pathologizing and critical/relational talk and practice in their work as part of health care teams. Secondly, the book does not contend that all aspects of the dominant paradigm are incompatible with an Islamic one, only parts of it. Therefore parts of that dominant discourse will be referenced where appropriate: for instance in the use of medicalized terminology such as 'treatment', 'clients', 'diagnosis', and diagnostic categories. Thus, the book approaches the topic of the construction of an Islamic psychology and psychotherapy from within and as an adaptation of contemporary psychology, in order to make such contemporary approaches more compatible with an Islamic ontological paradigm for use with Muslim service users.

Cultural adaptations of popular Western concepts of psychotherapy can only go so far in their effective application with Muslim service users with higher levels of religiosity (Abu-Raiya & Pargament, 2011). If therapists are working from within their Western training regarding conceptualizations of the person and of commonly accepted treatment goals, they may be undermining fundamental Islamic principles, ethics, or even laws (Abdullah, 1999; Skinner, 2010). For a person who identifies as Muslim and who wishes to hold their faith as the ultimate standard with which they use to guide their development and decision making and to determine their goals in life, it is crucial that the psychological approach used to help such people be informed by that set of values and concepts (Martinez, Smith, & Barlow, 2007; Worthington, Hook, Davis, & McDaniel, 2011). This is a matter of respecting and honouring service users' beliefs and it is a matter of acknowledging the potential for healing and growth that exists within the religious framework. In cases where the client's religious commitments lie at the heart of or enable the continuation of their distress (see Jaspal & Cinnirella, 2010), an approach that is grounded in a more informed and nuanced understanding of the person's religious philosophy, law, and virtues may be able to help bridge a client's feelings of incongruence between their religious ideals and their personal experience (Coyle & Lochner, 2011; Peteet, 2014).

Practitioners have reported that often the cause of a client's distress in connection with Islam stems from a misinterpretation, misrepresentation, or misuse of Islamic teachings and can often be alleviated or healed by correcting the person's misunderstanding through education based on guidance from the scholarly spiritual tradition of Islamic knowledge (Badri, 1979, 2014). The same has been discussed in the field of Christian counselling in which therapeutic interventions can involve invoking scripture to "correct" a client's beliefs, or cognitive restructuring (Tan, 2011). In a study investigating ways in which clinical psychologists understand and address spirituality within therapy, Crossley and Salter (2005) found that therapists reframe problematic spiritual or religious material in ways that are helpful but still consistent with client beliefs. However, this requires an extensive familiarity with the client's religious tradition in order for such interventions to be successful.

If a service user desires to live by the creed of their religion then ethical issues could be raised in the psychotherapist leading that person down a path that is not aligned with such beliefs, values, and assumptions, even when it appears to be the religion itself that is at the heart of the problem. While having an intimate understanding of a client's religious framework can be very useful in helping to direct them towards healthy growth from within that relative tradition, as Coyle and Lochner (2011) caution, "even when the psychologist has substantial background knowledge about a client's religious or spiritual tradition, it is still necessary to explore the client's interpretations of that tradition" (p. 268). While this is true, many service users, unaware of the intricacies of the philosophical underpinnings of either their Islamic faith or Western psychotherapy, may inadvertently fall prey to following guidance that is antithetical to their religious teachings, albeit unknown to the therapist as well. This presents a situation that on one hand becomes an ethical dilemma for the therapist and the field of Western psychology, and on the other hand a potential problem with potential spiritual consequences for the individual and Muslim communities in general within the context of their theological paradigm.

The problem with using a Western paradigm for approaches to psychotherapy with followers of the Muslim path is that, while many of the concepts and techniques correspond with traditional Islamic approaches (Badri, 2013), the assumptions and norms that are inherent to Western psychotherapy may not all align entirely with principal values, virtues, and concepts that are important to an Islamic paradigm (Haque, 2008). Certainly, there are safeguards for this phenomenon that are built into the professional ethics of the field of modern psychotherapy. While early conceptions of the ethical role of the therapist asserted a need for practitioners to have an unbiased stance that would not project their own beliefs and values onto the client, that conceptualization has been queried and critiqued in favour of a more realistic recognition that it is not possible for a therapist to have value neutrality in this sense within the therapeutic relationship. The American Psychiatric Association articulates corresponding ethical guidelines by (a) imploring practitioners to maintain respect for their patients' commitments (values, beliefs, and worldviews), (b) warning them against imposing "their own religious/spiritual, antireligious/

spiritual, or other values, beliefs and world views on their patients" and (c) recommending that they foster recovery by making treatment decisions with patients in ways that respect and take into meaningful consideration their cultural, religious/spiritual and personal ideals (APA 2006). While all of these safeguards help to create the potential for a therapist to be helpful and therapeutically effective with a client of a different religious affiliation than their own, it does not remove the potential for significant pitfalls.

Peteet (2014) asserts that a therapist's differing values and virtues, that are implicit in their perspective based on upbringing, theoretical orientation, religious affiliation, etc., "influence the direction of clinical work in recognizable ways" (p. 1195). He identifies specific virtues that are characteristic of popular traditions: "for Jews, communal responsibility and critical thought; for Christians, love and grace; for Muslims, reverence and obedience; for Buddhists, equanimity and compassion; for Hindus, appreciation of Dharma and Karma; and for secularists, respect for scientific evidence and intelligibility" (p. 1198). Thus it is easy to conceive that the relative positionality of the therapist can impact the direction that treatment goals take.

While every form of psychotherapy will involve challenging the client in some way, at a very fundamental level the basic ground upon which a Western approach to therapy is situated is a place that allows for and values all viewpoints as potentially valid, given that societies such as the United States and the United Kingdom are multicultural, democratic societies where the law of the land is assumed not to be overtly influenced by any one religious tradition. It can be said that the Western paradigm of psychotherapy honours and operates under an ideal that there are multiple truths, unlike an Islamic paradigm which asserts one Truth with multiple "right answers" or interpretations of how to align with that Truth. Thus in a Western psychotherapeutic context the only specific behaviour that a therapist can unequivocally have reason to guide a service user away from is when it involves either harming oneself or others. Outside those parameters, however, the service user is free to choose what they deem acceptable and appropriate and the therapist is, for the most part, expected to respect that behaviour as potentially being the best course of action for the person. It is not considered the therapist's place to judge whether a given behaviour is good or bad for the person, but rather their role is to facilitate reflection and exploration of the client's process (Gergen, 2015). There is however research which shows how, even when they espouse these commitments, therapists may signal their approval and disapproval of client responses in sessions (for example, Magaldi-Dopman, Park-Taylor, & Ponterotto, 2011).

There are indeed definite parallels to this stance of acceptance within an Islamic viewpoint, specifically with regards to judgement. It is a common Islamic value, and one that is mentioned multiple times in the Qur'an, that no human can pass judgement on another fellow human being (Q 4:94, 68:7).[1] This is because, from an Islamic viewpoint, God is the only One who knows what is in the heart of a person or, in other words, what the actual intention of that person is. Additionally, it says in the Qur'an that there is "no compulsion in religion" (Q 2:256), thus no person is obligated to follow the guidance set forth in Islam, including Muslims, even though obvious social influence can create a powerful perceived obligation that is connected to a person's identity and sense of belonging. Thus, based on this Islamic principle, there is certainly a justification for a therapist operating from within an Islamic paradigm to allow for the acceptance of a service user's choices regardless of whether they are aligned with Islamic values or not. However, it would be incongruent with the teachings of Islam for a therapist to encourage a Muslim service user to consider a behaviour that is *haram* (forbidden) as potentially equally valid to one that is *halal* (permitted). Yet this could be the result of common practices in a psychotherapeutic relationship situated within the Western paradigm where the therapist and/or client are unaware of such discrepancies. For example within a Western paradigm of psychotherapy, if a non-Muslim service user were to divulge to his or her therapist that he or she had premarital sexual relations there may not necessarily be a reason to see this as a problem, as it is very commonplace in the West for people to have sex outside of wedlock. Thus the general norm from within this context would be that this is acceptable behaviour. While the therapist likely would take into consideration the meaning that the behaviour held for the client and the way it functioned within the client's world view, depending on the client's position the therapist may very well assume that this behaviour may or may not have a negative consequence for the person. From within the Islamic paradigm though, not only is premarital sex forbidden because of its connection to a particular value, it is believed to have a detrimental effect on the soul of the person and an actual impediment to their healthy spiritual development (Yusuf, 2012).

Certainly, a culturally competent therapist could be well informed and know that premarital sex is considered forbidden and thus steer the client away from such behaviour, or bring the issue to their attention as it is incongruent with the service user's value system. However, if the therapist is not working from within an Islamic paradigm, he or she may simply be honouring the cultural context without understanding and being able to provide meaningful insight from a place that understands why premarital sex is forbidden and recognizes how it can have consequences for the person's soul and process of growth within an Islamic context. The distinction becomes a difference between a therapeutic approach that is sensitive to clients' religious values and one that is overtly grounded in the virtues, conceptualization of the person and ultimately the cosmological paradigm of a given client. Tan (1996, 2011) makes this distinction in the discussion of his approach to Christian counselling, which he calls "Christ centred, biblically based, and Spirit filled" (Tan, 2011, p. 325), by articulating two modes of approaching therapy: implicit and explicit integration. According to Tan (2011) implicit integration is when the therapist does not use distinctly Christian interventions, such as citing scripture or praying, and the Christian aspect of the therapy is thus "covert". Explicit integration is when the therapist integrates the psychotherapy "with spiritual guidance or direction to some extent" (Tan, 2011, p. 342). Hathaway (2009) discussed how explicit religious approaches may be more likely to be effective with certain clients, particularly those who are more religiously inclined, and that more research is needed in Christian counselling methods to further indicate the distinction between multicultural adaptations that are culturally sensitive and specifically Christian interventions to better determine what constitutes therapeutic effectiveness with certain Christian clients. In the case of Islam and psychotherapy, the pragmatic difference between the two paradigmatic approaches becomes fundamental to the nature of the guidance being given and can have a substantial impact on multiple factors of the person's development as viewed from within the Islamic view of the person in relation to their religion.

The development of a separate framework for a paradigm of an Islamic psychology, within which an Islamic approach to psychotherapy is situated, thus needs to be defined by values and concepts that are fundamental to the cosmological, philosophical, and theological worldview of Islam. More specifically the process needs to be aligned with the conceptualization of the person and the teachings from the Qur'an and Sunnah (the tradition based on the life and behaviours of the Prophet Muhammad) which detail the nature of the human condition and which explain the understanding of the human psyche from an Islamic perspective (Haque & Mohamed, 2008). These values and concepts should be derived from traditional scholarly sources that are in line with the religiously accepted framework for understanding and interpreting religious knowledge. While there exist many variant perspectives and interpretations of Islam when viewed from a cultural anthropological standpoint which recognizes and values multiplicity in the Islamic experience, much of that disparity in experience is confined to the experience of people and the study of sociological phenomena. While it is a valid and useful venture to study all of these aspects of human experience for understanding many different aspects of people and their relationship to religion, there can be so many different definitions of Islam that it can render the concept meaningless and reduce it to just a name (Ahmed, 2015). There does exist however a long history of religious scholarly teaching that has clearly defined parameters for what and how things can be subject to multiple interpretations (Winter, 2008). Thus there is an argument for the notion of an "Islamic perspective" as it is defined by the community of religious scholars (*'ulamā*) who adhere to such clearly defined parameters of religious knowledge. It is beneficial to acknowledge and utilize this source of knowledge as a guiding body for the understanding of Islam in the context of psychology as the majority of religious Muslims throughout the world do so and thus it is the most common ground foundation from which to derive conceptualizations about such a vast number of people who subscribe to the religion of Islam.

Throughout the history of Islamic thought and from within this context of a religiously defined body of Islamic knowledge, there have been many Muslim scholars who have written and taught about concepts of the human psyche from within the context of Islamic knowledge (Badri, 2013; Haque, 2004; Mohamed, 1996). Indeed there is such a great deal of scholarly work about the psychology of humankind as derived from Quranic and Prophetic tradition sources that it is perhaps inaccurate to speak of Islamic Psychology as an "emerging discipline". Indeed, most, if not all, of the concepts conceived of in Western psychology within the past one hundred years have their parallels with Islamic concepts that were written about hundreds of years before by established Muslim scholars (Haque, 2004). Thus there is no need to create new knowledge *"ex nihilo"* when it comes to an Islamic paradigm of psychology. There already exists enough material and teachings, although much of it is written in Arabic, to constitute a fully articulated theoretical orientation of Islamic psychology. However, as all of this knowledge comes from within a religious framework, it is divided among multiple branches of knowledge and not necessarily under one umbrella of study such as the field of psychology is in the Western academic and scientific disciplines. Some aspects of knowledge relevant to an Islamic understanding of psychology are derived from the realm of philosophy, while others are derived from the realm of Islamic law (*fiqh*) or creed (*'aqīdah*). One possible explanation for this is that the conceptualization of psychology, the study of the psyche, while not being absent of the influence of religious thought (see Richards, 2009) is one that has largely developed out of the context of a secular, scientific approach to understanding and making sense of the world. From the stance of an Islamic worldview, which makes sense of things in ways revealed in the Qur'an and from the Prophet Muhammad, there is no necessary distinction between what is considered psychology and what is considered theology.

It could be argued that Islam in itself is, or includes, a pathway to understanding the nature of the psyche and it could thus be considered that the study and practice of Islam are inherently an Islamic psychology. In other words, part of the path of Islam is understanding the teachings from the Qur'an and Sunnah which explain the nature of the soul or psyche and that the practices decreed in Islam are therapeutic methods for correcting maladaptive behaviour, solving interpersonal problems, and achieving self-growth – all primary aims of psychology. It could be conceived that psychology is seen through the lens of the religion (*deen*) of Islam and the *deen* of Islam seen through the lens of psychology. Both alternative perspectives have the potential for unique contributions to the Islamic understanding of the person as a well-articulated developmental path towards spiritual, moral, and mental health.

Need for the Study

Until now most research and writing on the topic of Islamic psychology has evaded any practical steps to make such an approach feasible and pragmatic for modern times. There is a need for studies that translate Islamic concepts of the person from philosophical and theological origins into practical applications in the familiar language of psychology and psychotherapeutic interventions. As has been the case with the development of Christian psychotherapy, practitioners have recognized the importance and utility of the mental health field in offering a fitting venue for carrying on the Christian tradition of "soul care" (Hathaway, 2009). Richards (2009) illuminates the fact that while the perception of psychotherapy as a science removed from the realm of religion may be prominent, the field has always had integral ties to religious thought and tradition. While the term "pastoral counselling" now refers to a much broader concept not necessarily connected with any particular religion or spiritual tradition, it has long been an integral part of the Christian tradition (Evans, 2000) and Christian mental health practitioners have been able to use that as a precedent for further developing a model of Christian counselling that utilizes the familiar language and concepts of psychotherapy (Hathaway, 2009). The Association of Pastoral Counsellors in America defines pastoral counselling as "a process in which a pastoral counsellor utilizes insights and principles derived from the disciplines of theology and the behavioural sciences in working with individuals, couples, families, groups, and social systems towards the achievement of wholeness and health" (Strunk, 1993, p. 15). The closest thing to this in the Islamic tradition is that of the role of a shaykh for Muslims to receive personal religiously oriented developmental and spiritual guidance; however, that is now mostly confined to Sufism (Abdullah, 1999; Jurich, 1998). Thus the most common outlet that mainstream Muslims have for receiving religiously oriented counsel is from Imams (Muslim religious leaders) in local Muslim communities, many of whom are not equipped for such responsibility and do not have an overt understanding of how to integrate Islamic teachings with personal "pastoral counselling" (Ali, Milstein, & Marzuk, 2005).

Although there have been efforts towards this aim, more research is needed in this area to support the further development of informed approaches to incorporating Islam into psychotherapy. There currently exists a significant gap in research concerning evidence for the efficacy of treatments and interventions that incorporate Islamic faith tenets into psychotherapy with Muslim clients (Beshai, Clark, & Dobson, 2013; Hamdan, 2008; Haque & Keshavarzi, 2014). Moreover, there has been little effort to incorporate into formal methodologies the existing religious wisdom and indigenous approach to psychology that has been established and is currently being practised by traditional religious healers and Muslim mental health practitioners. It would be of great benefit to the Muslim world and the field of mental health alike to establish an Islamically oriented approach to psychotherapy that is grounded in an Islamic paradigm from which to develop uniquely indigenous Islamic interventions and techniques of psychotherapy. Given that there have been no previous attempts to formalize any theory of Islamic psychology in this way, and therefore no theory to extend or build upon, the need for the construction of a new theory is warranted and is the aim of the research presented in this book. The case for this will be made in a much more developed way later in the following chapters.

Overview of Chapters

In what follows this introduction, this book will be presented in six more chapters. Chapter Two presents an overview of research in the domain of religion and psychology, literature that helps delineate a definition of Islam for the purposes of the book, research in the field of Islamic psychology and Islamically integrated psychotherapy, and analogous literature that helps paint a picture of the broader context of considerations in regards to the research topic. Chapter Three gives a brief overview of methodologies in qualitative research, discusses the chosen methodology for this research project, how and why it was chosen, and presents relevant criteria for evaluating the research findings. Chapter Four presents the findings of the first phase of the study on an Islamic model of the soul- theoretical foundations for Islamic psychology and psychotherapy. Chapter Five presents the first half of the findings from the second phase of the study; the nature and structure of the soul: therapeutic conceptualizations of Islamic psychotherapy. Chapter Six presents the findings from the second half of the second phase; the stages and development of the soul: the clinical scope of Islamic psychotherapy. And finally, Chapter Seven is a discussion of the findings from both phases and the research as a whole.

Note

1 "Q" indicates a passage from the Qur'an. The number before the colon indicates the *surah* (chapter) and the number after the colon indicates the *ayah* (verse).

References

Abdullah, S. (2008). Islamic counselling and psychotherapy: Trends in theory development. *Annual Review of Islam in South Africa*, 2. Retrieved 1 June, 2012 from, http://asertif.blogspot.co.uk/2008/11/islamic-counseling-psychotherapy-trends.html
Abu-Raiya, H., & Pargament, K. I. (2011). Empirically based psychology of Islam: Summary and critique of the literature. *Mental Health, Religion & Culture*, *14*(2), 93–115 23p. https://doi.org/10.1080/13674670903426482

Ahmed, S. (2015). *What is Islam?: The importance of being Islamic.* Princeton University Press.

Ali, O. M., Milstein, G., & Marzuk, P. M. (2005). The Imam's role in meeting the counseling needs of muslim communities in the United States. *Psychiatric Services, 56*(2), 202–205.

Amri, S., & Bemak, F. (2012).Mental health help-seeking behaviors of muslim immigrants in the United States: Overcoming social stigma and cultural mistrust. *Journal of Muslim Mental Health, 7*(1). DOI: http://dx.doi.org/10.3998/jmmh.10381607. 0007.104

Badri, M. (1979). *The dilemma of Muslim psychologists.* MWH London.

Badri, M. (2008). Human nature in Islamic psychology: An Islamic critique. In A. Haque & Y. Mohamed (Eds.), *Psychology of personality: Islamic perspectives* (pp. 39–60). Cengage Learning Asia.

Badri, M. (2013). *Abu Zayd al-Balkhi's sustenance of the soul: The cognitive behavior therapy of a ninth century physician.* International Institute of Islamic Thought.

Badri, M. (2014). Cognitive systematic desensitization: An innovative therapeutic technique with special reference to Muslim patients. *The American Journal of Islamic Social Sciences, 31*(4), 1–13.

Beshai, S., Clark, C. M., & Dobson, K. S. (2013). Conceptual and pragmatic considerations in the use of cognitive-behavioral therapy with Muslim clients. *Cognitive Therapy and Research, 37*(1), 197–206. https://doi.org/10.1007/s10608-012-9450-y

Coyle, A., & Lochner, J. (2011). Religion, spirituality and therapeutic practice. *Psychologist, 24*, 264–266.

Craven, M., & Coyle, A. (2007). Counselling psychologists' talk about 'psychopathology' and diagnostic categories: A reflective account of a discourse analytic study. In E. Lyons & A. Coyle (Eds.), *Analysing qualitative data in psychology* (pp. 235–247). Sage.

Crossley, J. P., & Salter, D. P. (2005). A question of finding harmony: A grounded theory study of clinical psychologists' experience of addressing spiritual beliefs in therapy. *Psychology and Psychotherapy: Theory, Research and Practice, 78*(3), 295–313. https://doi.org/10.1348/147608305X26783

Evans, G. R. (2000). *A history of pastoral care.* A&C Black.

Gergen, K. J. (2015). Relational ethics in therapeutic practice. *Australian & New Zealand Journal of Family Therapy, 36*(4), 409–418. https://doi.org/10.1002/anzf.1123

Hamdan, A. (2008). Cognitive restructuring: An Islamic perspective. *Journal of Muslim Mental Health, 3*(1), 99–116. https://doi.org/10.1080/15564900802035268

Haque, A. (2004). Psychology from Islamic perspective: Contributions of early Muslim scholars and challenges to contemporary Muslim psychologists. *Journal of Religion and Health, 4*, 357.

Haque, A. (2008). Psychology of personality: Islamic perspectives. In A. Haque & Y. Mohamed (Eds.), *Psychology of Personality: Islamic Perspectives* (pp. xv–xxv). Cengage Learning Asia.

Haque, A., & Keshavarzi, H. (2014). Integrating indigenous healing methods in therapy: Muslim beliefs and practices. *International Journal of Culture & Mental Health, 7*(3), 297.

Haque, A., & Mohamed, Y. (Eds.). (2008). *Psychology of Personality, Islamic Perspectives.* Cengage Learning Asia.

Hathaway, W. L. (2009). Clinical use of explicit religious approaches: Christian role integration Issues. *Part of a Special Issue: Theophostic Prayer Ministry, 28*(2), 105–112.

Jaspal, R., & Cinnirella, M. (2010). Coping with potentially incompatible identities: Accounts of religious, ethnic, and sexual identities from British Pakistani men who identify as Muslim and gay. *British Journal of Social Psychology, 49*(4), 849–870. https://doi.org/10.1348/014466609X485025

Jurich, J. (1998). *A Cross-Cultural Study of "The Conference of the Birds": The Shaikh/Disciple and Therapist/Patient Relationship in Sufism and Psychotherapy.*

Killawi, A., Daneshpour, M., Elmi, A., Dadras, I., & Hamid, H. (2014). Recommendations for promoting healthy marriages & preventing divorce in the American Muslim community. *Institute for Social Policy and Understanding.*

Leahey, T. H. (2012). *A history of psychology: From antiquity To modernity.* (7th ed.). Pearson.

Magaldi-Dopman, D., Park-Taylor, J. & Ponterotto, J. G. (2011). Psychotherapists' spiritual, religious, atheist or agnostic identity and their practice of psychotherapy: A grounded theory study. *Psychotherapy Research, 21*(3), 286–303.

Marie, M., Hannigan, B., & Jones, A. (2016). Mental health needs and services in the West Bank, Palestine. *International Journal of Mental Health Systems, 10*, 1–8. https://doi.org/10.1186/s13033-016-0056-8

Martinez, J. S., Smith, T. B., & Barlow, S. H. (2007). Spiritual interventions in psychotherapy: Evaluations by highly religious clients. *Journal of Clinical Psychology, 63*(10), 943–960. https://doi.org/10.1002/jclp.20399

Mayers, C., Leavey, G., Vallianatou, C., & Barker, C. (2007). How clients with religious or spiritual beliefs experience psychological help-seeking and therapy: A qualitative study. *Clinical Psychology & Psychotherapy, 14*(4), 317–327. https://doi.org/10.1002/cpp.542

Mohamed, Y. (1996). *Fitrah: The Islamic concept of human nature.* Ta-Ha Publishers.

Parker, I. (2018). *Psy-complex in question: Critical review in psychology, psychoanalysis and social theory.* John Hunt Publishing.

Peteet, J. R. (2014). What is the Place of Clinicians' Religious or Spiritual Commitments in Psychotherapy? A Virtues-Based Perspective. *Journal of Religion and Health, 53*(4), 1190–1198. https://doi.org/10.1007/s10943-013-9816-9

Richards, G. (2009). Psychology meets religion. In *Putting psychology in its place* (3rd ed., pp. 329–347). Routledge.

Rose, N. (1998). *Inventing our selves: Psychology, power, and personhood.* Cambridge University Press.

Skinner R. (2010). An Islamic approach to psychology and mental health. *Mental Health, Religion & Culture, 13*(6), 547–551. https://doi.org/10.1080/13674676.2010.488441

Strunk, O. (1993). A prolegomenon to a history of pastoral counseling. In R. J. Wicks, R. D. Parsons, & D. Capps (Eds.), *Clinical handbook of pastoral counseling* (pp. 14–25). Paulist Press.

Tan, S.-Y. (1996). Religion in clinical practice: Implicit and explicit integration. In *Religion and the clinical practice of psychology* (pp. 365–387). American Psychological Association. https://doi.org/10.1037/10199-013

Tan, S.-Y. (2011). *Counseling and psychotherapy: A Christian perspective.* Baker Academic.

Winter, T. (2008). *The Cambridge companion to classical Islamic theology.* Cambridge University Press.

Worthington, E. L., Hook, J. N., Davis, D. E., & McDaniel, M. A. (2011). Religion and spirituality. *Journal of Clinical Psychology*, *67*(2), 204–214. https://doi.org/10.1002/jclp.20760

Yusuf, H. (2012). *Purification of the heart: Signs, symptoms and cures of the spiritual diseases of the heart* (2nd ed.). Sandala.

2 Islam and Psychology: The Development of a New Field

Introduction

The Islamic tradition contains within it a detailed understanding of the human being from a Qur'anic ontological perspective. There exists a long and rich history, going back centuries, of *'ilm an nafs* (the knowledge/study of the soul). It is only recently that this body of knowledge within the Islamic intellectual heritage has been conceived of within the contemporary context of what is now known as the field of psychology and more specifically, the practice of psychotherapy. The integration of such traditional theological knowledge into a professional, academic context has given rise to the development of a new field: Islamic psychology. Given this relatively new development it is important to highlight some of the previous thought that has led to such an endeavour, what considerations are important with regards to both Islam and psychology, and how best practices in the field can inform the development of approaches to Islamic psychotherapy.

While there is a limited but growing amount of research and literature specifically on the integration of Islam and psychotherapy, there is a wealth of knowledge and information in relevant fields and analogous contexts. The aim of this chapter is to orient the discussion of the intersection of Islam and psychotherapy by elucidating some of the influences, challenges, and ideas that are crucial in understanding from a well-informed place how best to approach an investigation into the development of a theory of Islamic psychology that is grounded in such data. This will be accomplished by analyzing the literature according to the following themes: the integration of religion and spirituality in the field of psychotherapy, defining Islam, the integration of Islam in psychotherapy, defining an Islamic Psychology paradigm, and Islamic conceptions of the self/soul from the scholarly tradition.

The Integration of Religion and Spirituality in the Field of Psychotherapy

While academic and scientific inquiries into the intersection of psychotherapy and Islam may be recent and therefore not plentiful, there exists a great deal of research which examines the use of religion in psychotherapy in general (Richards, Sanders, Lea, McBride, & Allen, 2015). In order to put into perspective the greater context in which the development of an Islamic approach to psychology is situated within the larger professional discipline, it is useful to have a sense of the history of psychology and religion and to understand some of the intricacies of best practice in the discipline. The development of the intersection of psychology and religion throughout time has led to a flowering of interest and ideas in this area that makes it a ripe time in history to further advance specific religious and spiritual approaches to psychotherapy (Pargament & Saunders, 2007; Sperry & Shafranske, 2005).

The history of religion and spirituality within the discipline of psychology has had a circuitous path of development. At the beginning, it was a prominent feature in the understanding of human psychology but it fell out of focus for some time and now has recently had a resurgence in the field. At the very root of the word psychology is the ancient Greek word 'psyche', which originally meant 'soul or spirit' (Haque, 1998). Thus psychology was originally understood to be the 'study of the soul'. Only later in the 18th century did it begin to become more concerned with material science as there was a distinction drawn between rational and empirical psychology (Brown, 1985). And yet still, at the early stages of the development of psychology as a formal field of thought, in the 19th century, Biblical psychology was common with the works of Rausch, Delitzcsch, and Chambers (Rauch, 1844). Indeed many of the first psychologists in America in the late 19th century were heavily influenced by religious thought and affiliation (Richards, 2009) and it was out of this era that one of the first theorists of the psychology of religion arose, William James. James distinguished between institutional religion or 'extrinsic religion' and personal religion or 'intrinsic religion' (Main, 2008), which was later further developed by Gordon Allport (Allport, 1950). While previous preoccupation with religion had been mostly with people's affiliations and attachments to their respective religious groups, or 'extrinsic religion', most of James focus and interest was with that of a person's mystical experience or heartfelt sense of faith: 'intrinsic religion' (Brown, 1985).

As the field of psychology developed and its theorists and practitioners were concerned with being respected and established within the growing trend of empirical science, there was a shift away from the esoteric and immaterial dimension of the psyche and religious experience and a move towards a more secular and pragmatic positivist-empiricist framework (Brown, 1985; Main, 2008). This trend was perhaps most commonly seen in the popular founding work of Sigmund Freud and his psychoanalysis. Freud was antagonistic towards notions of religion and spiritual experience and viewed them as a cause of neuroses and regression (Freud & Gay, 1989; Ruitenbeek, 1973). As influential as Freud's theories and practice of psychoanalysis were, so too was his attitude towards religion as many psychoanalysts and others have since tended to regard religious beliefs and practices as impediments to healthy psychological growth and thus not as a potentially useful source of material within psychotherapy but moreover as pathology (King-Spooner, 2001). While this heavily influenced the entire field of psychology for quite some time throughout the early half of the 20th century, later developments in psychoanalysis resulted in some constructive integrations of religion as attitudes towards spirituality shifted (e.g., Rizzuto, 1981).

Towards the last half of the 20th century, as people became hungry for a deeper explanation of meaning in life and psychology had established itself as a reputable discipline enough to no longer need to rely quite as much on science wholeheartedly, there began a renewed interest in the intersection of psychology and religion and spirituality which brought about a surge in research in this area (Richards et al., 2015). This trend in research interest culminated in 1976 with the establishment of Division 36: *Psychology of Religion* within the American Psychological Association (Piedmont, 2013). Since then we have seen a wealth of inquiries, from primarily American and British sources, into notions of religion and spirituality within the context of psychology in theory and practice, with international contributions increasing (Pargament & Saunders, 2007). The momentum of interest in this research topic has continued throughout the recent past (Richards et al., 2015), with an increased interest in spirituality over religion (Heelas, Woodhead, Seel, Szerszynski, & Tusting, 2005; Tacey, 2004), leading the APA division to change its name in 2011 to the Society for the Psychology of Religion and Spirituality.

Within the context of professional ethics and best practice, it is perhaps necessary, if not at the very least clinically advisable, to address service users' relationships to the structures that they use to make meaning of their experience (Gonsiorek, Richards, Pargament, & McMinn, 2009; Richards & Bergin, 2014). Coyle (2010) said, "the domain's commitments to holism and egalitarianism require the practitioner to engage actively and openly with clients' meaning-making systems and life worlds" (p. 260). Awareness and consideration of the client's own personal relationship to spirituality and/or brand of religious belief is an important factor in understanding how the client makes sense of their experience. Bergin and Payne (1991) asserted that "ignorance of spiritual constructs and experience predispose a therapist to misjudge, misinterpret, misunderstand, mismanage, or neglect important segments of a client's life which may impact significantly on adjustment or growth" (p. 201). Thus, it could be considered best practice to at the very least acknowledge, inquire about and respect a client's spiritual and/or religious orientation, but in recognizing the potential benefit and clinical direction that religion and spirituality can offer to the psychotherapeutic encounter, some theorists and practitioners have developed and practice spiritually focused therapies (Pargament & Saunders, 2007).

Many of the studies conducted over the past few decades that examined spiritually focused therapies, in general, found that these types of approaches offer clients ways of connecting notions of hope and meaning-making to their experiences of mental health symptoms (Bowland, Edmond, & Fallot, 2012;

Ebrahimi, Neshatdoost, Mousavi, Asadollahi, & Nasiri, 2013; Hasanović, Sinanović, Pajević, & Agius, 2011). When a person is overwhelmed with the physical experience of their psychological symptoms, connecting to a source of healing and guidance that is beyond the realm of that physical dimension, which clients describe as their experience of spirituality (Pargament, 2011), can be empowering and transformative.

Studies have shown that in particular religiously oriented therapies have the most positive impact in treatment with clients who are more religiously committed or whose symptoms and treatment goals are related to religion (Martinez, Smith, & Barlow, 2007; Worthington, Hook, Davis, & McDaniel, 2011). Clients who identify as religious and seek treatment in secular psychotherapy tend to have difficulty connecting to and trusting the therapist's determination of treatment goals (Cragun & Friedlander, 2012). It is suggested, for both treatment effectiveness and ethical considerations, that therapists make efforts to adapt therapeutic approaches to fit within the particular faith perspectives of religious clients (Anderson, Heywood-Everett, Siddiqi, Wright, Meredith, & McMillian, 2015; Hook et al., 2010; Martinez et al., 2007; Mayers et al., 2007; Plante, 2007; Worthington et al., 2011). These research findings have paved the way for therapeutic developments in the integration of Islam and psychotherapy for use with Muslim service users. Given that these classifications are broad and there is some discrepancy as to different interpretations of what can be considered Islamic and whose experience of being Muslim is relevant, some distinctions and clarifications must be made as to which Islam and which Muslims an Islamically oriented approach to psychotherapy might be aimed at.

Defining Islam

In today's global socio-political landscape Islam is at the forefront of heated issues that dominate the news cycle in the West. Never before has Islam received so much attention and been so in focus than in the recent past (Powell, 2011). This is of course not due to any positive associations nor earned through admiration. On the contrary, much of the focus on Islam arises from fear and rejection of its perceived values (Cesari, 2012). These perceived values have been largely assumed by the general public and the media to be in line with the acts of violence and terrorism seen on TV being claimed to be motivated by Islam (Cesari, 2012; Jackson, 2007). Thus while people may be paying attention to Islam more than ever before, this does not necessarily mean that the collective level of knowledge of Islam has increased. Perhaps it would be more accurate to claim that there has been a gross miseducation of what exactly Islam stands for and what are the values that it asserts (Jackson, 2007). However, it can be difficult to determine exactly what values and concepts do in fact define Islam, as even among the global Muslim population there exists a number of different interpretations, ways of practising, and definitions of Islam.

While some claim that there is in fact a long standing tradition of religious law and interpretation that is well established and has definite parameters around what is sanctioned in Islam and what is not (Akram, 2014), others criticize the notion that there is a right way and a wrong way to interpret Islam and argue that instead of one unified Islam there are only multiple versions of "Islams" based on numerous experiences and interpretations (Ahmed, 2015; El-Zein, 1977). As with any subject matter, there are multiple angles and vantage points which influence a given person's outlook on the relative reality of a given experience or subject. With regards to religion, this is especially complicated as it involves not only the disparity of perceptions of followers of the religion and outsiders but multiple interpretations of what is actually happening and how it is defined, based on one's acknowledgement of a transcendent reality or a more materialist view of religion as strictly a social phenomenon (Mujiburrahman, 2001).

It can be said that there are two distinct and apparently opposing approaches to conceptualizing religion: the "anthropological" and the "theological" (El-Zein, 1977). Viewing religion through an anthropological lens takes an ethnographic look at the local customs and phenomenological experiences of the people in a given context who practise the religion, essentially focusing on the unique experience of the religion as it manifests within a local context of cultural experience. Given that over 1.5 billion people across the world identify as Muslim (Grim & Hsu, 2011), it is easy to see how many sociocultural versions of Islam could exist. Geertz (1975) studied Muslim cultures in different parts of the world and determined that each society transformed Islam to fit their own unique local context and historical situation. Islam is not a static thing unaffected by human experience. It is necessarily shaped and brought to life by people's lived experience of it (Varisco, 2005). Ahmed (2015) argues that Islam cannot be defined solely by either a "cultural" or "theological" viewpoint exclusively and that attempts to do so are unhelpful and misleading in truly understanding Islam as a living phenomenon. He asserts that popular determinations of what gets labelled "Islamic" are deficient unless they take into account the multitude of influences that have been a part of the development of Islam over time.

Islam is as difficult to define and pin down to a singular definition as is the Muslim identity of its followers. Given the great diversity of the Muslim experience due to the vast expanse of locations where such experience exists across cultures and geography, what one person identifies with in regards to their label as a "Muslim" may in fact be very different than that of another who identifies him or herself with the same label. Prentice, Miller, and Lightdale (1994) refer to this as a "common-identity" group, where a person's identification with the large group becomes more of a symbolic attachment than a personally defined experience.

Given the multiple factors at play in shaping both perceptions of Islam and relative experiences of Muslims, it becomes a difficult task to simply refer to "Muslims" or a "Muslim community" as well as "Islam" or what is considered

"Islamic" when clearly how those are defined can vary greatly. Thus, in the discussion of an "Islamic" psychology with "Muslim" service users it is important to acknowledge these nuances and to recognize the dynamics at play. For the purpose of our discussion we will be referring to Muslims in a broad generalization with the recognition that there are many different reasons and commitments that are involved for individuals who claim that common identity. Given that the focus here is on the theologically Islamic paradigm of the psychological understanding of the person, we are more concerned with the aspect of the theological viewpoint of defining Islam as opposed to the anthropological viewpoint of the social phenomena. As noted in the literature reviewed here we recognize that it is a dynamic interplay, and so our intention is not to deny the relative lived experience that defines a person's Islam, as certainly that has an important and sensitive role especially in the context of psychotherapy which ultimately centres around the individual's experience. But in defining an Islamic approach to psychotherapy it is necessary to understand the influence of Islam as a source of religious knowledge with a determinate cosmological paradigm. Thus to do so we are drawing on the theological view of Islam, with the assumption that the common denominator among the people who belong to the Muslim identity group is, at the heart, the religion of Islam.

In Geertz's (1975) study of different Muslim cultures, he discovered that the *'ulamā*, the religious body of Islamic scholars in a given community, attempt to separate Islam from the local cultural context and reflect upon the sacred tradition in order to focus on a more universal Islam that gets at the essence of the religious teachings. From this perspective then, the *'ulamā* represent a theological representation of Islam, as opposed to an anthropological one (El-Zein, 1977). El-Zein (1977) describes that while both phenomena exist simultaneously in any given context, the purely anthropological viewpoint excludes an important factor in understanding Islam as a religious reality, as represented in the viewpoint of the *'ulamā*:

> Their notion of Islam centers upon the reading of the Quran and the prophetic traditions which yield meanings intended to transcend any particular cultural idiom. Formal religious education becomes a process of repetition in which meanings are already defined and stabilized in the pretence of universality. These unchanging formulations of the essence of Islam and the folk concepts which change continually according to social usage in any particular circumstance exist simultaneously in all Islamic societies. The anthropologist taking a phenomenological approach focuses on the daily lived experience of the local Islams and leaves the study of theological interpretation to the Islamists. Therefore, he faces the problem of grasping meanings which are fluid and indeterminate. (p. 242)

The *'ulamā*'s focus on capturing the unchanging essence of Islam is useful for conceptualizing the philosophical underpinnings of what can be considered

Islamic from a purely spiritually based perspective that is rooted in the source of Qur'an and prophetic tradition. The concept of the *'ulamā* is one that is relatively unique to Islam, is an integral part of the preservation of theological integrity and a key factor in the transmission of religious knowledge over time (Akram, 2014).

In order to claim authenticity to an original source it makes sense that there would need to be some direct link to that source which would enable the integrity to hold up over time. El Shamsy (2008) explains that the early scholars of Islam (*'ulamā*) did this by devising specific cultures of learning based around knowledge that was passed down directly from the Prophet Muhammad and his companions (*ṣaḥābah*). In order to preserve the integrity of such knowledge, specialized modes of inquiry and standards of authenticity were established, such as hearing an oral transmission directly from the source or through authoritative transmission (*sama'*), or reading a copied text aloud to an authoritative teacher who could correct mistakes in understanding (*qira'a*) (Berkey, 2014; El Shamsy, 2008). Students who underwent such pedagogical traditions would then receive certificates of authoritative transmission (*isnad*) that linked the student to the original teacher and thus maintained a direct connection to a chain of transmission that traced back to the original teachings of the Prophet and his companions (Berkey, 2014). This method was considered to be unique to the Muslim community at the time and was a defining characteristic of the *'ulamā* (El Shamsy, 2008). Additional mechanisms of traditional learning that were crucial to the authentic preservation of knowledge were: *subh-* or companionship, where a student would live with a teacher to absorb not only knowledge but the context and application of such knowledge, and a later development; *ijaza*-where a teacher would grant official permission to a student to teach a branch of knowledge, which eventually enabled scholarship to spread more widely and aided in the development of an established orthodoxy which further helped to preserve Islamic theology (Berkey, 2014; El Shamsy, 2008).

In the discussion of what can be considered "Islamic" from a religious perspective, it is useful to understand religious definitions as defined by an established Islamic orthodoxy. Like Christianity and Judaism, the community of traditional Muslim religious scholars overtime developed an Islamic orthodoxy in order to establish an adherence to the teachings in the closest possible form to that of the original teachings of Islam as communicated by and through the Prophet Muhammad (Henderson, 1998). This tradition of Muslim orthodoxy helped to further establish a unique Islamic theology. Whereas early foci of the study of Islamic theology, influenced by Orientalism (Said, 1979), attempted to track influences from the Greek tradition, it has since been recognized that Islamic theology contains much that is indigenous and is rooted in the Qur'anic revelation (Winter, 2008). According to Winter (2008), in an attempt to preserve this unique Islamic brand of metaphysics, after witnessing the divisions among Jews and Christians caused by innate paradoxes in monotheism, "Muslim thinkers came to recognize the need for a formal discipline of argument and proof which could establish the proper sense of a scripture which turned out to be open to many different inter- pretations" (p. 6). While the multiplicity of interpretations persisted and de- veloped over time, the social construction of an orthodoxy acted as a mechanism to legitimize certain schools of thought, in order to allow for a structured, regulated and sanctioned avenue for disagreement while estab- lishing a basis for common understanding (Winter, 2008).

In attempting to understand and explain the formation and utility of or- thodoxy in the context of Islamic history, El Shamsy (2008) says:

Orthodoxy as a social phenomenon is not a "thing" but rather a process. For theological doctrines to become established as orthodox, they must find a place in the constantly changing net of social relations and institutions that constitute society. This is a two-way process: ideas can reconfigure these relations and institutions, but the social context also actively receives ideas and promotes, channels and/or suppresses them. Thus the history of orthodoxy cannot be simply a history of ideas, but a history of how, in particular situations, claims to truth came to be enshrined in social practices, such as rituals, and in institutions, such as the "community of scholars". (p. 97)

The community of Muslim scholars, which constituted the Sunni Islamic orthodoxy, had taken shape by the end of the 10th century and was structured around four schools of law, which were and are still considered to be equally valid: Maliki, Hanafi, Shafi'i, and Hanbali (El Shamsy, 2008). These schools of law (*fiqh*) defined right action while three main schools of theology (Ash'aris, Maturidis and traditionists) defined right belief (El Shamsy, 2008; Van Ess, 2006). El Shamsy (2008) contends that eventually "the ''ulamā' worked out a system of mutual tolerance that was based on universal agreement regarding the sacred sources, a pragmatic acceptance of and respect for differences of opinion, and an ideal of intellectual humility" (p. 107). The *'ulamā* referred to here is that of the majority Muslim denomination who believe that the in- heritors of the religion, or religious leadership, can be anyone who follows the *Sunnah*, or Prophetic tradition, and are therefore known as *Sunni* Muslims (Betts, 2013). The second largest denomination of Muslims are those who believe that only direct descendants of the Prophet can be the true inheritors of the religion (caliphate), who are known as *Shi'ite* (Betts, 2013). A Shi'ite version of orthodoxy developed later, as up until 940 there was a living re- ligious authority in the form of the "infallible Imams" (Mavani, 2013). The early development of Shiite orthodoxy saw two schools; the Akhbaris asserted that religious knowledge can potentially be understood by ordinary believers, while the Usulis asserted that only a select group of dedicated scholars should hold the keys to religious knowledge thus making it essential for ordinary believers to follow a religious authority, the latter of which is dominate still today (Mavani, 2013).

Whether it be larger fundamental divisions such as the Sunni-Shiite divide, smaller factions within Sunni Islam according schools of jurisprudence (*maḏhahib*), or smaller factions still such as Ahmediyah, Ismaili, and Ibadi, there are certain major fundamental "pillars" of Islam that most if not all who belong to the common identity group "Muslim" agree on (Betts, 2013). Namely these are: the creed (*shahadah*), daily prayers (*salat*), almsgiving (*zakāh*), fasting during Ramadan (*sawm*) and the pilgrimage to Mecca (*hajj*) (Glassé, 2013). The major unifying aspect then of what can be considered Islamic from this viewpoint is centred on the notion that guidance in life for those who follow an Islamic path (*Muslims*) revolves around the teachings from the Qur'an and the example of the Prophet Muhammad. This Islamic knowledge is disseminated from scholarly sources that adhere to the traditions of the *'ulamā* and include Qur'anic exegesis (*tafsīr*), dialectic theology (*kalām*), understanding of prophetic traditions (*aḥādīth*), and writings that expand on such knowledge from learned scholars who have followed the line of transmission as set out by the Muslim *'ulamā* (Van Ess, 2006). This then is what constitutes the "Islamic" part of an "Islamic psychology".

The Integration of Islam in Psychotherapy

As the trend of incorporating spiritual and religious concepts into psychotherapy has developed, there has been a more recent and increasing interest in the integration of Islam in psychotherapy with Muslim service users (Haque, Khan, Keshavarzi & Rothman, 2016). A recent increase in tragedies befalling Muslim communities in places like Syria and Palestine, which has forced refugees into new Western host countries, has brought an influx of Muslim service users into social services due to challenges adjusting to their new environment and coping with stress and trauma (Marie et al., 2016). In addition, many Muslims face identity and persecution issues due to a rise in Islamophobia in Western countries (Every & Perry, 2014). This situation has caused social service and mental health providers to bring into focus the question of how best to serve this population (Ahmed & Reddy, 2007; Haque, 1998; Rassool, 2015). Most of the literature in this area has been focused on adapting general Islamic concepts and beliefs to Western models of psychotherapy and efforts to make therapeutic approaches more culturally relevant to Muslim service users (Haque et al., 2016).

Awareness of the diversity in multicultural societies and its effects on the context of social services has been brought into acute attention within the field and cultural sensitivity has become a core component of the ethical delivery of psychotherapeutic intervention (Ponterotto, 2001). Recent models have emerged that are designed to offer more culturally sensitive approaches to therapy. Attempts at doing this include modifications of mainstream modalities and interventions to render them more culturally relevant to the beliefs of Muslims (e.g., Abdul-Hamid & Hughes, 2015; Ahmed & Amer, 2011; Ahmed & Reddy, 2007; Ali, Liu, & Humedian, 2004; Aloud & Rathur, 2009;

Amer & Jalal, 2012; Hasanović et al., 2011; Mahr, McLachlan, Friedberg, Mahr, & Pearl, 2015; Thomas & Ashraf, 2011). Given that Cognitive Behavioural Therapy (CBT) is one of the most popular, empirically researched and widely used approaches to psychotherapy in the field currently (Cuijpers et al., 2014; Hans & Hiller, 2013; Stewart & Chambless, 2009), much of the attention to the integration of Islam in therapy with Muslims has been focused on CBT.

The attention to specifically Islamic concepts in working with this population highlights the importance of knowing the Muslim psyche in the appropriate delivery of culturally congruent care. However, there can sometimes be difficulty in distinguishing between religious concepts and cultural sensibilities, as Muslims' identities are often a complex integration of their relative geographic culture and their connection to their Islamic religion, as discussed above. Dwairy (2009) highlights how attempts to reveal unconscious content and promoting self-actualization can be counterproductive for some Muslims who identify strongly with their culture and may become defensive when considering independent thought. Many mainstream approaches to psychotherapy are situated within an individualist perspective while many Muslim cultures are dominated by a collectivist perspective (Al-Krenawi & Graham, 2003). In order for clients to feel that the therapist respects and understands their perspective, it is important for the approach to honour the client's position of how Islam plays a role in their lives. Abu Raiya and Pargament (2010) studied how to integrate religion and psychotherapy for Muslim clients and make recommendations which include assessing the relative place that Islam has in the life of the client, how committed they are to practicing their faith, and how the clinician's approach should reflect these varying levels of commitment.

Perhaps more important than simply being sensitive to a service user's relative orientation to their Muslim religion, is the notion of adjusting therapeutic interventions to concur with and align with their level of religiosity. One development over the last fifteen years that can be useful in this distinction on whether to focus more on culturally sensitive concerns relevant to Muslim cultures or on uniquely religious concepts is the particular growth in the area of assessment scale development for use with Muslims. Many of these recently developed assessments aim to measure religiosity among Muslims (eg, Abdel-Khalek, 2007; Abu-Raiya, Pargament, Mahoney, & Stein, 2008; Alghorani, 2008; AlMarri, Oei, & Al-Adawi, 2009; Dasti & Sitwat, 2014; Francis, Sahin, & Al-Failakawi, 2008; Ghorbani, Watson, Geranmayepour, & Chen, 2014; Ghorbani, Watson, & Shahmohamadi, 2008; Jana-Masri & Priester, 2007). This can help practitioners to determine the degree to which Islam plays a part in the client's views and beliefs, thus indicating whether a therapeutic approach with more specifically Islamic interventions and approaches is necessary and could potentially be more effective in achieving treatment goals.

While identifying the level of religiosity is useful in determining the degree to which a client may need or could potentially benefit from more Islamically grounded interventions, there is currently very little for practitioners to access in terms of formalized models for such approaches (Haque et al., 2016). Most of the research into the integration of Islam into psychotherapy published in English has been focused on adapting known Western models with Islamic concepts, only a few authors have attempted to identify uniquely Islamic psychotherapy interventions (for example Haque & Keshavarzi, 2014).

Several research psychologists and Islamic scholars have presented how contributions from the Islamic scholarly tradition over the centuries have offered detailed insights and accounts into the psychological perspective found in the sources of Qur'an, *aḥādīth* and the *tafsīr* (exegesis) of such texts and traditions (Badri, 1979; Haque, 1998; Haque & Mohamed, 2008). While much of that literature was and is written in the Arabic language and thus unavailable to the English speaking community of researchers, still there is a significant amount that has either been translated or has had commentary in English publications. One of the most widely referenced such works, originally written in Arabic in the 20th century, is Abu Hamid al-Ghazali's Revival *of the Religious Sciences* (*Iḥyā' 'Ulūm al-Dīn*) (Al-Ghazali, 2014). The great jurist and *aḥādīth* scholar Imam Nawawi stated that "were the books of Islam all to be lost, excepting only the *Iḥyā'*, it would suffice to replace them all." (Lumbard, 2009, p. 291). Much of the subsequent writings of scholars on notions of the understanding of the person and the Islamic paradigm of psychology are derived from al-Ghazali's contributions in the *Iḥyā' 'Ulūm al-Dīn* and other works.

The richness of the scholarly work throughout Muslim history and tradition has not been studied as much as it is needed considering the wealth of material that exists. There still exist many texts that require translation and efforts to make sense of the meanings within the context of modern psychology. Much of the current research tends to focus on general Islamic themes or concepts, rather than a more sophisticated formulation of the human psyche that is likely to be found in the wealth of untouched literature in the Islamic sciences. Specifically, theoretical models that are grounded in the philosophy of Islamic thought and within the Islamic tradition need to be expanded. As mentioned, there are few models of psychotherapeutic care that are authentic to the Islamic tradition that does not begin with *a priori* Eurocentric assumptions or reflect such notions of human psychology. These models require the sophistication to answer the questions of defining psychopathology and laying out a coherent framework of intervention that naturally emerges out of an understanding of human psychology in Islamic terms, within an Islamic paradigm of psychology.

Defining an Islamic Psychology Paradigm

As the need and desire for psychotherapy services rises among Muslim communities, practitioners have responded with efforts to reach out to potential Muslim service users and make their services more accessible to this population (Abdullah, 2007; Ahmed & Amer, 2011; Ahmed & Reddy, 2007;

Weatherhead & Daiches, 2010). While some of that attention has been paid by non-Muslim psychotherapists who mostly attempt to provide culturally sensitive therapy to Muslim service users, many Muslim psychotherapists and psychologists have made attempts to leverage their position as insiders in the community to help bridge the gap between the level of need and the level of uptake of mental health services among Muslims (Abu Raiya & Pargament, 2010; Beshai, Clark, & Dobson, 2013; Hamdan, 2008). These practitioners may have the intention of helping their own community and feel a sense of responsibility to use their skills and training to support the Muslim community (*ummah*). This benevolent intention can manifest in two quite different ways; The Muslim psychologist can use their identity as a Muslim, along with their familiarity with Muslim customs and practices, to essentially offer perhaps more in depth culturally sensitive therapy than a non-Muslim could offer, or the Muslim psychologist can approach psychotherapy from a religious Islamic perspective, utilizing the beliefs, philosophy, and religious edicts to inform treatment goals (Beshai, Clark, & Dobson, 2013; Hamdan, 2008; Keshavarzi & Haque, 2013). While the latter is increasingly gaining interest and attention, most Muslim mental health practitioners take the former approach.

While good intentioned Muslim psychologists may have the honourable desire to use their psychology education and training to help their fellow Muslim brothers and sisters, what they oftentimes are not fully aware of is how that education and training can in some ways be misaligned with the guidance offered in the client's Islamic faith. This is due to the popular notion that the field of psychology, as it is taught and practised in the academic and scientific community, is based in a materialist paradigm that prioritizes objectivity and takes a neutral, some would say atheist, stance on religion or any form of transcendent experience of humans (Pasqualini & Martins, 2015; Schermer, 2003). Notions of what is considered normal and abnormal behaviour are bound by cultural phenomena and thus subject to multiple perspectives, and yet most of Western psychology has defined such norms from one perspective (Nevid, Rathus, & Greene, 2017; Wegrocki, 1939). In many ways, in order to be consistent with his or her religious orientation, a Muslim would have to fundamentally reject some Western notions as they may contradict some Islamic values and beliefs, as is a potential with other religions in the context of therapy. Thus the very foundation of such a psychological paradigm could be said to be unfit for and out of alignment with an Islamic paradigm (Badri, 1979). This phenomenon also arises in the implementation of other alternative therapeutic approaches. For example, existential psychotherapists will query and use alternatives to orthodox diagnostic categories (Milton, Craven, & Coyle, 2010), and thus there may be a great deal of insight that Muslim therapists can benefit from in learning from colleagues who are practitioners of such approaches.

While many people jump in mid-stream and try to adapt pre-existing Western psychotherapeutic approaches to Muslim service users, few may fully understand the underlying implications of such an approach. While the

English speaking academic world has only fairly recently seen the development of writings and research on Islamic psychology, and the latter thus could
be considered to be in its infancy (Haque, 1998; Hodge & Nadir, 2008), this
remains to be one of the most pressing and seemingly most unaddressed issues
within the burgeoning field of Islamic psychology. Malik Badri appears to
have been ahead of his time when he published his book in 1979 titled, "The
Dilemma of Muslim Psychologists". Badri discusses the situation of the
Muslim psychology community, primarily in the Arabic speaking Muslim
world at the time, in light of the saying of the Prophet Muhammad (*ḥadīth*),
"You would tread the same path as was trodden by those before you inch by
inch and step by step so much so that if they had entered into the hole of the
lizard, you would follow them in this also" (Sahih Muslim 2669 a: Book 47,
Hadith 7). Badri uses the words of the Prophet to drive the point of his critique of many Muslim psychologists and to point out that such an approach is
a known pitfall in the path of a Muslim, so much so that it was cautioned
against in the religious tradition. Thus not only is it something to consider as a
psychologist but, perhaps more importantly from his perspective, as a Muslim.
Badri (1979) opens his book with the following words:

> Unthinking repetition of Western theories and practices in the discipline
> of psychology probably presents one of the most serious threats to the
> status of Islamic ideology among our Muslim scholars and laity. Western
> psychologists propound theories about man's personality, motivation and
> behaviour which are in many ways contradictory to Islam. These theories
> and their applications are carefully sugar-coated with the attractive cover
> of "science". Muslim psychologists, like their colleagues in other parts of
> the world, have an anxious zeal to be introduced under the prestigious
> umbrella of the sciences. (p. 2)

Muslim psychologists may be tempted to forgo their religious orientation and
worldview in a desire to be accepted by the Western dominated field of
psychology, thus in extreme cases essentially abandoning their own paradigm
for another, even in the case that it is counter to their religious views. In the
introduction to the collection of essays that he edits, "Epistemological Bias in
the Physical and Social Sciences", Abdelwahab Elmessiri (2006) claims that
Muslim scientists adopt everything wholeheartedly and parrot the same terminology and methodology of the West. But these methodologies are not
entirely neutral as he says:

> Instead they are seen as expressing a system of values that define the field
> of investigation and the direction of research, and which very often
> determine their results in advance. This is what we call bias ie; the totality
> of latent values underlying the paradigm, and the procedures and
> methodologies that guide researchers without their necessarily being
> aware of them. (p. xii)

What is often missed by Muslim psychologists in their efforts to serve their Muslim community from within their academic and professional discipline is the concept of an underlying paradigm. Surely the Western field of psychology has a tremendous amount to offer in terms of therapeutic approaches, insights and studies of human behaviour. But when at the heart of the foundational perspective is a view of the world that does not include and embrace the notion of God, the drives, motivations and even treatment goals can be completely different, and at times antithetical (Pasqualini & Martins, 2015; Schermer, 2003).

As the field of psychology transformed from its original state as a field of inquiry into the study of the soul to its new identity as one of the fields of science, the theoretical foundations from which the approaches and techniques emerged are entrenched in the scientific paradigm (Hergenhahn & Henley, 2013; Leahey, 2012). The pillars of which the scientific community purports to be the foundation of its paradigm are objectivity, neutrality and empirical evidence. Scientists claim to study the human being objectively and claim to have a neutral stance on religion. However, this is not necessarily the case. While the roots of Western psychology and its founding assumptions lie in the Judeo-Christian tradition, as the discipline has developed over time it has veered from its origins (Richards, 2009). According to Badri (1979), scientists' view of the human being is from the lens of atheism and thus this stance of the observer affects what is observed. While many psychologists may in fact believe in God and claim that a scientific approach does not necessitate an atheist perspective, many thinkers have pointed out that while science and religion may not necessarily be at odds which each other, the social representations of science as they are collectively conceived of often do not make room for religious experience or phenomena (Polkinghorne, 1998; Ward, 2008). By definition, the realm of the divine, or spiritual dimension, is characterized by the nature of being unseen. Thus the scientific paradigm could be seen to be biased against the spiritual realm of God, religion, and such matters. Elmessiri (2006) articulates this as such:

> There is a bias toward the perceptible, the measurable and the quantitative against the imperceptible, the qualitative, and that which cannot be measured. Western science has limited the scope of research to the world of the five senses. This explains its relative disregard for the complex, the qualitative and the indefinite. That which cannot be observed by the five senses, easily measured and subjected to statistical quantification thus falls outside the scope of modern science. Moral and teleological issues should then be discarded and neglected, for they don't fit in that mould. (p. 35)

This Western scientific paradigm tends towards the simple and one dimensional and tends to avoid the more complex and multifaceted realm of experience because it is difficult to measure and find hard and fast answers.

Polkinghorne (2005) says "for science describes only one dimension of the many-layered reality within which we live, restricting itself to the impersonal and general, and bracketing out the personal and unique" (p. ix). Thus there is a tendency towards "causal monism", explaining phenomena in terms of one decisive cause, rather than multiple elements that may have less obvious effects on outcomes (Elmessiri, 2006; Russo & Williamson, 2007). This is evidenced in the preference within the scientific and academic community of quantitative over qualitative research, which although has been making great progress in acceptance and uptake within research, still retains a lower grade status (Beck, 1993; Guba & Lincoln, 1994).

Of course, one can strike a balance between the scientific approach and a religious perspective and find a middle path from which to operate from. And many researchers of late have done this, as evidenced by the increase in qualitative studies that explore existential phenomena (Gaist, 2013; Pargament, 2011; Sperry, 2016). Ward (2008) asserts that science and theology can actually work together in harmony and that such an approach can "offer the consilience of personal and scientific explanation and the integration of many diverse data within one coherent framework" (pp. 155). Ward (2008) emphasizes the importance of personal experience and cautions against over reliance on impersonal data as the driving factor in what we consider reliable evidence. However, as Badri (1979) asserts, Muslim psychologists often neglect to embrace this approach. Habib (2006) echoes this stance and adds that the Muslim world adopts "radical empiricism", even more so than the current Western scientific community itself does. From an Islamic perspective, as with most spiritual traditions, diagnosing and treating mental health with only biological and cognitive models of the self is dangerous and potentially damaging without consideration of the soul. From this perspective there are other potential causes and experiences beyond simply biological and cognitive that are valid parts of the growth process that should not be ignored (Skinner, 2010). According to Habib (2006), the Muslim world tends to import the Western scientific field with its alleged objectivity and he asserts that what is needed is the abandonment of the illusion of neutral scientific objectivity in favour of a new ideological stance. In parts of the world where religious paradigms are not as counterintuitive to the dominant psychological paradigm, and where clients and clinicians operate under more similar notions of mental health, studies have shown better outcomes of therapeutic interventions due to this paradigmatic alignment (Callan & Littlewood, 1998; Skinner, 2010; Thomas, Shah, & Thornton, 2009).

Without an established Islamic paradigm that the psychologist is rooted in and operating from, he/she can have such blind spots to in fact compromise the most fundamental of beliefs such as the striving for the afterlife as the end goal. This is the result of not having an all-encompassing approach to the merging of religious concepts and Western psychological ones and instead engaging in the process haphazardly and inconsistently. Elmessiri (2006) speaks directly to this pitfall:

Our theoretical effort to discover bias should never stop at the partial level of practice, but must include the whole theoretical structure of Western philosophy. We end up "patching up", that is, borrowing concepts from here and there, where the modern Western outlook is applied in one field and not in another. This sometimes takes the form of borrowing Western concepts while modifying only some aspects of their moral and epistemological and at others, trying to prove that the borrowed Western concept has a parallel version in our heritage so as to justify its adoption. This is a process of retroactive Westernization, since it leads to a wholesale adoption of Western epistemological paradigms, though the terminology has been changed and the rationale for adoption has been altered. (pp. 50–51)

Looking at psychology from an Islamic perspective necessitates a better understanding of what an Islamic perspective actually is. A distinction must be made between Islamic religious cosmological philosophy which would constitute and necessitate a paradigm shift from Western psychology, and what is a very different thing entirely in adapting Western psychology to fit within the cultural context of Muslims' sensibilities. Without such a distinction attempts to discuss "Islamic Psychology" can often in reality be instead discussions of "Muslim Psychology" in that rather than a paradigm shift it is an adaptation of the Western paradigm to understand and apply to Muslim people.

The general approach to attempts at understanding psychology in the context of Islam, even amongst Muslims, has been to view it from the outside in, as an anthropologist who does not actually believe in the natives' strange ways and foreign beliefs as they are outside of their Western paradigm (Thomas & Ashraf, 2011; Vasegh, 2009). Similarly, some researchers adopt a viewpoint known as social constructionism (Burr, 2015) to assess the psychology of Muslims, and by doing so miss out on a great deal of information that would be helpful in understanding their subjects. Criticisms of the social constructionist approach in the study of religious phenomena point out that such an approach cannot appropriately consider people's religious experiences (Coyle, 2008). More appropriate methods of inquiry need to be adopted which allow for the assessment of underlying motivations from within the Islamic religious paradigm.

In order to move towards the development of or adoption of a truly Islamic model of psychology, the practitioner must step outside of the Western paradigm within which their psychological training is rooted and entertain the notion that Islam may in fact operate under a very different paradigm of understanding the human experience. Badri (1979) terms this *phase three*, "the phase of emancipation". In this phase the Muslim psychologist sees his/her limited power and knowledge and sees himself as a Muslim first and then a psychologist. He then understands that Islam contains the answers and frameworks for understanding the human condition and that his Western psychology training can be used to serve the Muslims from within this paradigm

(Badri, 1979). Habib (2006) also articulates a series of stages that speak to this same process among Muslim and Arab psychologists, only he adds a fourth, perhaps idealistic as he puts it, stage where the new ideology and paradigm are established and a new scientific perspective is achieved, thus effecting a new culture and thus a new professional and academic field entirely.

Some argue that there is no need for a totally new approach to psychology and that the practice of psychology is open and accessible to being adapted without any fundamental changes. They assert that the paradigmatic frameworks are transferable to any therapeutic approach as needed to fit the client's individual worldview (Bartoli, 2007; Post & Wade, 2009). Thus their approach is adaptation and not an overhaul of the fundamental principles that drive and formulate a conception of human psychology. With this type of perspective what these psychologists are in fact often doing in reality is merely adapting language and cultural sensibilities without actually importing a new or unique paradigm. They are often unaware of the bias inherent in their theoretical orientations and mistakenly view them as fact or scientifically proven (Badri, 1979; Elmessiri, 2006). The realm of psychology; the understanding of the nature of the inner experience of the human being, is subject to vastly different perspectives based on the cosmological, existential, or simply epistemological framework with which humans are being viewed from. One cannot claim that their theory does not have a bias and that it is purely dealing with the nature of members of humanity "as they are", because there exist many explanations of why, how and even if humankind actually is the way in which a given theory explains. Up until now the dominant theories of psychology have predominantly been those that are situated within a Western paradigm (Haque, 1998). In a time when societies are made up of greatly diverse groups of people who hold vastly different paradigmatic perspectives, it may be prudent to embrace multiple views of human psychology relevant to a given paradigm of the human predicament.

Throughout the development of the field of psychology there have risen endeavours to reconsider psychology from within the perspective of a given religious, cultural, gender/sexuality or other framework. In many ways these endeavours have been successful in making psychotherapy more relevant to the respective population. This plurality of psychologies offers people the ability to understand the human experience as it relates to the specifics of the corresponding worldview. This allows for the practitioner and service user alike to perceive of the treatment goals as they relate to the shared cultural, religious or other paradigmatic view of humankind. This is an important feature of successful psychotherapy as it allows for treatment goals to align with philosophical perspectives authentically (Coyle, 2010; Pargament, 2011). There are many lessons to be learned from the previous efforts of other alternative psychologies that apply to the process that an Islamic psychology will need to endeavour in order to develop into a defined theoretical perspective.

Once this process is further developed and integrated into shared practice, the emancipated Muslim psychologist, in Badri's view, would then need to stand firm in their Islamic beliefs and frameworks and not feel the need to hide, compromise or be ashamed of such philosophical alignments. In Badri's (1979) own words, "Muslim behavioural scientists should not be apologetic about their ideology and belief" (p. 13). This stance of Badri is one that can be seen in much of his writing and appears to be rare in the growing field of Islamic Psychology, which is still in its infancy in the Western world of academia. Perhaps the field was not developmentally ready to take these steps at the time of his writing 40 years ago. Badri's (1979) call to response to this 'dilemma of Muslim psychologists' is not to completely reject psychology as a discipline, as he says essentially that would be throwing out the baby with the bathwater, or more specifically as he puts it "throwing out the bath water with a number of healthy babies; valuable gems with much trash." (p. 73). Badri (1979) lists all of the useful contributions of the field of Western psychology such as psychometric testing, behavioural studies, conditioning, and many useful bodies of knowledge and asserts that any Muslim society would be missing out on a great deal of useful knowledge just based solely on the notion that they are "Western" or "non-Muslim". Elmessiri (2006) agrees with the sentiment and adds:

> We no longer have to accept it wholesale with all its positive and negative aspects (as advocated by some Westernizers), nor do we have to reject it wholesale (as some rigid fundamentalists would have us do); rather, we can study Western civilization as having its share of positive and negative points. We can then open up to it in a way which is at once creative and critical just as we would open up to other cultural formations. We can then benefit from the fruits of human knowledge, Western knowledge included, separate the elements imported from the paradigm that underlies it, then assimilate it into our own system after adapting it to our values and world outlook. (p. xix)

What is now known as modern psychology is not all completely Western nor modern. Much of it is comprised of ponderings and philosophies of useful ideas from ancient Greek philosophers such as Aristotle, and moreover many Islamic thinkers, including Ibn Sina in the areas of psychotherapy and psychiatry, Ibn Khaldun in sociology and social psychology, Ibn Sirin in the field of dream interpretation, and al-Ghazali and al Muhasibi offering insight to personality studies (Badri, 1979; Haque, 1998; Haque, 1998; Mohamed, 1996), as outlined in Table 2.1. In the collective development of a well-articulated theory of Islamic Psychology, the Muslim psychology community has the potential to look to the past for their own traditions that are rich with explanation and direction of Islamic psychological theory. There may not be much need to postulate new theories from current thinkers' own understanding. What perhaps is needed is an effort to collect and collate the existing knowledge of the Islamic science of the soul from traditional sources, organize that knowledge into a systematic theoretical orientation which is familiar to

Table 2.1 Comparison of Classic Islamic Literature on Conceptualizations of the Person and 'Western' Literature in Psychology and Related Disciplines on Parallel/Analogous Concepts

"Islamic" Authors	*Topics (from a "Western" perspective)*	*"Western" Authors*
At-Tabari (9th century) Ar-Razi (9th century) Ibn Sina (11th century)	Psychotherapy, Psychiatry	Johann Weyer (16th century) Thomas Sydenham (17th century) Sigmund Freud (19th century) Wilhelm Wundt (19th century)
At-Tabari (9th century)	Child Development	Jean Piaget (19th century) Lev Vygotsky (19th century)
Al-Balkhi (9th century)	Cognitive Therapy	Albert Ellis (20th century) Aaron Beck (20th century)
Al-Farabi (9th century) Ibn Khaldun (14th century)	Sociology, Social Psychology	Norman Triplett (20th century) Kurt Lewin (20th century)
Al-Kindi (9th century) Al-Balkhi (9th century)	Depression	Robert Burton (17th century) Emil Kraepelin (19th century)
Ibn Sirin (7th century) Al-Kindi (9th century) Al-Farabi (9th century)	Dream Interpretation	Sigmund Freud (19th century) Carl Jung (19th century)
Al-Majusi (10th century) Ibn Sina (10th century) Ibn Zarbi (12th century)	Mental Illness	Emil Kraepelin (19th century)
Ibn Miskawayh (10th century)	Moral Psychology	Jean Piaget (19th century) Lawrence Kohlberg (20th century)
Ibn Sina (11th century) Mulla Sadra (16th century)	"Mind-Body Problem"	Aristotle (4th century BCE) René Descartes (17th century) Immanuel Kant (18th century) Karl Popper (20th century)
Al-Ghazali (11th century) Al-Muhasibi	Personality Studies	Gordon Allport (20th century)
Al-Ghazali (11th century)	Self Actualization	Abraham Maslow (20th century)
Ibn Tufayl (12th century)	Transpersonal Psychology	William James (19th century) Abraham Maslow (20th century) John Rowan (20th/21st century)

the modern ways of thinking and subject it to relevant empirical scrutiny. Elmessiri (2006) talks about needing to come up with a comprehensive theory; the work of a team or teams of scholars to develop a paradigm in a way that organizes thought and knowledge in a way familiar to these other paradigms of knowledge. As Elmessiri (2006) says "'stemming from our own heritage' is by no means synonymous with the literal transcription of earlier contributions; rather, it denotes the ongoing, creative attempt to apprehend the paradigms implicit in different Islamic texts and phenomena" (p. 68). The development of an Islamic paradigm of psychology can thus be gleaned and distilled from the knowledge that has been passed down through scholarly understandings of the teachings based on the Qur'an and Prophetic traditions. Within this body of knowledge and wisdom the understanding of the person and conceptions of the self/soul from an Islamic perspective are the foundational philosophical frameworks that an Islamic paradigm of psychology can be built upon.

Islamic Conceptions of the Self/Soul from the Scholarly Tradition

In the course of developing a theoretical framework for the practice of an Islamic Psychology, there are certain foundational elements that need to be elucidated in order to articulate a fully formed paradigm of Islamic psychology (Badri, 1979; Haque, 1998). One of the more foundational aspects of any theory of psychology is the relative viewpoint on the psychology of the person. The psychology of the person is fundamental to philosophical underpinnings of theoretical approaches in psychotherapy and determines much of the outlook on how we understand the human being and make sense of behaviour and motivation (Coon & Mitterer, 2008). However, a theory of the person that is grounded in the philosophical paradigm of Islam requires a framework that differs from the historical and popular trends in the field of psychology as theorized in the West. While some of the general theories on the psychology of the person can relate across worldviews and cosmological philosophies, other aspects of the way the person is defined need to be understood more originally from within the lens of a given religious paradigm.

While religious models of the person or "self" have not been widely researched, it would appear that there has been more attention paid to this in Buddhism than there has been in regards to Islam. In many ways the popular approach to the understanding of personality does not align with notions of the self and the nature of the person from a Buddhist perspective (De Silva, 2005; Izutsu, 1982,). In his book *An Introduction to Buddhist Psychology* Padmasiri De Silva (2005) says in regards to the Buddhist concept of self:

> The dynamic continuum is not limited to one life span but is affected by numerous past lives. Therefore the western models do not work entirely for this paradigm as not only is it an issue of acknowledging the sacred or spiritual, but notions of the self are completely rooted in different philosophies than that of Judeo Christian thought. Conscious and unconscious mind that has residues of not only childhood but past lives. (p. 83)

In Buddhism, the conceptualization of the self is considered an illusion that we cling to and the goal is thus to essentially let go of the idea of the self altogether rather than to understand it and define it in the form of personality (De Silva, 2005). Similar to the idea that Buddhism has a fundamentally different perspective in understanding the nature of the human being, so too does the Islamic orientation merit its own unique framework of the self that is based on a religious philosophical paradigm (Abu-Raiya, 2012; Haque & Keshavarzi, 2014; Haque & Mohamed, 2008).

While there are a multitude of traditional religious scholarly work that expounds on subject matter that essentially defines a theory of the person, like other Islamic psychology sources, the majority of those works are written in the Arabic language and not necessarily structured in a way that is familiar to the contemporary field of psychology (Badri, 2008). The development of a uniquely Islamic theory of the self has recently been gaining interest among researchers and clinicians who are realizing that it is a necessary foundational element for the building of a larger context of an Islamic psychological orientation within which practitioners can operate (Abu-Raiya, 2012, 2014; Ali, 1995; Haque & Mohamed, 2008; Othman, 2016; Smither & Khorsandi, 2009). However, at this point in time that research has been minimal and mostly confined to introductory papers and suggested potential models and approaches and there is a call for more thorough and empirical research to be undertaken in this particular area (Haque et al., 2016).

In Islamic religious teaching the concept of self involves the notion that the human being is connected first and foremost to God as the creator and source of everything (Izutsu, 1982). Huq (2008) contends that from an Islamic perspective, the primary medium for a Muslim to connect to God is via the heart. There is an often quoted, yet untraceable, saying in the Islamic tradition where God says "The heavens and the earth cannot contain Me, but the heart of My believing slave hath room for Me". The heart is where a Muslim connects with the transcendental consciousness of Allah (Huq, 2008). While most modern approaches to psychology focus on the mind or brain of the person as central to their concept of self, similar to other religious traditions (Odorisio, 2014) Islam views the heart as the central seat of regulation of the person and thus the centre of the self (Ahmad, 2008; Ali, 1995; Huq, 2008). The significance of the heart in connection with the overall state of the human being is again exemplified in the *ḥadīth* of the Prophet Muhammad that states "There is a piece of flesh in the body. If it is healthy, the whole body is healthy. If it becomes unhealthy, the whole body gets unhealthy- that is the heart" (Sahih Bukhari Vol. I, Hadith No. 47). Thus the importance of the state of the heart is stressed in regards to the overall optimal functioning of the person, both physical and spiritual, in turn the state of the self, or soul, is linked with the relative connectedness of the person to Allah (Ahmad, 2008; Ali, 1995; Huq, 2008).

The well respected 11th century Islamic scholar Abu Hamid al-Ghazali used the term *qalb*, which means heart in English, to refer to the aspect of the human being that is the essence of the person's spiritual self (Ali, 1995; Al-Ghazali, 2014). In al-Ghazali's explanations of this spiritual self, based on Qur'anic sources, he uses four terms to describe qualities of the nature of the self; *nafs* (ego or 'lower self'), *'aql* (mind/perception), *qalb* (heart) and *rūḥ* (spirit). While al-Ghazali describes seemingly distinct attributes of these four qualities of the self, he also often used the terms interchangeably, alluding to the integral nature of the self and the idea that these terms may be more for our benefit in understanding the esoteric reality of the spiritual self which is complex and beyond our capability of understanding fully in linear thought rather than a delineation of separate parts of the self (Al-Ghazali, 2014). This conceptualization of the self, using these four terms, is the most widely referenced framework in the literature on Islamic Psychology (Abu-Raiya, 2012; Al-Attas, 2008; Badri, 1976; Haque, 1998; Haque & Keshavarzi, 2014; Haque & Mohamed, 2008; Huq, 2008; Keshavarzi & Haque, 2013; Utz, 2011). Al-Ghazali discussed these four 'aspects' of the human being as interconnected and having an interdependent relationship with one another to where together they make up the whole person, or soul of the human being as one entity (Haque & Keshavarzi, 2014).

The Arabic word *nafs* is best translated simply as 'soul' and indeed the word is used to refer to the entire soul of the human being, or their spiritual essence. However, in the discussions of the four aspects of the soul mentioned above the word *nafs* is also used to describe the "lower" part of the self/soul and is similar to the concept of 'ego' in that it reacts to the environment. However it is not innately bad, as the ego is sometimes deemed, as it can be trained towards good habits and can ultimately be purified and perfected. The *'aql* is often referenced in the literature on Islamic psychology (for example, Haque, 1998; Haque & Keshavarzi, 2014) as the intellect of the human and the seat of rationality, logic and reason. However, the word *'aql* is derived from the word *ya'qiluna* that is used in the Qur'an (Q 22:46), to describe a type of perceiving that is done by the heart, which is closer to a spiritual 'seeing' or knowing than the rational faculty of the mind or brain. The *rūḥ* (similar to its Semitic language cousin; *ruach* in Hebrew) is the spirit, which al-Ghazali (2014) sometimes did not differentiate from the heart as it is the essence of the person, which God breathed into the human being (Q 15:29). And the *qalb* is the heart, which is described as the 'king' or central command centre of the other integrated aspects (Al-Ghazali, 2014). Al-Ghazali asserted that the heart is the central aspect of the human being which differentiates him/her from non-humans in that they have a special connectedness to God which defines the nature of what it means to be human (Ali, 1995; Bakhtiar, 2008). Thus the heart plays a central role in the Islamic concept of the self or soul, as it is seen as the seat of human consciousness and is considered inextricably linked to concepts of human nature from an Islamic perspective (Haque, 2008).

One of the longest contended and continued philosophical debates is what is known as "the mind-body problem" (Crane & Patterson, 2012). The debate is one of ontology and epistemology and centres around the nature of the soul and its relation to the body (Popper, 1979). The name of this philosophical problem reflects the tendencies of the two dominant camps in the debate, the materialist and dualist, to envision the essence of the self or consciousness as mental activity and therefore refer to the word "mind" where an Islamic paradigm would tend to use the term "soul" (Rahman, 2008). The materialist view sees the "mind" or "soul" as a function of the physical brain and physical states (Chalmers, 2002). The dualist view holds that the "mind" or "soul" is distinct from the brain and, in turn, the physical or body as well (Chalmers, 2002; Crane & Patterson, 2012). Within Western philosophy either of these views are generally based upon one of three frameworks; the Aristotelian paradigm, the Cartesian paradigm, and the scientific materialist paradigm (Crane & Patterson, 2012).

Ibn Sina, also known as Avicenna, was an early Islamic scholar and contributor to this philosophical discourse with his "floating man" experiment. Ibn Sina posited that if a man were floating in air without any physical sense perception of his bodily limbs, he would still have consciousness of himself, which he asserted is proof that the soul exists independent of the body without any logical dependency between them (Avicenna, 1952, 1959, 1975; Druart, 2000; Marmura, 1986). This view fits within the Aristotelian paradigm and is a reflection of the materialist affirmation of the primacy of quiddity over existence (Druart, 2000). However, Ibn Sina's view on this does not represent the majority of scholars in the history of Islamic thought, as the views of later scholars favoured positions that were thought to be in closer alignment with Qur'anic principles (Al-Attas, 2001).

Al-Attas (2001) argues that Ibn Sina contradicts not only himself in his other works in regards to his "floating man" concept, but moreover that this position contradicts the Qur'an itself, which speaks in detail about the soul's existence prior to life in the temporal world *dunya*. Ibn Sina's influence led some early *kalām* (study of Islamic doctrine) thought to assert a rejection of the body and the worldly realm as a requirement for spiritual elevation (Rahman, 1981). However this seems to have been an influence of an influential strand of Christian theology which sees the world as being broken because of original sin and therefore the body must be wholly rejected (Crisp, 2015). The majority position in Islamic thought, based on a uniquely Islamic paradigm as derived from the Qur'an, views the body and soul as integrated and therefore the body itself is seen as a vehicle for purification of the soul and moreover, not necessarily wholly separate from the soul (Al-Attas, 2001). This Islamic solution to the "mind-body problem" is a unique one that, while sharing some attributes with the Aristotelian paradigm represents a distinct position in this age-old philosophical debate and is perhaps best represented in the work of the 16th/17th century Iranian Shi'a philosopher, Mulla Sadra (Rahman, 1975).

Both Ibn Sina and Mulla Sadra believed that the soul is an immaterial substance and that this substance is a category of quiddity, a substance that itself has properties rather than being a property of the body, brain or physicality (Rahman, 1975, 1981). Where Mulla Sadra parts from Ibn Sina, and thus becomes more central to the development of Islamic thought in this area, is in the conviction that the whole debate is that of quiddity not existence (Kamal, 2016). In other words, the debate is not about the reality of the soul but about consideration and perspective, in that existence is only the domain of God and the quiddity of anything in the created realm is always a matter of perspective and not intrinsically real in and of itself, for that "realness" only belongs to God (Kamal, 2016; Rahman, 1981). This position allows for multiple perspectives, each true from their relative perspective and negates the possibility of distinct dualities, such as what happened with Cartesian dualism which posited the mind as distinct from the body and as separate substances (Foster, 1991). Sadra viewed the body not as something distinctly separate from the soul but rather as nothing other than the soul in an extremely dense state. For Sadra the existence of the soul at its weakest point, in its earthly manifestation, results in its corporealization and that throughout the course of life in the *dunya* the soul slowly emerges, eventually shucking off the body in its earthly death (Kamal, 2016).

Within this Islamic view of the "mind body problem", different levels of perception exist simultaneously, allowing for a paradox of apparent multiplicity in the physical separateness of corporeal bodies, which the great 18th century scholar ibn Ibn Ajiba (2004) calls the "illusion of physicality" (p. 270). This illusion of physicality and the simultaneously absolute Oneness of God governing it all creates the paradox. The relationship between the soul and the body can in this view be seen as the portion of God that desired to be known. This portion is not the summation of God but rather represents God's self-disclosure in as much as God displays God's Self to human beings (ibn Ajiba, 2004). In this view the body is then not to be wholly rejected as it is seen as a gateway to arriving at deeper levels of experiencing reality, through the embracing and understanding of human nature.

In many of the discussions among thinkers in the field, the study of Islamic psychology in relation to theology inevitably links to notions and definitions of human nature (Brown, Murphy, & Malony, 1997; Ingram, 1996; Jeeves, 1997; Spilka & Bridges, 1989). According to Haque (2008) "if a correct perception and conceptualization of human nature is lacking, any attempt at explaining human personality will be flawed, inaccurate, and perhaps misleading. A theory is as good as the premises and assumptions on which it is based" (p. xvi). Mohamed (2008) therefore begins the discussion of where to start in the development of an Islamic personality theory by focusing on the Islamic concept of *fiṭrah*; human nature. The Arabic word *fiṭrah*, while often translated as "human nature", "primordial nature", or "innate disposition", literally means to bring forth or originate and God is referred to in the Qur'an as the *faṭir* or creator of the heavens and earth (Murata & Chittick, 1998). As initially explored in his (1996) book *Fiṭrah; The Islamic Concept of Human Nature*, Mohamed (2008) continues with relaying theories and concepts of the Islamic view of human nature directly from well-known Muslim scholars of old. His discussion of *fiṭrah* involves three dimensions; the religious dimension, the pre-existential dimension, and the dualistic dimension. Unlike Abu Raiya (2012, 2014), who sees the Qur'anic theory of personality as having a negative view of human nature like Christian theological thought (Crisp, 2015), Mohamed (2008) describes these scholars' view of the *fiṭrah* of human beings as positive, in that all human children, regardless of religious affiliation, when they are born are pure, whole and essentially "good". The religious dimension of *fiṭrah*, as Mohamed (2008) relates, is based on the idea of *tawḥīd*, the oneness of God. In this scholarly view, since humankind's *fiṭrah* is to be pure from God, all humans have the potential to witness this oneness and that the *fiṭrah* is characterized by this oneness, as it is engraved on every human soul. Therefore the thinking that follows from this for these religious scholars is that humans are born with a natural inclination towards God and His oneness and to thus recognize God, and to have faith in Him. The mission of the prophets, and in turn religion, is to remind humankind of God's oneness and to remind them of their *fiṭrah*, to strive and eventually return to God and their true nature (Al-Attas, 2001; Mohamed 1996, 2009).

Ibn Khaldun and al-Tustari, among other early Muslim scholars, all generally agreed on the innate dualistic dimension of *fiṭrah* as the tension between the inclination towards either good or evil within the human being and the dynamic interplay that happens throughout the human experience. However, this dualistic nature only exists in the physical life of this world (*dunya*) and thus all along humans still possess the innate purity of their original human nature (*fiṭrah*), which was present in pre-existence (Dhaoudi, 2008; Mohamed, 2008). Thus the nature of the human struggle and dynamic of the personality is very much defined by this process of perceived duality and the striving of the individual to live from the state of *fiṭrah*, thus the test of this life and ultimately the guidance in navigating this process is what is known as Islam (Dhaoudi, 2008; Mohamed, 2008). Ibn Khaldun the following two verses from the Qur'an to support the idea of the duality of human nature (Mohamed, 2008), "And guided him on the two highways [of good and evil] (Q. 90:10)"; and "And the soul and that which shaped it. And inspired it [both] to lasciviousness and to consciousness of Allah. Successful is the one who purifies it. And failed is the one who buries it [in sins] (Q. 91-7-10)". Thus according to Ibn Khaldun the human being is in a fluctuating state of tension between two opposing forces within his/her nature; namely one that is oriented towards animalistic urges and potentially sin, or covering over (*kafara*) the truth of its nature, and one that is oriented towards purity and a God-like state (Dhaoudi, 2008; Mohamed, 2008), a concept that has parallels in both Christianity as well as some aspects of Western psychology that were influenced by such thought (Richards, 2009). The animalistic aspect is one that is only tied to humans' worldly manifestation in this life and thus the original state or human nature is to be fully embodied by this more pure God-like nature (Al-Attas, 2001; Dhaoudi, 2008; Mohamed, 2008).

The Islamic view of the person seems to be intimately linked with spiritual development. There is a running theme in the literature as almost any discussion of a theory of the person within an Islamic framework is integral to a discussion of how the person develops towards a higher state of being or functioning or towards a perfected character. Whereas this is not traditionally seen as part of personality development and instead has more direct parallels with Christian models of spiritual development like the 7th century CE *Ladder of Divine Ascent* by John Climacus (1982), it seems to be that in Islamic thought the two are inseparable. This can be seen most acutely in another of al-Ghazali's early conceptualizations with regards to the *nafs* discussed earlier. Al-Ghazali referred to three stages of the *nafs*, based on traditional knowledge and scholarly interpretation of the Qur'an, namely; *nafs al-ammārah bi-l-su*, *nafs al-lawāmmah*, and *nafs al-muṭma'innah* (Al-Ghazali, 2014; As-Shadhuli, 1994). The *nafs al-ammārah bi-l-su*, which can be found referenced in the Qur'an (12:53) is a developmental state of being in which the self "exhorts one to freely indulge in gratifying passions and instigates to do evil (Haque, 1998, p. 367)". The *nafs al-lawāmmah* (Q 75:2) is a relatively 'higher' state of being that attempts to choose right over wrong and guides towards more constructive decisions (As-Shadhuli, 1994; Haque, 1998; Haque & Keshavarzi, 2014). The *nafs al-muṭma'innah* (Q 89:27) is an even higher state of being wherein the self is situated in the good and correct, no longer inclines towards evil, and achieves ultimate peace (As-Shadhuli, 1994; Haque, 1998; Haque & Keshavarzi, 2014). The third stage does not however mean that the personality has reached perfection, as self-actualization and personality development is a lifelong process and the soul is in a constant state of flux (Hamid, 2008). While many Sufi authors write about more than three stages of the soul, sometimes five and sometimes seven (As-Shadhuli, 1994), these three stages of spiritual development are most commonly referenced and are central to the foundations of an Islamic psychological framework (Haque, 1998).

In traditional Islamic thought, at his/her highest level of realization of *fiṭrah*, or primordial nature, the human being has the potential to embody the essence of The Universal Man (*al-Insān al-Kāmil*), or Perfect Man, which is a manifestation of the divine light, also referred to as the "Light of Muhammad (*nūr-al-Muhammad*)" (Mohamed, 2008; Nasr, 1991; Nicholson, 1984; Schimmel, 2011). The Prophet Muhammad is considered to be the perfected man who was a living manifestation of this potentiality in the human being (Mohamed, 1996, 2008). Perhaps a better way to understand the concept of *al-Insān al-Kāmil* is as an integrated human being, rather than a "perfect" one, as the Prophet Muhammad was indeed human, but was one whose personality was integrated with the divine realities, which are perfect. His essence, the "Light of Muhammad (*nūr-al-Muhammad*)", is one that is considered to be both a living reality and a source of inspiration for all humankind to emulate as the ultimate goal of development towards perfection in this life (Abdullah, 2005). According to Mohamed (2008), "man's perfection and knowledge of God depends on his faithfulness to the pre-existential covenant, to his *fiṭrah*, by emulating Prophet Muhammed, the primal manifestation of divine names" (p. 8). In the Qur'an, God communicates that the believers are to follow the example of the Prophet (Q 33:21) and this plays such a central role to the practice of Islam, that for most Muslims the only legitimate sources of religious guidance are either the words directly from the Qur'an, or the sayings and traditions (*aḥādīth*) of the Prophet (Abdalati, 2011; Murata and Chittick, 1998). The concept of following the "*sunnah*", or practice of the Prophet, involves the attempt on the part of the believer to behave, think and act as much as possible like the Prophet did; to emulate him as the ideal goal of the human persona (Abdalati, 2011; Ali, 1995; Murata and Chittick, 1998). While this is a commonly accepted practice and one that is at the heart of what it is to be a practising Muslim (Ali, 1995), Sufis are known to focus on praising, honouring and emulating the Prophet more than most (Murata and Chittick, 1998). Murata and Chittick (1998) said, "the Sufis attempted to bring about perfect practice and faith by developing the inner qualities implied, but not necessarily actualized, by correct activity and correct thinking. In their view, these inner attitudes and character traits marked the Prophet's personality" (p. 246).

According to Ibn Abbas, the Arabic term used for human in the Qur'an (Q 20: 115), *insan*, is derived from the word *nasiya* (to forget) and this is because the human is in a state of forgetfulness, having once known his/her true nature in pre-existence but forgetting it once entering into the life of this material world (*dunya*) (Al-Attas, 2001; Haque, 1998). Thus forgetfulness is the reason for humans' divergence from their *fiṭrah* state and thus remembrance of their true nature is the path of Islam (Al-Attas, 2001). If the purpose of an Islamic path in life is to remember the *fiṭrah* state and return to it by developing the personality to the point of more closely resembling the perfected example of humanity as exemplified by the Prophet Muhammad, then it would follow that the life of a Muslim should presumably be to attempt to attain increasingly higher stages of this example. While Islam views the Prophet as the highest spiritual being out of all of God's creations, and therefore no other person can ever reach his level, the Muslim is encouraged to attempt to reach as high a level as possible, using the ultimate example of the prophet as the goal (Rahman, 2008). Thus the Prophet Muhammad, in addition to being the messenger of Islam, is considered to be the "living Qur'an" and the example of humanity that a Muslim should strive to be like, not a figure who will necessarily bring salvation to all who believe in him (Murata & Chittick, 1998). Thus it is up to the individual to take personal responsibility to actively endeavour to develop and grow to be a better person, or to achieve a higher state of spiritual being.

The articulation of an Islamic understanding of the self can be a core philosophical viewpoint upon which an Islamic paradigm of psychology can be conceived. However, given that most of the literature on this subject is contained within different branches of knowledge within the Islamic tradition, as the conception of psychology as a separate discipline is a relatively new development in human thought, and that the majority of that literature is written in the Arabic language, creative attempts must be made to access these sources. The present research does not aim to create a *new* conceptualization of the person/soul from an Islamic perspective but rather one that is accessible to an English-speaking audience that is unable to engage with the relevant extensive, dispersed classical sources in Arabic. What is novel here are the *consolidation* of core insights from this dispersed literature in Arabic and the presentation of it in English. This task is approached by incorporating the input of scholars from various branches of knowledge and background within the Islamic tradition who have read and understood these sources and are therefore in a position to explain the Islamic thought as it pertains to the conception of a theory of Islamic psychology. As no such theory has previously existed this research took on the task of developing new theory from the input of these scholars as part of the construction of a theory that is grounded in data, which called for the employment of an appropriate methodology for this specific purpose.

References

Abdalati, H. (2011). *Islam in focus* (2nd ed.). American Trust Publications.

Abdel-Khalek, A. M. (2007). Assessment of intrinsic religiosity with a single-item measure in a sample of Arab Muslims. *Journal of Muslim Mental Health, 2*(2), 211–215. https://doi.org/10.1080/15564900701614874

Abdul-Hamid, W. K., & Hughes, J. H. (2015). Integration of religion and spirituality into trauma Psychotherapy: An Example in Sufism? *Journal of EMDR Practice and Research, 9*(3), 150–156.

Abdullab, S. (2007). Islam and counseling: Models of practice in Muslim communal life. *Journal of Pastoral Counseling, 42*, 42–55.

Abdullah, M. (2005). *The ocean of mercy*. Sidi Muhammad Press.

Abu Raiya, H., & Pargament, K. I. (2010). Religiously integrated psychotherapy with Muslim clients: From research to practice. *Professional Psychology: Research and Practice, 41*(2), 181–188. https://doi.org/10.1037/a0017988

Abu-Raiya, H. (2012). Towards a systematic Qura'nic theory of personality. *Mental Health, Religion & Culture, 15*(3), 217–233. https://doi.org/10.1080/13674676.2011.640622

Abu-Raiya, H. (2014). Western psychology and Muslim psychology in dialogue: Comparisons between a Qura'nic theory of personality and Freud's and Jung's ideas. *Journal of Religion & Health, 53*(2), 326–338 13p. https://doi.org/10.1007/s10943-012-9630-9

Ahmad, A. (2008). Pathology of the heart in the Qur'an: A metaphysico-psychological explanation. In A. Haque & Y. Mohamed (Eds.), *Psychology of personality: Islamic perspectives* (pp. 183–194). Cengage Learning Asia.

Ahmed, Sameera, & Amer, M. M. (Eds.). (2011). *Counseling Muslims: Handbook of mental health issues and interventions*. Routledge.

Ahmed, Sameera, & Reddy, L. A. (2007). Understanding the mental health needs of American Muslims: Recommendations and considerations for practice. *Journal of Multicultural Counseling & Development, 35*(4), 207–218.

Ahmed, Shahab. (2015). *What is Islam?: The importance of being Islamic.* Princeton University Press.

Akram, M. (2014). The authority of Ulama and the problem of anti-state militancy in Pakistan. *Asian Journal of Social Science, 42*(5), 584–601. https://doi.org/10.1163/15685314-04205006

Al-Attas, S. M. N. (2001). The nature of man and the psychology of the human soul. In *Prolegomena to the metaphysics of Islam: An exposition of the fundamental elements of the worldview of Islam* (pp. 143–176). International Institute of Islamic Thought and Civilization.

Al-Attas, S. M. N. (2008). The nature of man and the psychology of the human soul: A brief outline and framework for an Islamic psychology and epistemology. In A. Haque & Y. Mohamed (Eds.), *Psychology of personality: Islamic perspectives* (pp. 131–157). Cengage Learning Asia.

Al-Ghazali, A. H. (2014). *Imam Al-Ghazali Mukhtasar Ihya Ulum Ad-din* (2nd ed.). Spohr Publishers.

Alghorani, M. A. (2008). Knowledge-practice measure of Islamic religiosity (KPMIR): A case of high school Muslim students in the United States. *Journal of Muslim Mental Health, 3*(1), 25–36. https://doi.org/10.1080/15564900802035169

Ali, A. H. (1995). The nature of human disposition: Al-Ghazali's contribution to an Islamic concept of personality. *Intellectual Discourse, 3*(1), 51–64.

Ali, S. R., Liu, W. M., & Humedian, M. (2004). Islam 101: Understanding the religion and therapy implications. *Professional Psychology: Research and Practice, 35*(6), 635–642. https://doi.org/10.1037/0735-7028.35.6.635

Al-Krenawi, A., & Graham, J. R. (2003). Principles of social work practices in the Muslim Arab world. *Arab Studies Quarterly, 25*(4), 75–91.

Allport, G. W. (1950). *The individual and his religion, a psychological interpretation.* Macmillan.

AlMarri, T. S. K., Oei, T. P. S., & Al-Adawi, S. (2009). The development of the short Muslim practice and belief scale. *Mental Health, Religion & Culture, 12*(5), 415–426. https://doi.org/10.1080/13674670802637643

Aloud, N., & Rathur, A. (2009). Factors affecting attitudes toward seeking and using formal mental health and psychological services among Arab Muslim populations. *Journal of Muslim Mental Health, 4*(2), 79–103. https://doi.org/10.1080/15564900802487675

Amer, M., & Jalal, B. (2012). Individual psychotherapy/counseling: Psychodynamic, cognitive-behavioral, and humanistic-experiential models. In S. Ahmed & M. Amer (Eds.), *Counseling Muslims: Handbook of mental health issues and interventions.* Routledge.

Anderson, N., Heywood-Everett, S., Siddiqi, N., Wright, J., Meredith, J., & McMillan, D. (2015). Faith-adapted psychological therapies for depression and anxiety: Systematic review and meta-analysis. *Journal of Affective Disorders, 176*, 183–196.

As-Shadhuli, S. M. (1994). *Music of the soul.* Sidi Muhammad Press.

Badri, M. (1976). Muslim psychologists in the lizard's hole. In *From Muslim to Islamic, 2* (pp. 6–35). Assoc of Muslim Social Scientists.

Badri, M. (1979). *The dilemma of Muslim psychologists.* MWH London.

Badri, M. (2008). Human nature in Islamic psychology: An Islamic critique. In A. Haque & Y. Mohamed (Eds.), *Psychology of personality: Islamic perspectives* (pp. 39–60). Cengage Learning Asia.

Bakhtiar, L. (2008). Traditional Islamic psychology. In A. Haque & Y. Mohamed (Eds.), *Psychology of personality: Islamic perspectives* (pp. 195–209). Cengage Learning Asia.

Bartoli, E. (2007). Religious and spiritual issues in psychotherapy practice: Training the trainer. *Psychotherapy: Theory, Research and Practice, 44*(1), 54–65. https://doi.org/10.1037/0033-3204.44.1.54

Beck, C. T. (1993). Qualitative research: The evaluation of Its credibility, fittingness, and auditability. *Western Journal of Nursing Research, 15*(2), 263–266. https://doi.org/10.1177/019394599301500212

Bergin, A. E., & Payne, I. R. (1991). Proposed agenda for a spiritual strategy in personality and psychotherapy. *Journal of Psychology and Christianity, 10*(3), 197–210.

Berkey, J. P. (2014). *The transmission of knowledge in medieval Cairo a social history of Islamic education.* Princeton University Press.

Beshai, S., Clark, C. M., & Dobson, K. S. (2013). Conceptual and pragmatic considerations in the use of cognitive-behavioral therapy with Muslim clients. *Cognitive Therapy and Research, 37*(1), 197–206. https://doi.org/10.1007/s10608-012-9450-y

Betts, R. B. (2013). *The Sunni-Shi'a divide.* University of Nebraska Press.

Bowland, S., Edmond, T., & Fallot, R. D. (2012). Evaluation of a spiritually focused intervention with older trauma survivors. *Social Work, 57*(1), 73–82. https://doi.org/10.1093/sw/swr001

Brown, L. B. (1985). *Advances in the psychology of religion.* Pergamon.

Brown, W. S., Murphy, N. C., & Malony, H. N. (1997). *Whatever happened to the soul?: Scientific and theological portraits of human nature.* Augsburg Fortress Publishers.

Burr, V. (2015). *Social constructionism.* Routledge.

Callan, A., & Littlewood, R. (1998). Patient satisfaction: Ethnic origin or explanatory model? *International Journal of Social Psychiatry, 44*(1), 1–11. https://doi.org/10.1177/002076409804400101

Cesari, J., 2,3. (2012). Securitization of Islam in Europe. *Welt Des Islams, 52*(3/4), 430–449. https://doi.org/10.1163/15700607-201200A8

Chalmers, D. J. (2002). *Philosophy of mind: Classical and contemporary readings.* Oxford University Press.

Climacus, J. (1982). *The ladder of divine ascent.* Paulist Press.

Coon, D., & Mitterer, J. O. (2008). *Introduction to psychology: Gateways to mind and behavior* (12th ed.). Wadsworth Publishing.

Coyle, A. (2008). Qualitative methods and "the (partly) ineffable" in psychological research on religion and spirituality. *Qualitative Research in Psychology, 5*(1), 56–67. https://doi.org/10.1080/14780880701863583

Cragun, C. L., & Friedlander, M. L. (2012). Experiences of Christian clients in secular psychotherapy: A mixed-methods investigation. *Journal of Counseling Psychology, 59*(3), 379. https://doi.org/10.1037/a0028283

Coyle, A. (2010). Counselling psychology contributions to religion and spirituality. In M. Milton (Ed.), *Therapy and beyond: Counselling psychology contributions to therapeutic and social issues* (pp. 259–276). John Wiley & Sons, Ltd.

Crane, T., & Patterson, S. (2012). *History of the mind-body problem.* Routledge.

Crisp, O. D. (2015). On original sin. *International Journal of Systematic Theology, 17*(3), 252–266. https://doi.org/10.1111/ijst.12107

Cuijpers, P., Sijbrandij, M., Koole, S., Huibers, M., Berking, M., & Andersson, G. (2014). Psychological treatment of generalized anxiety disorder: A meta-analysis. *Clinical Psychology Review, 34*(2), 130–140. https://doi.org/10.1016/j.cpr.2014.01.002

Dasti, R., & Sitwat, A. (2014). Development of a multidimensional measure of Islamic spirituality (MMS). *Journal of Muslim Mental Health, 8*(2). http://dx.doi.org/10.3998/jmmh.10381607.0008.204.

De Silva, P. (2005). *An introduction to Buddhist psychology.* Palgrave Macmillan.

Dhaoudi, M. (2008). The place of human nature in Ibn Khaldun's thinking. In A. Haque & Y. Mohamed (Eds.), *Psychology of personality: Islamic perspectives* (pp. 91–111). Cengage Learning Asia.

Druart, T.-A. (2000). The human soul's individuation and its survival after the body's death: Avicenna on the causal relation between body and soul. *Arabic Sciences and Philosophy*, *10*(2), 259–273. https://doi.org/10.1017/S0957423900000102

Dwairy, M. (2009). Culture analysis and metaphor psychotherapy with Arab-Muslim clients. *Journal of Clinical Psychology*, *65*(2), 199–209. https://doi.org/10.1002/jclp.20568

Ebrahimi, A., Neshatdoost, H. T., Mousavi, S. G., Asadollahi, G. A., & Nasiri, H. (2013). Controlled randomized clinical trial of spirituality integrated psychotherapy, cognitive-behavioral therapy and medication intervention on depressive symptoms and dysfunctional attitudes in patients with dysthymic disorder. *Advanced Biomedical Research*, *2*. https://doi.org/10.4103/2277-9175.114201.

El Shamsy, A. (2008). The social construction of orthodoxy. In T. Winter (Ed.), *The Cambridge companion to classical Islamic theology* (pp. 97–118). Cambridge University Press. /core/books/cambridge-companion-to-classical-islamic-theology/social-construction-of-orthodoxy/C4797757A376275590D69B13D8696C8F

Elmessiri, E. A. M. (2006). *Epistemological bias in the physical & social sciences* (A. M. Elmessiri, Ed.). International Institute of Islamic Thought.

El-Zein, A. H. (1977). Beyond ideology and theology: The search for the anthropology of Islam. *Annual Review of Anthropology*, *6*, 227–254.

Every, D., & Perry, R. (2014). The relationship between perceived religious discrimination and self-esteem for Muslim Australians. *Australian Journal of Psychology*, *66*(4), 241–248. https://doi.org/10.1111/ajpy.12067

Foster, J. (1991). *The immaterial self: A defence of the Cartesian dualist conception of the mind* (1st ed.). Routledge.

Francis, L. J., Sahin, A., & Al-Failakawi, F. (2008). Psychometric properties of two Islamic measures among young adults in Kuwait: The Sahin-Francis scale of attitude toward Islam and the Sahin index of Islamic moral values. *Journal of Muslim Mental Health*, *3*(1), 9–24. https://doi.org/10.1080/15564900802035201

Freud, S., & Gay, P. (1989). *The future of an illusion* (J. Strachey, Ed.; The Standard edition). W. W. Norton & Company.

Gaist, B. (2013). Understanding religion and spirituality in clinical practice. *International Journal of Jungian Studies*, *5*(1), 103–105. https://doi.org/10.1080/19409052.2012.711625

Geertz, C. (1975). *Islam observed: Religious development in Morocco and Indonesia*. University of Chicago Press.

Ghorbani, N., Watson, P. J., Geranmayepour, S., & Chen, Z. (2014). Measuring Muslim spirituality: Relationships of Muslim experiential religiousness with religious and psychological adjustment in Iran. *Journal of Muslim Mental Health*, *8*(1). http://dx.doi.org/10.3998/jmmh.10381607.0008.105.

Ghorbani, N., Watson, P. J., & Shahmohamadi, K. (2008). Afterlife motivation scale: Correlations with maladjustment and incremental validity in Iranian Muslims. *The International Journal for the Psychology of Religion*, *18*(1), 22–35. https://doi.org/10.1080/10508610701719314

Glassé, C. (2013). *The new encyclopedia of Islam*. Rowman & Littlefield.

Gonsiorek, J. C., Richards, P. S., Pargament, K. I., & McMinn, M. R. (2009). Ethical challenges and opportunities at the edge: Incorporating spirituality and religion into psychotherapy. *Professional Psychology: Research and Practice*, *40*(4), 385–395. https://doi.org/10.1037/a0016488

Grim, B. J., & Hsu, B. (2011). Estimating the global Muslim population: Size and distribution of the world's Muslim population. *Interdisciplinary Journal of Research on Religion, 7,* 1–19.

Guba, E. G., & Lincoln, Y. S. (1994). Competing paradigms in qualitative research. In *Handbook of qualitative research* (pp. 105–117). Sage Publications, Inc.

Habib, R. (2006). Modernizing vs. westernizing the social sciences: The case of psychology. In A. M. Elmessiri (Ed.), *Epistemological bias in the physical and social sciences* (pp. 126–144). International Institute of Islamic Thought.

Halimah, A. M. (2014). Translation of the holy Quran: A call for standardization. *Advances in Language and Literary Studies, 5*(1), 122–133.

Hamdan, A. (2008). Cognitive restructuring: An Islamic perspective. *Journal of Muslim Mental Health, 3*(1), 99–116. https://doi.org/10.1080/15564900802035268

Hamid, R. (2008). The concept of personality in Islam. In A. Haque & Y. Mohamed (Eds.), *Psychology of personality: Islamic perspectives* (pp. 257–281). Cengage Learning Asia.

Hans, E., & Hiller, W. (2013). A meta-analysis of nonrandomized effectiveness studies on outpatient cognitive behavioral therapy for adult anxiety disorders. *Clinical Psychology Review, 33*(8), 954–964. https://doi.org/10.1016/j.cpr.2013.07.003

Haque, A. (1998). Psychology and religion: Their relationship and integration from an Islamic perspective. *American Journal of Islamic Social Sciences, 15*(4), 97–116.

Haque, A. (2004a). Psychology from Islamic perspective: Contributions of early Muslim scholars and challenges to contemporary Muslim psychologists. *Journal of Religion and Health, 4,* 357.

Haque, A. (2004b). Religion and mental health: The case of American Muslims. *Journal of Religion & Health, 43*(1), 45–58.

Haque, A. (2008). Psychology of personality: Islamic perspectives. In A. Haque & Y. Mohamed (Eds.), *Psychology of personality: Islamic perspectives* (pp. xv–xxv). Cengage Learning Asia.

Haque, A., & Keshavarzi, H. (2014). Integrating indigenous healing methods in therapy: Muslim beliefs and practices. *International Journal of Culture & Mental Health, 7*(3), 297.

Haque, A., Khan, F., Keshavarzi, H., & Rothman, A. E. (2016). Integrating Islamic traditions in modern psychology: Research trends in last ten years. *Journal of Muslim Mental Health, 10*(1), 75–100.

Haque, A., & Mohamed, Y. (Eds.). (2008). *Psychology of personality, Islamic perspectives.* Cengage Learning Asia.

Hasanović, M., Sinanović, O., Pajević, I., & Agius, M. (2011). The spiritual approach to group psychotherapy treatment of psychotraumatized persons in post-war Bosnia and Herzegovina. *Religions, 2*(3), 330–344. https://doi.org/10.3390/rel2030330

Heelas, P., Woodhead, L., Seel, B., Szerszynski, B., & Tusting, K. (2005). *The spiritual revolution: Why religion is giving way to spirituality* (1st ed.). Wiley-Blackwell.

Henderson, J. B. (1998). *The construction of orthodoxy and heresy: Neo-confucian, Islamic, Jewish, and early Christian patterns.* SUNY Press.

Hergenhahn, B. R., & Henley, T. (2013). *An Introduction to the History of Psychology.* Cengage Learning.

Hodge, D. R., & Nadir, A. (2008). Moving toward culturally competent practice with Muslims: modifying cognitive therapy with Islamic tenets. *Social Work, 53*(1), 31–41.

Hook, J. N., Worthington, E. L., Davis, D. E., Jennings, D. J., Gartner, A. L., & Hook, J. P. (2010). Empirically supported religious and spiritual therapies. *Journal of Clinical Psychology, 66*(1), 46–72. https://doi.org/10.1002/jclp.20626

Huq, M. (2008). The heart and personality development. In A. Haque & Y. Mohamed (Eds.), *Psychology of personality: Islamic perspectives* (pp. 159–181). Cengage Learning Asia.

Ibn Ajiba, S. A. (2004). *The basic research: Arabic title: "Al Futuhat Al Ilahiyya Fi Sharh Al Mabaahith Al-Asliyya"* (1st ed.). Madinah Press.

Ingram, J. A. (1996). Psychological aspects of the filling of the holy spirit: A preliminary model of post-redemptive personality functioning. *Journal of Psychology and Theology*, *24*(2), 104–113. https://doi.org/10.1177/009164719602400203

Izutsu, T. (1982). *Toward a philosophy of Zen Buddhism*. Prajñā Press.

Jackson, L. (2007). A veil of ignorance: Public perceptions of Islam in the United States and their educational implications. *International Journal of the Humanities*, *5*(4), 157–164.

Jana-Masri, A., & Priester, P. E. (2007). The development and validation of a Qur'an-based instrument to assess Islamic religiosity: The religiosity of Islam scale. *Journal of Muslim Mental Health*, *2*(2), 177–188. https://doi.org/10.1080/15564900701624436

Jeeves, M. A. (1997). *Human nature at the millennium: Reflections on the integration of psychology and Christianity*. APOLLOS/Inter-Varsity Press.

Kamal, M. (2016). *Mulla Sadra's transcendent philosophy*. Routledge. https://doi.org/10.4324/9781315596211

Keshavarzi, H., & Haque, A. (2013). Outlining a Psychotherapy Model for Enhancing Muslim Mental Health Within an Islamic Context. *International Journal for the Psychology of Religion*, *23*(3), 230–249. https://doi.org/10.1080/10508619.2012.712000

King-Spooner, S. (Ed.). (2001). *Spirituality and psychotherapy*. PCCS Books.

Küng, H. (1990). *Freud and the problem of God, Enlarged ed.* Yale University Press.

Leahey, T. H. (2012). *A history of psychology: From antiquity to modernity* (7th ed.). Pearson.

Lumbard, J. E. B. (2009). *Islam, fundamentalism, and the betrayal of tradition: Essays by western Muslim scholars*. World Wisdom.

Mahr, F., McLachlan, N., Friedberg, R. D., Mahr, S., & Pearl, A. M. (2015). Cognitive-behavioral treatment of a second-generation child of Pakistani descent: Ethnocultural and clinical considerations. *Clinical Child Psychology and Psychiatry*, *20*(1), 134–147. https://doi.org/10.1177/1359104513499766

Main, R. (2008). Psychology of religion: An overview of its history and current status. *REC3 Religion Compass*, *2*(4), 708–733.

Marie, M., Hannigan, B., & Jones, A. (2016). Mental health needs and services in the West Bank, Palestine. *International Journal of Mental Health Systems*, *10*, 1–8. https://doi.org/10.1186/s13033-016-0056-8

Marmura, M. (1986). Avicenna's "Flying Man" in context. *The Monist*, *69*(3), 383–395. https://doi.org/10.5840/monist198669328

Martinez, J. S., Smith, T. B., & Barlow, S. H. (2007). Spiritual interventions in psychotherapy: Evaluations by highly religious clients. *Journal of Clinical Psychology*, *63*(10), 943–960. https://doi.org/10.1002/jclp.20399

Mavani, H. (2013). *Religious authority and political thought in Twelver Shi'ism from Ali to post-Khomeini*. Routledge.

Mayers, C., Leavey, G., Vallianatou, C., & Barker, C. (2007). How clients with religious or spiritual beliefs experience psychological help-seeking and therapy: A qualitative study. *Clinical Psychology & Psychotherapy*, *14*(4), 317–327. https://doi.org/10.1002/cpp.542

Milton, M., Craven, M., & Coyle, A. (2010). Understanding human distress: Moving beyond the concept of 'psychopathology.' In M. Milton (Ed.), *Therapy and beyond* (pp. 57–72). John Wiley & Sons, Ltd. https://doi.org/10.1002/9780470667279.ch4

Mohamed, Y. (1996). *Fitrah: The Islamic concept of human nature.* Ta-Ha Publishers.

Mohamed, Y. (2008). Human natural disposition (Fitrah). In A. Haque & Y. Mohamed (Eds.), *Psychology of personality: Islamic perspectives* (pp. 3–18). Cengage Learning Asia.

Mujiburrahman. (2001). The phenomenological approach in Islamic studies: An overview of a Western attempt to understand Islam. *Muslim World, 91*(3/4), 425–450. https://doi.org/10.1111/j.1478-1913.2001.tb03725.x

Murata, S., & Chittick, W. (1998). *Vision of Islam* (1st ed.). Paragon House.

Nasr, S. H. (Ed.). (1991). *Islamic spirituality: Foundations.* The Crossroad Publishing Company.

Nevid, J. S., Rathus, S. A., & Greene, B. (2017). *Abnormal psychology in a changing world* (10th ed.). Pearson.

Nicholson, R. A. (1984). *Sufi doctrine of the perfect man* (New edition). Holmes Pub Group Llc.

Odorisio, D. M. 1. (2014). The alchemical heart: A Jungian approach to the heart center in the upaniṣads and in Eastern Christian prayer. *International Journal of Transpersonal Studies, 33*(1), 27–38.

Othman, N. (2016). A preface to the Islamic personality psychology. *International Journal of Psychologic al Studies, 8*(1), 20–27.

Pargament, K. I. (2011). *Spiritually integrated psychotherapy: Understanding and addressing the sacred.* Guilford Press.

Pargament, K. I., & Saunders, S. M. (2007). Introduction to the special issue on spirituality and psychotherapy. *Journal of Clinical Psychology, 63*(10), 903–907. https://doi.org/10.1002/jclp.20405

Pasqualini, J. c. (1, 2), & Martins, L. m. (1, 2). (2015). Dialectics between singularity-particularity-universality: The implications of the materialist dialectical method to psychology. *Psicologia e Sociedade, 27*(2), 362–371.

Piedmont, R. L. (2013). A short history of the psychology of religion and spirituality: providing growth and meaning for division 36. *Psychology of Religion and Spirituality, 5*(1), 1–4. https://doi.org/10.1037/a0030878

Plante, T. G. (2007). Integrating spirituality and psychotherapy: Ethical issues and principles to consider. *Journal of Clinical Psychology, 63*(9), 891–902. https://doi.org/10.1002/jclp.20383

Polkinghorne, J. (2005). *Exploring reality: The intertwining of science and religion* (edition). Yale University Press.

Polkinghorne, J. C. (1998). *Science and theology: An introduction.* Augsburg Fortress Publishers.

Ponterotto, J. G. (2001). *Handbook of multicultural counseling.* Sage Publications.

Popper, K. R. (1979). *Objective knowledge: An evolutionary approach.* Clarendon Press.

Post, B. C., & Wade, N. G. (2009). Religion and spirituality in psychotherapy: A practice-friendly review of research. *Journal of Clinical Psychology, 65*(2), 131–146. https://doi.org/10.1002/jclp.20563

Powell, K. A. (2011). Framing Islam: An analysis of U.S. media coverage of terrorism since 9/11. *Communication Studies, 62*(1), 90–112. https://doi.org/10.1080/10510974.2011.533599

Prentice, D., Miller, D., & Lightdale, J. (1994). Asymmetries in attachments to groups and to their members—Distinguishing between common-identity and common-bond groups. *Personality and Social Psychology Bulletin, 20*(5), 484–493.

Rahman, F. (Ed.). (1981). *Avicenna's psychology*. Hyperion Pr.

Rahman, Fazlur. (1975). *The philosophy of Mulla Sadra Shirazi*. SUNY Press.

Rahman, S. (2008). Nature of soul: The philosophy of Mulla Sadra. In A. Haque & Y. Mohamed (Eds.), *Psychology of personality: Islamic perspectives* (pp. 115–130). Cengage Learning Asia.

Raiya, H. A., Pargament, K. I., Mahoney, A., & Stein, C. (2008). A psychological measure of Islamic religiousness: Development and evidence for reliability and validity. *The International Journal for the Psychology of Religion, 18*(4), 291–315. https://doi.org/10.1080/10508610802229270

Rassool, G. H. (2015). Cultural competence in counseling the Muslim patient: Implications for mental health. *Archives of Psychiatric Nursing, 29*, 321–325. https://doi.org/10.1016/j.apnu.2015.05.009

Rauch, F. A. (1844). *Psychology: Or, a view of the human soul; including anthropology*. M.W. Dodd.

Richards, G. (2009). Psychology meets religion. In *Putting psychology in its place* (3rd ed., pp. 329–347). Routledge.

Richards, P. S., & Bergin, A. E. (Eds.). (2014). Toward religious and spiritual competency for mental health professionals. In *Handbook of psychotherapy and religious diversity* (2nd ed., pp. 3–19). American Psychological Association. https://doi.org/10.1037/14371-001

Richards, P. S., Sanders, P. W., Lea, T., McBride, J. A., & Allen, G. E. K. (2015). Bringing spiritually oriented psychotherapies into the health care mainstream: A call for worldwide collaboration. *Spirituality in Clinical Practice, 2*(3), 169–179. https://doi.org/10.1037/scp0000082

Rizzuto, A.-M. (1981). *Birth of the living God: A psychoanalytic study* (New edition). University of Chicago Press.

Ruitenbeek, H. M. (1973). *Freud as we knew him*. Wayne State University Press.

Russo, F., & Williamson, J. (2007). Interpreting causality in the health sciences. *International Studies in the Philosophy of Science, 21*(2), 157–170. https://doi.org/10.1080/02698590701498084

Sahin, A. (2013). Reflections on the possibility of an Islamic Psychology. *Archive for the Psychology of Religion, 35*(3), 321–335.

Said, E. W. (1979). *Orientalism*. Vintage Books.

Schermer, V. L. (2003). *Spirit and psyche: A new paradigm for psychology, psychoanalysis, and psychotherapy*. Jessica Kingsley Publishers.

Schimmel, A. (2011). *Mystical dimensions of Islam* (2 ed.). The University of North Carolina Press.

Skinner R. (2010). An Islamic approach to psychology and mental health. *Mental Health, Religion & Culture, 13*(6), 547–551. https://doi.org/10.1080/13674676.2010.488441

Smither, R., & Khorsandi, A. (2009. The implicit personality theory of Islam. *Psychology of Religion and Spirituality, 1*(2), 81–96.

Sperry, L., & Shafranske, E. P. (Eds.). (2005). *Spiritually oriented psychotherapy*. American Psychological Association. https://doi.org/10.1037/10886-000

Sperry, M. (2016). From theory to clinical practice: Psychoanalytic complexity theory and the lived experience of complexity. *International Journal of Psychoanalytic Self Psychology, 11*(4), 349–362. https://doi.org/10.1080/15551024.2016.1213096

Spilka, B., & Bridges, R. A. (1989). Theology and psychological theory: Psychological implications of some modern theologies. *Journal of Psychology and Theology, 17*(4), 342–349. https://doi.org/10.1177/009164718901700404

Stewart, R. E., & Chambless, D. L. (2009). Cognitive–behavioral therapy for adult anxiety disorders in clinical practice: A meta-analysis of effectiveness studies. *Journal of Consulting and Clinical Psychology*, *77*(4), 595–606. https://doi.org/10.1037/a0016032

Tacey, D. (2004). *The spirituality revolution: The emergence of contemporary spirituality*. Routledge. https://doi.org/10.4324/9780203647035

Thomas, J., & Ashraf, S. (2011). Exploring the Islamic tradition for resonance and dissonance with cognitive therapy for depression. *Mental Health, Religion & Culture*, *14*(2), 183–190. https://doi.org/10.1080/13674676.2010.517190

Thomas, P., Shah, A., & Thornton, T. (2009). Language, games and the role of interpreters in psychiatric diagnosis: A Wittgensteinian thought experiment. *Medical Humanities*, *35*(1), 13–18. https://doi.org/10.1136/jmh.2008.000422

Utz, A. (2011). *Psychology from the Islamic perspective*. Intl Islamic Pub House.

Van Ess, J. (2006). *The flowering of Muslim theology*. Harvard University Press.

Varisco, D. M. (2005). *Islam obscured: The rhetoric of anthropological representation*. Palgrave Macmillan.

Vasegh, S. (2009). Psychiatric treatments involving religion: Psychotherapy from an Islamic perspective. In P. Huguelet & H. G. Koenig (Eds.), *Religion and spirituality in psychiatry* (pp. 301–316). Cambridge University Press.

Vasegh, S. (2014). *Religious cognitive behavioral therapy: Muslim version*. http://www.spiritualityandhealth.duke.edu/images/pdfs/RCBT%20Manual%20Final%20Muslim%20Version%203-14-14.pdf

Ward, K. (2008). *The big questions in science and religion*. Templeton Foundation Press.

Weatherhead, S., & Daiches, A. (2010). Muslim views on mental health and psychotherapy. *Psychology & Psychotherapy: Theory, Research & Practice*, *83*(1), 75–89.

Wegrocki, H. J. (1939). A critique of cultural and statistical concepts of abnormality. *The Journal of Abnormal and Social Psychology*, *34*(2), 166–178. https://doi.org/10.1037/h0056841

Winter, T. (2008). *The Cambridge companion to classical Islamic theology*. Cambridge University Press.

Worthington, E. L., Hook, J. N., Davis, D. E., & McDaniel, M. A. (2011). Religion and spirituality. *Journal of Clinical Psychology*, *67*(2), 204–214. https://doi.org/10.1002/jclp.20760

Reflection 1: A Journey of the Soul, a Journey to Islam

As a young boy around the age of 14 I realized that I was different than most of my high school peers. I was less interested in sports and being in the popular group and more interested in questioning what is real and exploring the mystery of the human condition. I spent my time philosophizing about truth and identity, reading books on counter culture and Eastern religions, and spending time alone in nature. When I went to college I decided to continue my explorations in academic subjects that seemed to match my interests and was drawn to consider majoring in psychology.

The thing that initially attracted me to psychology was the idea that it studies the psyche or soul of the human being. I was always intrigued by the notion that we as human beings have a deeper, perhaps more authentic part of ourselves that is beyond or beneath the external identities that we construct and operate from in our worldly lives. I always thought of psychology in this way, that it looked at the true, more hidden and more real aspects of the self and that it was about understanding that deeper aspect that would allow for increasing levels of capability or potential. I suppose I was taking the word psychology quite literally, in that it means the study of the psyche, or soul. However, what I found in most of my psychology courses was that the focus was on studying the brain, behaviour, and attributes of the human being that are tangible and measurable, with very little discussion or exploration of the concept of the soul.

I wound up not majoring in psychology because of this seemingly ironic absence of the human experience in the study of human beings that was characteristic of all but one course I took. However, it was in this one course where I found precisely what I was looking for and that course was *psychology and religion*. I was captivated by the subject matter because it addressed the spiritual aspect of the human experience. Although I had always been intrigued and interested in religious concepts and ideas for this reason, I was turned off by the idea of following a religion. At the time, I saw religion as something that restricted the self rather than expanded it, as that was how I saw many people's relationship to religion. But what I found fascinating was that the subfield of Humanistic psychology drew on the wisdom and insight from many of the great world religions and spiritual traditions and applied it in an active way of developing the self without the confines of the adherence to one path. Abraham Maslow's notion that the goal of psychological growth and development is "self-actualization" resonated with me and for that reason I took a keen interest in this subfield of psychology.

At the same time that my interest had been peaked in this new direction and had taken it upon myself to read and learn more about Humanistic psychology, I discovered that my own grandfather, Leonard Schneider, had been one of the pioneers of the subfield. He had studied directly under Abraham Maslow and later went on to become a colleague and close personal friend of Fritz Perls, among other pioneers of the field. Thus I suppose you could say that I had a hereditary disposition to be inclined toward Humanistic Psychology. In one of the last conversations I had with my grandfather before he died he told me that he wished he would have paid more attention to religion and spiritual traditions and how they can be of great use within the therapeutic encounter for providing structure to people's understanding of themselves and their own personal growth.

Throughout my college years and beyond I was actively involved in the study of various religious traditions and travelled around the world living, studying and practising with different spiritual and faith communities. Amidst this experiential education I decided to pursue a Masters degree in psychology to continue my passion and turn it into a career. I was as eclectic in my theoretical approach to psychology as I was in my theological approach to spirituality: I couldn't bring myself to commit to just one path. In my early career I often claimed to have an "eclectic" orientation, which in the field of psychotherapy is often seen as a cop out. Similarly with regards to spirituality and religion, I claimed to be spiritual but not religious. I studied and admired all religions and incorporated aspects of them into my own personal path, but did not subscribe to a religion, or even perhaps the idea of religion. Like some who are turned off by or skeptical of conventional notions of God but consider themselves spiritual, my sense was that there was a universal power that connects all living things. Whereas some people tend to reject the idea of God in opposition to how others perceive God, I was comfortable with the idea that there are many different ways to understand and relate to the spiritual, Divine reality. My own feeling was that what I call God is in essence the same thing as what another may describe in other terms. Therefore, belief in God was never a question for me. I liked to quote Carl Jung in my answer to whether I believed in God by saying "I do not believe, I know" (Jung, 1959). To me, the existence of God was a given, and I believed that our task in this life is to become closer to God, which I interpreted as in essence what self-actualization really was – God-consciousness. Essentially, my relationship to psychology was infused with my spiritual journey.

With the last words of my grandfather in my mind, coupled with my own experiences with religious spiritual devotion, I came to the acute realization that without a dedicated path I was hitting a glass ceiling in my own growth. I came to see that I could not advance further on my path of personal growth unless I committed to a path that disciplined myself to allow for deeper transformation and expansion of consciousness by working through my psychological imbalances in a systematic and successive way. I came to believe that the eclectic approach to both a theoretical orientation to psychology as well as to a theological orientation to spirituality suffered from lack of structure and theoretical grounding that is situated within one paradigm. I eventually determined that in order to continue on my inner quest I needed to commit to a path. This was simultaneously true of my approach to psychotherapy and my personal spiritual discipline. Thus my ultimate landing on a theoretical orientation to psychology is inextricably linked to my eventual embracing of a religious path. In fact, the two were one and the same.

In my search for a path that would primarily orient me toward spiritual self-development, I discovered a deeply intricate science to the conceptualization of the soul, and it was grounded in Islam. Given the way in which I came to embrace it, there is very little separation for me between Islam as a religion and psychology/psychotherapy as different disciplines that I am adapting or integrating with Islam. For me the spiritual work and the psychological work are inextricably interconnected. I see Islam as a psychology and believe that psychology (the study of the psyche) can be realized in full through the Islamic tradition. I went on to study Islam and was guided by several teachers in the tradition who helped me understand this science of the soul from the tradition and how I could contextualize it within my work as a developing psychotherapist. I spent ten years making my way at integrating these Islamic concepts into my own therapeutic practice with Muslim clients. It was at this point that I came to realize that several other Muslim clinicians were doing the same and that there lacked a clear, structured framework for developing this as a cohesive theoretical orientation. Thus my position in approaching this research topic is as an insider on multiple levels, as a psychotherapist, a practising Muslim, and a practising Islamic psychotherapist.

3 Grounded Theory and Theology: A Methodological Approach to Constructing a Religiously Inspired Theoretical Framework

What is currently missing from the research in this field is the foundational theoretical orientation upon which to build applications of Islamic psychology in therapeutic practice. Rather than to add to the numbers of ideas and suggestions about what an Islamic psychology could potentially be and disagreements about what it is, it is time for a theory to emerge that is grounded in the actual data that exist. This research proposes to take a step in that direction by developing a grounded theory of Islamic psychology and, from there, of Islamic psychotherapy.

The methodological choice for a research project should be reflective of the aim of the research, the contextual reality of the phenomena being studied and how the research questions can best be answered. Research methodologies are situated in epistemological and ontological paradigms and philosophy of science (Haverkamp & Young, 2007). The Islamic paradigm has its own epistemology and ontology, which from an outside perspective could be perceived not to be an interpretive/constructivist one. However, the lived reality of Islam, as is believed to be embodied in the life of the Prophet Muhammad and extended through the scholarly tradition of the Muslim *ummah* (global community), certainly can be said to have elements of constructivist approaches to social phenomena as Muslims work to make sense of how to apply religious tenets to daily life (Al-Sharaf, 2013). This is reflected in the numerous *madhahib* (schools of thought) which are considered equally acceptable within the tradition and the historical precedent of multiple interpretations of and perspectives on Islamic principles in practice (Al-Alwani, 1993). This reality of the phenomena being investigated in this research justifies the incorporation of a variety of Islamic scholarly voices in the development of a theory of Islamic psychology and makes constructivist grounded theory a fitting choice of methodology for the two studies that make up the research in the following presentation of findings.

In order to develop a religiously appropriate model that effectively incorporates key elements from the Islamic tradition, grounding a framework for an Islamic paradigm of psychology in the direct input from Islamic psychology thinkers, scholars of Islam and source texts is crucial. Those individuals who have dedicated their lives to studying and understanding the meanings and knowledge from Islamic sources and those who work closely with the Muslim community and who understand mental health in the context of Islam hold keys to information and insight that comes from their unique experience. Currently, this particular brand of insight and understanding is not found elsewhere as the field of Islamic psychology and Muslim mental health is a relatively new development in the academic and scientific communities. Consequently, there is no pre-existing theory to build upon in the development of this specialized field. Therefore a systematic way of constructing a theory that is grounded in these sources is needed to better situate the further development of the field of Islamic psychology and to pave the way for future research in the development of indigenous interventions. This work is part of an ongoing process of disciplinary awakening to the value and necessity of engaging actively with indigenous wisdoms beyond the Western canon (Baggini, 2018). This process has been unfolding in other disciplines, such as Christian theology, for some time (for example, Magesa, 2013) but is only just beginning in the domain of psychology. As a contribution to this effort, the objective of this study is to develop an emergent theory of Islamic psychology that is grounded in data, in other words a 'grounded theory' of Islamic psychology.

Qualitative Research in Psychology

Whereas methodology is the justification for the use of a particular approach to research, a method is a research tool that is employed, such as a survey or an interview (McGregor & Murnane, 2010). Qualitative research methods, such as interviews, are well suited for the study of spiritual and religious phenomena as they have the capacity to capture the complexity and fluidity of people's experiences that are often difficult to capture in suitably contextualized ways through quantitative approaches (Coyle, 2008). Consequently, many studies involving the intersection of spirituality and religion in the context of psychology have used qualitative methods to ask questions about people's experiences and processes (for example, Golsworthy & Coyle, 1999; Murray, Kendall, Boyd, Worth, & Benton, 2004; Walton, 1999; Wright, 2003). Although quantitative research methods were advocated in epistemological debates early in the history of the domain of psychology (Henwood & Pidgeon, 1994), for quite some time qualitative research in psychology was all but non-existent. This was largely due to the propensity within the psychology community to align the discipline with the rest of the scientific community and thus to favour quantitative approaches that were believed to be able to measure objective reality (Coyle, 2016). There was a buying into the assumption that psychological realities can be objectively measured. However, given the content and context within which the field of psychology is situated, with many aspects of it focused on the study of the inner world of the human being, qualitative methods have come to be more accepted within psychology research due to the fit that such methods have with the types of data that need to be obtained or interpreted in psychology (Coyle, 2016).

Qualitative research methods all share the basic assumption that psychological and social 'realities' are multiple and contextually determined (Lyons, 2000). Human beings are complex and their experiences are affected by multiple factors both from within their internal psychological experience and their unique external experiences. In addition to humans mostly being the subject of qualitative research, those doing the research are always human beings, thus creating even more permutations of relative experience within a given research setting. Thus, qualitative methods are those methods which take all of these factors into consideration and recognize that people, social structures, social allegiances, ideologies, and context all contribute to the realities of the subjects being studied (Dallos & Draper, 2010; Harre & Secord, 1972; Lyons, 2000). Rather than aiming to understand what a certain experience is from an entirely outside perspective, qualitative methods aim to ask questions such as "What is it like?" to have a given lived experience (Willig, 2001), or in the case of social constructionist qualitative research, "How is this phenomenon understood and represented in society?" (Coyle, 2008).

Within the domain of qualitative research there exist a number of different methods all of which are based on varying ideas of how to produce knowledge in psychology and how to go about doing so (Denzin & Lincoln, 2011; Henwood & Pidgeon, 1994; Willig, 2001). This multiplicity of qualitative research methods is due to differences in epistemological commitments across methods, in other words the particular sets of assumptions about how knowledge is produced (Coyle, 2016). Quantitative methods were historically underscored by the epistemology of positivism which assumes that researchers can take an impartial stance and thus determine objective conclusions about subjects; empiricism which favours the categorization of observations; or hypothetico-deductivism which develops and tests hypotheses from theories (Coyle, 2016). In contrast, qualitative methods are generally underscored by epistemologies that assume a more subjective reality in the production of knowledge.

Perhaps what most distinctly identifies a qualitative method is its consideration and inclusion of the influence of context on a given subject matter. The ways that different qualitative methods deal with or understand the role of context in the production of psychological knowledge can be seen in their epistemological focus in how they approach research and such methods can be chosen for certain studies based on their fit. Phenomenological methods are focused on "obtaining detailed descriptions of experience as understood by those that have that experience in order to discern its essence" (Coyle, 2016, p. 15), an example of which is interpretative phenomenological analysis (IPA). Social constructionism is based on the epistemological assumption that human experiences are products of particular cultural and historical contexts and is concerned with how social realities are constructed from within those contexts (Coyle, 2016; Willig, 2001), an example of which is discourse analysis. Grounded theory is another distinct form of qualitative research that takes context into account in a specific way and has been chosen for this particular study based on its fit with the research aims. However, even within the qualitative research subcategory that is known as grounded theory, there exist various versions of the approach.

Grounded Theory

Grounded Theory is a qualitative research approach that was developed in the 1960s by two American sociologists, Barney Glaser and Anselm Strauss (Kenny & Fourie, 2014). The impetus for the creation of the approach came out of the two researchers' disappointment with the overemphasis in their field at the time of researchers verifying theories as opposed to the actual process of theory generation (Kenny & Fourie, 2014). In their seminal work on the development of the approach, *The Discovery of Grounded Theory*, Glaser and Strauss (1967) observed that "since verification has primacy on the current sociological scene, the desire to generate theory often becomes secondary, if not totally lost, in specific researches" (p. 2). They were also critical of the lack of empirical research in the development of social theories and remarked that there was an "embarrassing gap between theory and empirical research" (Glaser & Strauss, 1967, p. 2). This led the two to pioneer a new methodology that would bridge this gap.

Glaser and Strauss (1967) advocated "developing theories from research grounded in data rather than deducing testable hypotheses from existing theories" (p. 4). Two major advantages to this approach are that the theory is emergent in that it is developed as a result of the findings from collected data and not from a synthesis of previous research findings, and that it is particularly useful in developing new theory in relation to a phenomenon or question on which "existing theory is incomplete, inappropriate or absent" (Henwood & Pidgeon, 1994, p. 102). In grounded theory, theory development is the explicit, central concern of the research endeavour from the outset rather than something that is achieved from existing resources in a post hoc fashion. Some researchers have used the grounded theory approach as a systematic way of analyzing qualitative data without aiming to generate new theory (Kenny & Fourie, 2014). The rationale for this is unclear as, given the labour-intensive, detailed analytic engagement associated with a grounded theory approach, there are many other less demanding ways of analyzing qualitative data if theory generation is not the aim of the research. For example, one very popular contemporary method is thematic analysis (Braun & Clarke, 2006).

Although there are several people in the field who have written on and speculated about a potential theory of Islamic psychology, no such theory currently exists or has been formally presented. In the preceding chapter, the case was also made that contemporary conceptualizations of psychology and psychotherapy do not align effectively with core Islamic commitments. Thus grounded theory was chosen as the methodological approach for this research study as theory development was the central aim of the project. No other qualitative approach has the generation of theory as its *explicit* core endeavour.

Constructivist Grounded Theory

There are three main versions of grounded theory: realist-positivist (Glaser, 1992), post-positivist (Strauss & Corbin, 1990), and constructivist-interpretivist (Charmaz, 2014). Perhaps due to its being the original form of grounded theory and therefore emerging out of a time when positivist-empiricist epistemological orientations were favoured, realist-positivist grounded theory tends to assume that a single truth can be discerned from data and that knowledge thus emerges from that data (Glaser, 1992; Madill, Jordan, & Shirley, 2000; Rennie, 1996; Thomas & James, 2006). Post-positivist grounded theory, as the name infers, attempts to move away from the notion that everything can be directly measured and instead it embraces the incorporation of interpretations of the experiences of people who are studied (Strauss & Corbin, 1994). However, the post-positivist approach shares the realism of its predecessor in that it is concerned with objectivity and the removal of bias (Annells, 1996; Charmaz, 2014). As a development in the evolution of grounded theory the constructivist-interpretivist approach "rejects the notion of objectivity and focuses on the meanings that can be constructed from interpretations of the data" (Weed, 2017, p. 5). In taking into consideration the nature of the subject matter of this research study, being that of the highly subjective and interpretive realm of religious experience and the soul, the constructivist approach to grounded theory was chosen as the best methodological fit for this purpose.

Data Generation in Grounded Theory

Rather than a typical research question being driven by a hypothesis drawn from pre-existent theory, the questions asked in the research are process-oriented in order to facilitate the emergence of answers that are genuine to the process under investigation. This approach is also reflected in the approach to data generation. Data are not gathered in the same way as you would gather fruit from a tree; rather it is an active process where the researcher and the interviewees are deeply involved in generating the data together in dialogue. In Magaldi-Dopman et al.'s (2011) grounded theory study, the researchers took into consideration their own orientation to spirituality and how that may have influenced and interacted with the responses from participants in the data generation process of interviewing. They said, "the researchers relied on the participants' views of the topic being studied while recognizing the influence of their own background on the research they were conducting" (p. 289).

Data in grounded theory research can involve interviews, qualitative surveys, participant observation, documents, diagrams, maps, and photographs

(Charmaz, 2014) but semi-structured interviews or observations are most common (Payne, 2016). In the present research, qualitative data were generated from participants' responses to individual interview questions in a procedure known as "Key informant interviewing" (Gilchrist, 1992). Gilchrist (1992) defines key informants by virtue of their position in a culture (understood here as a group and/or context characterized by particular experiences, outlooks and/or values). Key informants possess "special knowledge, status, or communication skills" (p. 75) and are willing to share their experience-based insights with the researcher. They act as expert mediators and communicators of the experiences of members of their culture, although of course the researcher needs to be mindful that key informants will also have their own personal investments in the research topic. Key informant interviewing has been used fruitfully in the mental health field in the past. For example, Potter and Coyle (2017) used this data generation approach to gain expert insights into the efficacy of using mindfulness in the treatment of Obsessive-Compulsive Disorder.

Given that Muslim mental health and Islamic psychology is a highly specialized field with very little academic research and writing, and the fact that most of the textual source material is written in Arabic, most of the sources of knowledge in this area are experiential in nature and lie within the personal and professional experiences of individual practitioners and scholars. Although there currently is no formal or operationalized approach to Islamically-oriented psychotherapy, some practitioners currently practise similar interventions in their work with Muslim service users (for example, Abdullah, 1999), while many scholars are familiar with the theoretical underpinnings of psychology from the Islamic perspective. Thus generating data in the form of insights and first-hand accounts from such informants is perhaps the best if not the only way to produce the type of data required for the development of an Islamic theory of psychology and psychotherapy.

In reference to the type of interviewing that solicits the type of data that are relevant to the emergence of theory, Charmaz (2014) said that intensive qualitative interviewing and grounded theory methods are "open ended yet directed, shaped yet emergent, and paced yet unrestricted" (p. 28). The structure of the interview schedules used in this research followed a format intentionally constructed to encourage responses from the interviewee that allow for open-ended answers that elicit rich data in the form of reports of personal experience. The interview begins with descriptive questions that invite the informant to describe their experience, followed by structural questions that focus the responses towards the research aims, and finally contrast questions which further clarify the responses (Gilchrist, 1992). In the present research, two separate interview schedules were used in the two different studies The development of each interview schedule will be discussed later in Chapters Four and Five where the respective studies are reported.

Sampling in Grounded Theory

Unlike quantitative studies that often use random sampling, qualitative research often uses "purposeful" sampling, where the researcher actively selects the most productive sample to address the research question (Marshall, 1996), or "criterion-based" sampling, where participants are selected based on defined characteristics relevant to the research question. According to Marshall (1996), "an appropriate sample size for a qualitative study is one that adequately answers the research question" (p. 523). The number of participants initially chosen for a qualitative study is based on the range of diversity of opinions and experiences from the pool of potential participants. The aim is to achieve a sample that can answer the research question while acknowledging that attaining a comprehensive answer to that question will usually entail more than one phase of the study with each employing complementary samples that progressively extend the emergent research picture (Marshall, 1996).

Saturation is the aim of grounded theory work, while acknowledging that the scope of some research questions and also resource limitations may constrain the possibility of attaining saturation in any given study (Marshall, Cardon, Poddar, & Fontenot, 2013). In the context of grounded theory, Payne (2016) defines saturation as the gathering of "further examples of meaningful units as one proceeds through the transcripts until no new instances of a particular category emerge" (p. 78). After initial data generation, fieldwork and analysis occur simultaneously in grounded theory work. The analysis of the data that have been gathered is used to develop an emergent theory and this then directs subsequent sampling and fieldwork. Thus the sampling evolves as the emergent theory evolves and further input is needed from additional sources in order to reach saturation. This approach is called "theoretical sampling" and is the characteristic sampling method for grounded theory (Glaser & Strauss, 1967). In this approach the sample is emergent in that as data are generated from the interviews, the resulting analysis is reflected upon by the researcher in light of the emergent theory which then informs the next steps of data generation. In this process the researcher attempts to discern those perspectives that have not yet been included in the data set but that might enrich, extend, or challenge the emergent theory. They then seek to recruit participants who are likely to hold and be able to share such perspectives. As Weed (2017) proclaims "research designs which complete data collection prior to proceeding to analysis compromise one of the key tenets of GT methodology" (p. 6). Whereas the initial sample is based on practical concerns by choosing obvious candidates, subsequent selection criteria are "data driven" as additional participants may be deemed necessary in light of the data collected from previous interviews (Johnson, 1990).

In the present research the process of recruiting scholars of Islam for the initial phase of the study began by identifying potential participants who by nature of their education, training and experiences possess knowledge of the

Islamic conception of human nature as derived from traditional sources. This initial selection process was purposeful in that participants were chosen based on their ability to offer insight into Islamic conceptions of human psychology and it was criterion based in that the specific focus of study or research of the scholars was taken into consideration in the selection process. Due to the researcher's education and professional experience being in the field of psychology and not theology, it was difficult to know exactly where and from whom to sample. Therefore the initial sample was small, as there was not yet an idea of what was needed to expand the not-yet-emerging theory. With each of these initial interviews, it became clear what was needed to develop the data generation. Each interview also provided the opportunity to learn about other potential scholars, by referral and discussion with participants as they themselves began to understand more about the research question.

In phase two of the research, theoretical sampling continued with a different group of participants: practising psychotherapists who believed that they integrate Islamic principles into their therapy with Muslim clients. Four of the participants in phase one who were recruited for that phase based on their academic study of Islamic psychology, also had clinical experience that involved incorporating their knowledge of Islamic psychology into therapeutic practice. These individuals also took part in phase two (in a separate interview some time after the phase one interviews) as they met the inclusion criteria for both phases. They provided the starting point for sampling in phase two and a 'springboard' from which further theoretical sampling took place as they were able to recommend where and with whom to sample next based on the emerging theory.

Data Analysis in Grounded Theory

The method of analysis used in grounded theory begins with rigorous reading and close examination of interview transcripts. In this research, transcription was done by the researcher for the majority of interviews, with the few interviews conducted with a translator in Arabic being transcribed and translated by a hired professional. During this initial stage of reading through transcripts, the researcher made note of points of interest, important concepts, and ideas particularly relevant to the research question. Within the grounded theory process, these notes are referred to as 'memos' (Charmaz, 2014). Memos were continually made throughout the analysis and, later in the process, were used as resources in the construction of theory.

After transcription, the data were then coded in an initial process of "open coding" which involves identifying and labelling units of text that are meaningful relative to the research question, for example, a word, phrase, sentence or larger section of text (Payne, 2016). These codes were the fundamental building blocks of the emergent theory of Islamic psychology and psychotherapy in that they addressed concepts about human nature (in the first phase) or descriptions of approaches with clients (in the second phase).

As codes were generated in this way, they were compared to other previously-generated codes and were grouped according to the similarity of what they concerned. In a process known as "focused coding", new, higher-level codes were produced that captured the concerns shared by groups of lower-level codes. The set of higher-level codes was then clustered and organized into relevant categories and subcategories – in other words, overarching themes that represent the ideas contained in the codes, based on the research interest as well as data-driven categories in what is called 'axial coding' (Charmaz, 2014; Payne, 2016). During axial coding, possible relationships between categories are noted, hypothesized, and tested against data obtained in ongoing theoretical sampling. Axial codes are then organized into selective codes which represent overarching or main categories of the emergent theory (Creswell, 2007) in what is known as selective or theoretical coding. These theoretical codes are what became the main components in the construction of the theory of Islamic psychology and psychotherapy presented in the preceding chapters. The emergent theory was 'grounded' in that it was developed from the data through increasingly higher-level coding but with constant movement back to the data to validate the output of each level of analysis against the data (Payne, 2016). In this consistently data-grounded way, a grounded theory of Islamic psychology was developed.

As a result of the methodological procedure in phase one – including data collection, line by line coding, open coding, constant comparison, axial coding, theoretical sampling, and selective coding – an Islamic model of the soul was generated through theoretical integration of the emergent theory (shown in Figure 4.1 in Chapter 4). This resultant model from phase one was then built upon in phase two of the project as participants in that phase were shown the model and were asked to reflect on how it can be interpreted and understood in the context of psychotherapy. Thus, phase two extended the scope of the outcome of phase one by considering the model's therapeutic application with the input from psychotherapists working in clinical contexts. The methodological procedure used in the study, including phase one and phase two, is illustrated in Figure 3.1 below.

In the context of the Islamic tradition, as was illustrated in Chapter 2, there are multiple interpretations of what some may consider to be 'Islamic' as well as variations of how such definitions are realized in practice. Therefore it may be unrealistic to make claims about having produced 'the' theory of Islamic psychology and instead more plausible to represent the outcome of any such attempt as 'a' theory of Islamic psychology. The constructivist approach to grounded theory embraces the notion that what is produced as a result of this research is one possible variation of what could potentially be conceived as Islamic psychologies. Nonetheless the theory developed here was based on a systematic analysis of data generated with well-placed key informants whose expertise in the research topic was based on scholarship and experience. It therefore has credibility and systematicity. As Weed (2017) said "realist approaches will regard the substantive theory generated as 'the truth', whereas

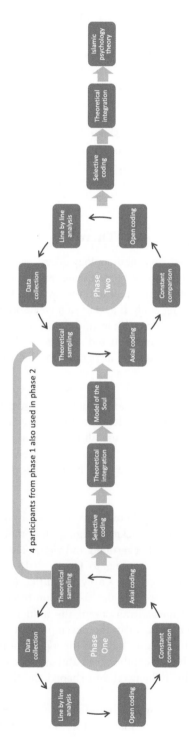

Figure 3.1 Methodological Procedure of the Study.

constructivists will see it as 'a truth' among many" (p. 10). Constructivism assumes that aspects of the substantive theory are not necessarily universal but that some elements of it will be more relevant to some participants than others (Weed, 2017), thus producing a theory that, while accurate and relevant to some, may not hold true for all. The focus in grounded theory work is on capturing and explaining the phenomenon in as much of its diversity and complexity as possible, not on individual people who will only have experience of aspects of the phenomenon. In distinguishing between so-called 'realist' approaches and others, Charmaz (2014) asserts that there is in fact a difference between 'real' and 'true' and says that constructivist grounded theory "remains realist because it addresses human realities and assumes the existence of real worlds" (p. 523).

Representation: Representing 'Us' and 'Them'

The constructivist approach to grounded theory methodology takes a relativist position, acknowledging the constructed nature of human experience and the multiplicity of possible standpoints of both participants and researchers. Thus, it views the participants' input and resulting analysis as part of a collaborative process of constructing and developing theory. While traditional positivist-empiricist research methods often evaluate studies based on their ability to diminish or remove the influence of the researcher, in regards to qualitative methods Coyle (2007) states:

> "The impression may be created that many qualitative methods somehow provide access to the pure and unadulterated subjectivities of research participants. This is not the case because all research products are the result of a dynamic and inescapable interaction between the accounts offered by participants and the interpretive frameworks of the researchers." (p. 20)

Qualitative methods ideally should attempt to acknowledge and take account of the 'speaking position' of the researcher, acknowledging that the researcher's stance, including but not limited to background and viewpoint, will influence the analytic outcome. However, according to Coyle (2016), this attempt is often underwhelming and does not necessarily do justice to the degree to which such positionality interacts with the data. Constructivist grounded theory not only accepts and makes transparent the influence of the researcher but actively embraces it as a factor in the development of the theory. The researcher of the present study is an insider to the topic on three levels; as a practising Muslim, a practising psychotherapist, and as an Islamic psychotherapist. Reflections on how this influenced and shaped the theory construction are offered in Reflection 2.

Whereas classic grounded theory, as practised by both Glaser and Strauss, embodies the rather tokenistic approach to making the stance of the researcher known that is often seen within qualitative research, the constructivist approach, as articulated by Charmaz, puts greater emphasis on the researcher's input in the development of theory. Charmaz (2014) says:

> "In typical grounded theory practice, you follow the leads in your data, as you see them – and constructivist grounded theory takes you one step further. With it, you try to make everyone's vantage points and their implications explicit – yours as well as those of your various participants." (p. 339)

From this approach the traditional line that often gets arbitrarily drawn between participants and researchers is removed as the research design infuses transparency within it by explicitly exploring just how the researcher(s) have impacted and even shaped the emergent theory. The distinction between 'us', the researchers, and 'them', the participants, in this case becomes a utilitarian label to offer clarity about which input is coming from what source rather than to insinuate that only the participants' input makes up the theory while the researchers simply observe and package it.

Providing such delineation and clarity with regards to the collaborative construction of the developed theory is useful for more than just transparency. Charmaz (2014) says:

> "Not only does a constructivist approach help you to remain clear about the antecedents of your constructed theory, this approach helps other researchers and policy-makers to establish the boundaries of the usefulness of your grounded theory and, possibly, to ascertain how and where to modify it." (p. 339)

The constructivist approach takes measures to highlight just where and how the theory developed can faithfully be utilized with most relevance. It allows for potential consumers of such theory to be discerning in terms of the evaluation not just of the quality of the research but of the fit of the research product – the theory – to the appropriate scenario. Given the sensitive and nuanced nature of the religious context that this research topic is situated in and the need for such context, worldview and belief to be taken into consideration carefully, it was evident that the utilization of the constructivist grounded theory approach by a Muslim researcher was a good fit for the methodological approach to the project.

Most research builds upon previously established theory or foundational knowledge and offers a new perspective or new angle or component of a theory, or testing the theory in different contexts and scenarios. In the case of this research topic, there is no previously established theory or even foundational research to build upon within a theoretical framework for an Islamic psychology. Thus the methodological choice of grounded theory was required in order to generate new theory where none exists. This scenario calls for commencing the project at the very beginning, the ontological framework of how the human being is conceived at a foundational level. Only once this has been established can we further theorize about how an Islamic psychology might be applied in psychotherapy. Therefore, the first phase of the study that made up the present research was a grounded theory of the self or soul in an Islamic paradigm. After this was established then a second phase of the grounded theory study was undertaken to develop those theoretical foundations into practical application. In the chapter that follows the findings from the first of those two phases is presented, with the input of 18 scholars of Islam to provide the knowledge and insight from the Islamic tradition to construct an Islamic model of the soul.

References

Abdullah, S. (1999). Islamic counselling and psychotherapy: Trends in theory development. *Annual Review of Islam in South Africa, 2*.

Al-Alwani, T. J. (1993). *Ijtihad.* International Institute of Islamic Thought.

Al-Sharaf, A. (2013). Developing scientific thinking methods and applications in Islamic education. *Education, 3*(11), 272–282.

Annells, M. (1996). Grounded theory method: Philosophical perspectives, paradigm of inquiry, and postmodernism. *Qualitative Health Research, 6*(3), 379–393. https://doi.org/10.1177/104973239600600306

Baggini, J. (2018). *How the world thinks: A global history of philosophy.* Granta Books.

Braun, V., & Clarke, V. (2006). Using thematic analysis in psychology. *Qualitative Research in Psychology, 3*(2), 77–101. https://doi.org/10.1191/1478088706qp063oa

Charmaz, K. (2014). *Constructing grounded theory: A practical guide through qualitative analysis.* Sage Publications.

Coyle, A. (2007). Introduction to qualitative psychological research (1st ed.). In E. Lyons & A. Coyle (Eds.), *Analysing qualitative data in psychology.* SAGE Publications Ltd.

Coyle, A. (2008). Qualitative methods and "the (partly) ineffable" in psychological research on religion and spirituality. *Qualitative Research in Psychology, 5*(1), 56–67. https://doi.org/10.1080/14780880701863583

Coyle, A. (2016). Introduction to qualitative psychological research (2nd ed.). In E. Lyons & A. Coyle (Eds.), *Analysing qualitative data in psychology* (pp. 9–30). SAGE Publications Ltd.

Creswell, J. W. (2007). *Qualitative inquiry and research design: Choosing among five approaches.* Sage Publications, Inc.

Dallos, R., & Draper, R. (2010). *An introduction To family therapy: Systemic theory and practice.* McGraw-Hill Education.

Denzin, N. K., & Lincoln, Y. S. (2011). *The SAGE handbook of qualitative research.* SAGE Publications Ltd.

Gilchrist, V. J. (1992). Key informant interviews. In B. F. Crabtree & W. L. Miller (Eds.), *Doing qualitative research* (pp. 70–89). Sage Publications, Inc.

Glaser, B. G. (1978). *Theoretical sensitivity: Advances in the methodology of grounded theory* (1st ed.). The Sociology Press.

Glaser, B. G. (1992). *Emergence vs forcing: Basics of grounded theory analysis.* Sociology Press.

Glaser, B. G., & Strauss, A. L. (1967). *Discovery of grounded theory: Strategies for qualitative research*. Routledge. https://doi.org/10.4324/9780203793206

Golsworthy, R., & Coyle, A. (1999). Spiritual beliefs and the search for meaning among older adults following partner loss. *Mortality, 4*(1), 21–40. https://doi.org/10.1080/713685964

Harre, R., & Secord, P. F. (1972). *The explanation of social behaviour*. Rowman & Littlefield.

Haverkamp, B. E., & Young, R. A. (2007). Paradigms, purpose, and the role of the literature: formulating a rationale for qualitative investigations. *The Counseling Psychologist, 35*(2), 265–294. https://doi.org/10.1177/0011000006292597

Henwood, K., & Pidgeon, N. (1994). Beyond the qualitative paradigm: A framework for introducing diversity within qualitative psychology. *Journal of Community & Applied Social Psychology, 4*(4), 225–238. https://doi.org/10.1002/casp.2450040403

Johnson, J. C. (1990). *Selecting ethnographic informants* (Vol. 22). Sage Publications, Inc.

Kenny, M., & Fourie, R. (2014). Tracing the history of grounded theory methodology: From formation to fragmentation. *The Qualitative Report; Fort Lauderdale, 19*(52), 1–9.

Lyons, E. (2000). Qualitative data analysis: Data display model. In G. M. Breakwell, S. Hammond, & C. Fife-Schaw (Eds.), *Research methods in psychology* (pp. 269–280). SAGE Publications Ltd.

Madill, A., Jordan, A., & Shirley, C. (2000). Objectivity and reliability in qualitative analysis: Realist, contextualist and radical constructionist epistemologies. *British Journal of Psychology, 91*(1), 1–20. https://doi.org/10.1348/000712600161646

Magaldi-Dopman, D., Park-Taylor, J., & Ponterotto, J. G. (2011). Psychotherapists' spiritual, religious, atheist or agnostic identity and their practice of psychotherapy: A grounded theory study. *Psychotherapy Research, 21*(3), 286–303. https://doi.org/10.1080/10503307.2011.565488

Magesa, L. (2013). *What is not sacred?: African spirituality*. Orbis Books.

Marshall, B., Cardon, P., Poddar, A., & Fontenot, R. (2013). Does sample size matter in qualitative research?: A review of qualitative interviews in is research. *Journal of Computer Information Systems, 54*(1), 11–22. https://doi.org/10.1080/08874417.2013.11645667

Marshall, M. N. (1996). Sampling for qualitative research. *Family Practice, 13*(6), 522–526. https://doi.org/10.1093/fampra/13.6.522

McGregor, S. L. T., & Murnane, J. A. (2010). Paradigm, methodology and method: Intellectual integrity in consumer scholarship. *International Journal of Consumer Studies, 34*(4), 419–427. https://doi.org/10.1111/j.1470-6431.2010.00883.x

Murray, S. A., Kendall, M., Boyd, K., Worth, A., & Benton, T. F. (2004). Exploring the spiritual needs of people dying of lung cancer or heart failure: A prospective qualitative interview study of patients and their carers. *Palliative Medicine, 18*(1), 39–45. https://doi.org/10.1191/0269216304pm837oa

Payne, S. (2016). Grounded theory. In *Analysing qualitative data in psychology* (pp. 119–146). SAGE Publications Ltd.

Potter, K. & Coyle, A. (2017). Psychotherapeutic practitioners' views of the efficacy of mindfulness for the treatment of obsessive compulsive disorder: A qualitative key informant analysis. *European Journal of Psychotherapy & Counselling*, 19(2), 124–140. https://doi.org/10.1080/13642537.2017

Rennie, D. L. (1996). Fifteen years of doing qualitative research on psychotherapy. *British Journal of Guidance & Counselling, 24*(3), 317–327. https://doi.org/10.1080/03069889608253016

Rudi, D., & Ros, D. (2010). *An introduction to family therapy: Systemic theory and practice.* McGraw-Hill Education (UK).

Strauss, A. L., & Corbin, J. (1994). Grounded theory methodology. In *Handbook of qualitative research* (pp. 273–285). Sage Publications, Inc.

Strauss, A. L., & Corbin, J. M. (1990). *Basics of qualitative research: Grounded theory procedures and techniques.* Sage Publications.

Thomas, G., & James, D. (2006). Reinventing grounded theory: Some questions about theory, ground and discovery. *British Educational Research Journal, 32*(6), 767–795. https://doi.org/10.1080/01411920600989412

Walton, J. (1999). Spirituality of patients recovering from an acute myocardial infarction: A grounded theory study. *Journal of Holistic Nursing, 17*(1), 34–53. https://doi.org/10.1177/089801019901700104

Weed, M. (2017). Capturing the essence of grounded theory: The importance of understanding commonalities and variants. *Qualitative Research in Sport, Exercise and Health, 9*(1), 149–156. https://doi.org/10.1080/2159676X.2016.1251701

Willig, C. (2001). *Introducing qualitative research in psychology: Adventures in theory and method.* Open University Press.

Wright, V. L. (2003). A phenomenological exploration of spirituality among African American women recovering from substance abuse. *Archives of Psychiatric Nursing, 17*(4), 173–185. https://doi.org/10.1016/S0883-9417(03)00088-8

Reflection 2: A Believer and a Scholar

Within constructivist grounded theory it is posited that the researcher inevitably brings his or her own epistemological frameworks and various interpretative lenses or predispositions to the analysis. From this approach to research not only are such assumptions and lenses considered an inevitable and indeed necessary component of the research process but researchers are encouraged to make them explicit and to reflect upon the ways in which these commitments have contributed to shaping the research process and the research product. The notion is that the researcher is not simply observing and capturing what is there in some objective, detached way but that she or he is actively constructing the analysis and any theory that comes from it in active dialogue with the data. Accordingly, as part of the grounded theory process, I made memos that included both reflections on the data and the connections I was seeing, and also reflections on how and why I was seeing what I saw.

The very first thing that became clear to me in the process of this research was my belief in Islam and the cosmological paradigm that the religion sets forth. As a believer who is convinced of the truth of the philosophy and revelation in the Islamic tradition, I found it very difficult to write from a purely academic stance which is often characterized both as an attempt to be objective and questioning and deconstructing every potential position. While I did want to approach the research as an academic and for my work to be received with credibility in the academic community, I also had a strong resolve not to compromise my position as a person of faith. I accept that a part of having faith or prescribing to "a faith" is about accepting things that you may not understand or be able to explain. For me, one of the biggest transformations in embracing a religion was a shift in my paradigm which allowed me to actually feel comfortable and confident in fully trusting in a tradition based on a feeling, even though I didn't fully intellectually understand it all.

As both a person raised in a secular culture of relativism and someone who was previously non-religious or areligious, I can appreciate the notion that a person speaking from a place of conviction in faith can often sound naïve or narrow minded, seemingly not allowing her or himself to entertain ideas that are outside their paradigm. And yet now, as a deeply committed and practising religious person, I still have that same sense when it comes to people speaking from their viewpoint. While I have found myself to be a believer in Islam, it apparently did not come at the cost of sacrificing this value of honouring and allowing for different viewpoints. My own stance is that I can both simultaneously have my own convictions about what is "The Truth" and genuinely respect, honour and allow for others' differing positions. I do not feel the need to have others believe what I believe nor do I believe that people with differing beliefs are necessarily lost or gone astray. One of the things that struck me most deeply with the way that I learned Islam was the Islamic principle that only God knows what is in each person's heart and that a non-Muslim could potentially be closer to God than a person who abides by the religion of Islam, all based on the inner state of their heart.

Having said that, I believe what I believe, and that is the epistemological and ontological paradigm of Islam. As a researcher I did not want to deny that about myself and my perspective and felt that I did not have to in order to produce high-quality research in an academic capacity. This is why the constructivist approach to grounded theory seemed most suited to my needs. Not only is it a tool for developing theory where there is no theory, as in the case with my topic, it also allows for and utilizes the stance of the researcher, seeing it not as a potential distraction from truth to be managed and minimized but as a strength to tap into. However, I did not experience that until getting into the analysis of the data, where it was clear that my knowledge of and conviction about the Islamic paradigm was an advantage and helped to draw connections and understand from an insider perspective the complex, interwoven paradigmatic framework that I was trying to elucidate for the purpose of the research aims. Earlier on in the research process my religious convictions certainly did feel like an obstacle which I had to learn how to navigate, as I found my own tendency to make "straw man" arguments that were not grounded in sources but constructed from my own musings of conviction on a given topic. For example making claims that in spite of the diversity of interpretations and approaches to Islam there is an "essence" of what Islam is that justifies using the term "Islamic" without using sources to convey a practical aspect of this sentiment. Through the process of reflection however, I came to see that not only did this not come off as credible or good quality academic work, it was actually not reflective of how I wanted to engage in the discourse. So in place of this "straw man" I did the due diligence to discover what aspects about that statement were founded and demonstrated with the literature how an Islamic Sunni orthodoxy has been established and preserved in the scholarly tradition, which can lead to a legitimate use of the term "Islamic" that actually has meaning.

Thus, this was not only a learning process for me in becoming a good academic, it was a growth experience that helped me to be more congruent with my own values and to find a harmonious balance between my religious convictions and my desire to engage meaningfully in conversations about the human condition with any and all people who share my interest in and passion for understanding and maximizing human potential.

4   An Islamic Model of the Soul: Theoretical Foundations for Islamic Psychology and Psychotherapy

Introduction

The understanding of human nature and the relative conception of structural aspects that make up the human psyche or "soul" determine much of how we make sense of behaviour and motivation and are fundamental to the philosophical underpinnings of theoretical approaches to psychology and psychotherapy (Coon & Mitterer, 2008). It is inappropriate to adopt the theoretical orientations that underpin contemporary Western psychology because most of these have been influenced by concepts of human nature other than those derived from Islam (Delaney & DiClemente, 2005). Thus, as Badri (1979) illustrated, adapting Western models by adding Islamic concepts and terminology is akin to applying a fresh coat of paint to an architecturally unfit structure. Without first constructing a fundamentally distinct conceptual framework of human nature with Islamic integrity, defining the discipline of Islamic psychology in an Islamically meaningful way would be impossible (Mohamed, 1996). While it is argued whether the Islamization of knowledge (Al-Attas, 1978; Al-Faruqi, 1982) is necessary for fields like economics and science, when dealing with subjective experience in the way that psychology does it is important to recognize that an Islamic paradigm maintains significantly different ontological assumptions relative to that of psychology's secular paradigm (Badri, 1979; Haque, 2004). In light of this, rather than merely Islamizing modern secular psychology, this study approaches the task from the perspective that the foundation of the "building" must be solidly laid, by defining an Islamic paradigm of the psyche/soul, upon which the structure can be built, in the form of psychotherapeutic approaches. This will be realized by presenting and analyzing the input of scholars from diverse disciplines of Islamic thought in the form of qualitative interview data and, through this analysis, developing an Islamic model of the soul.

In addressing the need to develop a comprehensive theory within an Islamic epistemological paradigm, Elmessiri (2006) asserts that the project must be a collaborative effort by a team of scholars who organize relevant thought and knowledge in a "creative attempt to apprehend the paradigms implicit in different Islamic texts and phenomena" (p. 68). This range of perspectives is necessary due to the variety of interpretations and definitions of

Islam (Ahmed, 2015; El-Zein, 1977; Mujiburrahman, 2001), as well as the numerous branches of knowledge within the Islamic tradition that offer critical insight and explanation of relevant teachings and concepts in regards to human psychology. Given that Islamic psychology is a highly specialized field with very little academic research and writing and the fact that most of the textual source material is written in Arabic, many of the resources in English relevant to this endeavour exist within the knowledge and experiences of individual practitioners and scholars from a diversity of Islamic disciplines.

This first phase of the study presents a data-grounded, consensual model of the soul from within an Islamic paradigm. Qualitative interviews with a wide range of leading scholars from a multitude of disciplines within the Islamic tradition and with relevance to Islamic psychology provided the necessary input from which to construct a uniquely Islamic paradigm. The research question that underpinned this phase of the study was: "What are the core principles and concepts regarding the conceptualization of the person from within an Islamic paradigm?" The model produced in this phase constitutes the foundation for an Islamic theory of human psychology and Islamic approaches to psychotherapy which are explored in the subsequent phase reported later in this book.

Method

Participants

Participants were sought who had academic or religious expertise related to Islamic conceptions of human psychology and who could therefore act as "key informants", sharing their own views and commenting from their informed positions on the views of others in their field (Gilchrist, 1992). Forty individuals were ultimately identified and were invited to take part. Most were authors of books or articles relevant to the research question but others were identified through personal recommendations and "snowballing". All were experts in their field and many were leading thinkers in topics related to Islamic psychology.

Eighteen people agreed to participate: 17 men and one woman who ranged in age from 39 to 89 years. Participants came from nine countries across four continents. The sample included practising Muslims, non-practising Muslims, and non-Muslims. Five participants were Islamic psychologists involved in research and/or clinical work; four were scholars in Islamic spirituality who were based in academic contexts; three were academic scholars in Islamic philosophy; three were non-academic Islamic religious scholars; three were traditional Islamic spirituality practitioners. Not all participants were recruited at the same time. Instead recruitment occurred progressively in the process of "theoretical sampling" as explained in the discussion of methodology in Chapter Three.

Except for the Islamic psychologists, many participants had little background in psychology and most were not previously familiar with the concept of Islamic psychology per se. While participants with an academic background provided historical and often interdisciplinary perspectives on Islamic thought, participants

Table 4.1 Participant Inclusion Category and Location – Phase 1

Pseudonym	Location	Inclusion Category
Abaas	India	Islamic Psychologists (clinical/research)
Enas	Saudi Arabia	
Hamit	United States of America	
Mustafa	Turkey	
Rahim	United Kingdom	
Kyle	United States of America	Islamic Philosophy Scholars (academic)
Tarkki	United Arab Emirates	
Yahya	South Africa	
Shaykh Khalil	Sudan	Traditional Islamic Spirituality Practitioners
Shaykh Abdalbarr	Saudi Arabia	
Shaykh Aziz	Sudan	
Abdelsalam	United Arab Emirates	Islamic Religious Scholars (non-academic)
Iqbal	United Kingdom	
Yaqoub	United Arab Emirates	
Cesar	United States of America	Islamic Spirituality Scholars (academic)
Gareth	United Kingdom	
John	United Arab Emirates	
Muataz	Canada	

with a traditional religious background were able to provide context to practical applications of such knowledge (Table 4.1).

Data Generation

Data were generated through individual semi-structured interviews conducted by the author/researcher. The interview schedule featured open-ended questions that were developed to elicit participants' personal views and opinions on what might constitute an Islamic psychological understanding of the human being, based on their relevant knowledge and study of related fields. Charmaz (2014) says "by creating open-ended, non-judgmental questions, you encourage unanticipated statements and stories to emerge" (p. 65). Considerable time and attention were paid to constructing an interview schedule that both allowed for rich data to come out of the interaction with the participant and that followed a progressive development of the interview itself. The first part of the schedule posed general questions about participants' relevant work and experience, such as "What is your role in relation to Islamic scholarship?" This was designed to ease the participants into the interview and to develop rapport with the researcher to create a comfortable conversational interaction from the onset in order to set the tone for the participant's willing engagement (Charmaz, 2014). In the second part of the interview schedule, once a comfortable conversation had been established, the topic of an Islamic conception of human psychology was introduced, and the participants' personal stance and ideas were explored without specific direction from the interviewer: for example, "What are the key principles and concepts that might characterize an Islamic conception of psychology?" This part of the interview schedule was designed to elicit the participant's own views on the subject without much leading or direction from the researcher and to allow them to offer insights that may not have been expected or anticipated. The third part of the interview schedule then focused on the particular principles that the participants identified as central, such as "How do virtues and vices come into play in the process of purification of the soul?" At this point in the interview, once the participant had the chance to give input without much influence from the researcher, the questions then became more interactive and reflective of both the ideas brought up by the participant earlier in the interview and/or similar ideas and concepts that came up in previous interviews with other participants (Charmaz, 2014). For example, the researcher may have said "This concept came up in other interviews but with a different explanation. What are your thoughts on this?" The idea of the arc of the interview schedule was to create an atmosphere that enabled rich conversations, allowed for participants to bring their own views to the table, and then interact with those views in the context of the research aims and the nascent grounded theory (Charmaz, 2014).

Analytic Procedure

Transcripts were analyzed using constructivist grounded theory, formulated by Charmaz (2014), as introduced in the previous discussion on methodology.

Results

The analysis produced eight categories relevant to the research question. These categories and the relationships discerned between them constituted a coherent model of the soul, which is presented diagrammatically in Figure 4.1 later in this chapter (it is not presented here because it includes terms that will be introduced in the presentation of analysis). The concepts that make up the categories reflect the participants' reliance on *tafsīr* (exegesis) of the Qur'an and *aḥādīth* in their interview responses, drawing upon writings of both modern and early scholars of Islamic theology and philosophy.

Although diverse insights were offered from different branches of knowledge and variations in interpretation were apparent, there was consensus about the distinct foundational elements of an Islamic conception of the soul. While all eight of the categories were noteworthy, four reflect more foundational aspects of the emergent model, namely "Nature of the soul", "Structure of the soul", "Stages of the soul", and "Development of the soul" (see Table 4.2).

Nature of the Soul

Concept of Fiṭrah

Beginning the task of defining such a vast and abstract concept as a paradigm of human psychology, as this study set out to do, seemed to require starting at the very root of defining the human condition. When asked to express their views, opinions, understandings and interpretations of what the major principles are that might define and characterize an Islamic psychology, all 18 participants identified the concept of *fiṭrah*, which is defined as human nature or natural disposition, as being central to the conceptualization. Abaas said:

> "So, unless we have that knowledge … ah … that what is the nature of man, that God has given us, and a solid knowledge on the concept of *fiṭrah* from an Islamic perspective, I don't think that we would be able to really get to the roots of Islamic psychology."

It was a shared sentiment that in general any psychological theory on humans must begin by stating its conception about what humans are. Yet participants put extra emphasis on the idea that in relation to Islam, the concept of *fiṭrah* is of particular importance in that there is a great deal of focus on this within the Islamic tradition, even though the word *fiṭrah* only appears once in the Qur'an (Q 30:30), as one participant pointed out.

The consensus among participants was that *fiṭrah* posits that all human beings are born with the same, natural, sound nature, which is pure and which comes from and has a direct link to God. Yaqoub explained, "In other words there's an imprint in every human being and that's why Allah says *fatrallah* [nature of Allah]. The *fiṭrah* is an allusion to the original imprint of this *tawḥīd*". The Arabic word *tawḥīd* refers to the oneness of God and the Islamic principle that all things come from and eventually return to God, and are sustained by God. The notion is that all human beings start out in the same pure form with this divine imprint and then his or her parents turn them into a Jew, Christian or Zorastrian etc., according to a *ḥādīth* (saying of the Prophet Muhammed) that was quoted by both John and Iqbal during their interviews.

Participants explained that from the moment of conception, the human being comes hardwired with this pure nature and that time is when the process of corruption begins as the person makes their way through the trials

Table 4.2 Theoretical Categories and Subcategories – Phase 1

Main Categories	Subcategories
Nature of the Soul	Concept of *fiṭrah* Different paradigm – innate goodness Primordial nature of knowing God Becoming out of alignment – *dunya* as distraction *Fiṭrah* exists underneath the projected self *Fiṭrah* as internal compass – realignment
Structure of the Soul	Concept of self, conception of soul Distinct features of the soul Soul as whole – integral nature of the soul *Nafs* (lower self) *Qalb* (heart) • Qalb as centre of the self • Distinct features of the *qalb* • The cognizant heart *'Aql* (intellect) • Lack of distinction between *qalb* and *'aql* • *'Aql* as cognition aspect of *qalb* • *'Aql* needs to be trained *Rūḥ* (spirit) • Concept of *rūḥ* • *Rūḥ* as life breath, life source • Divine nature of the *rūḥ* • *Rūḥ* as access to direct connection to God
Stages of the Soul	Changing nature/fluctuation of the *nafs* Comparison to Freudian model Three main stages Movement through the stages *Nafs al-ammārah bil su* (soul that commands to evil) *Nafs al-lawwāmah* (self reproaching soul) *Nafs al-muṭma'innah* (soul at rest)

Development of the Soul	The human project of development
	 Tazkiyat an nafs (purification of the soul)
	 Jihād an nafs (struggle of the soul)
	 Tahdhīb al-akhlāq (reformation of character)
	 • Need for moral reform
	 • *Muhlikat* and *Munjiyat* (Vices and Virtues)
	    ○ As illness and treatment
	    ○ *Muhlikat*
	    ○ *Munjiyat*

of the *dunya* (temporal world), which begins to distance them from their pure nature. Muataz remarked:

"Before you came in this world there was nobody, right, it wasn't an actualized or localized will and intelligence came from another source, it came from God. From like a spark of light, that divine light. And enters into this world and it acquires certain attributes and then they have to like make sense of this world so it learns intelligence and then acts will."

Muataz went on to say that the human being possesses "intelligence so they can discern truth from falsehood, right from wrong, and then a will so that they can act on what they've been able to discern". Several participants expressed that the human journey from the very beginning is posited in the Islamic paradigm as a process of the human being using their special purpose, and resulting in God-given qualities to uncover and to realize that pure nature and divine spark that the preoccupation with life in the temporal world tends to cover up. Abdelsalam explains the related notion shared by all of the Abrahamic traditions of humans being created "in God's image" by saying:

"Allah *subhana wa ta'ala* [the most glorified, the most high] created man in his image, but what we mean by image here, or his own form, is not like form meaning the physical form but it is form in the sense that he has made us such that we can rule over ourselves."

While most of the participants seemed to agree that the Islamic paradigm views the *fiṭrah* as being innately pure and good, Mustafa points out that there exists some variation on this idea within the Islamic tradition:

"Here we find ourselves facing various interpretations from the holy Qur'an, the Sunnah and the authenticated *aḥādīth* of our Beloved Prophet and the Islamic scholarly heritage of our early scholars. For example, our Islamic theory will stress the spiritual and the physical and animalistic nature of man. But does this combination of mud and God's Divine breath result in a creature with a good nature or *fiṭrah* that can be distorted by parents and evil environmental influences or is he born with a neutral nature that has the freedom of choice to accept Islam or kufr [unbelief]?"

Different Paradigm – Innate Goodness

Regardless of which interpretation of *fiṭrah* one settles on, with regards to it being neutral or innately good, participants made it clear that it is distinctly different from the widely accepted notion of human nature that has influenced Western psychology. In remarking on this aspect, and in referring to humans in general, Tarkki said:

"They have everything that they need to sort of be in an appropriate kind of dialogue and relation with their environment both, both natural and sort of human/social. That's a sort of a given and it certainly stands in marked contrast to the sort of the Christian theories of the fall and so on and so forth."

Tarkki's use of the phrase "Christian theories of the fall" is in reference to "the fall of man", a term used in Christian theological thought to refer to Adam and Eve's "fall" from innocence and obedience to blameworthiness and disobedience (Williams, 1927). While the Western psychological paradigm is not necessarily overtly Christian in its outlook, there has been a great deal of speculation, including by those who participated in this study, that indeed modern psychology is influenced by the Judeo-Christian tradition particularly with regards to ideas of human nature (Delaney & DiClemente, 2005). Yahya pointed out how this marked contrast also extends beyond what would be considered 'Western' by saying, "in Islam we have *tawḥīd*, which is the concept of the transcendent God and that's what makes innate human nature in Islam distinctly different from the Eastern philosophies such as Confucianism".

Primordial Nature of Knowing God

One aspect of *fiṭrah* that seemed to be significant for most of the participants was the idea that within this natural state of the human there exists a primordial nature of knowing God. In relation to this, 12 of the participants referenced a passage in the Qur'an which explains that before humans come into this world God asks all souls "Am I not your Lord" (Q 7:172) and they say "yes, we witness", witnessing God's reality and thus their natural state is to know God. John said:

"In its natural state, the human being is observing its covenant with God. A covenant that was made before time, and living as an *abd Allah*, a servant of God. And it is a *Moahed*, one that believes in the oneness of God."

John went on to explain that because of this deeper part of ourselves that knows God we are somehow naturally drawn back to that knowledge, or as Rahim described it, that there is "a force inside the self that pulls us back towards Allah *subhana wa ta'ala* [the most glorified, the most high]". And in Abdelsalam's words, "we have this primordial disposition to want to know Him so he is building us to that, and that's how we are hardwired".

Becoming Out of Alignment – Dunya as Distraction

A common theme for participants in describing the *fiṭrah* was to connect it directly with the idea that we all naturally become swayed away from that natural disposition and become out of alignment with that naturally pure self. This was primarily understood to be a result of our predicament here in this world within the *dunya*. Life in the *dunya* is considered to be a temporary state of existence where God's reality is hidden from humans and instead of witnessing the reality of *tawḥīd*, we perceive duality and separation as a part of this material world where we exist in perceived separation from God. Iqbal said, "The modern world has basically knocked us out of sync with our bodies and we're so out of tune with our very nature". This idea is that essentially in between the pre-existence state of witnessing and knowing God and the *akhirah* (afterlife) where humans again are open to the awareness of God's reality, people become distracted with the life in the *dunya* and forget about God. Muataz said:

> "It's very difficult especially amongst us contemporary people because there are so many devices that distract us, there's our phones, right, 'ding ding ding' everything and then there's just the images that we've created of ourselves through, usually through social media, things like this that like compound in our soul. Now we're trying to get at this like more primordial part of our selves but there are like literally layers and layers and layers of just problems."

He went on to say "It's a veil like or something that's like just literally blocking what should be there".

Participants seemed to agree that the primary reason for psychological problems that we acquire is this misalignment. Thus, the project of human life from an Islamic paradigm is attempting to realign with *fiṭrah*. Yahya asserted "Your psychological state has to be harmonious, your psyche, your mind ... has to be harmonious with your *fiṭrah*".

Fiṭrah Exists Underneath the Projected Self

The state of distraction in the *dunya* was not seen as one that is necessarily doomed to such misalignment with *fiṭrah*, nor was it seen as impossible to get back to or uncover that *fiṭrah* state. Participants made reference to the clear understanding that humans never actually lose their essence of that divine spark, that it exists always within the soul, even if deep inside hidden from the person. John explained:

> "Surat Al-Qiyamah 75, ... it says, truly the human being bears witness to himself as a nature, even if he is giving excuses, no sorry, no matter what excuses he gives. It's like, you know deep down you actually know, and that we could say lends to the *fiṭrah*. The *fiṭrah* that you are actually, inside, deep inside yourself, you actually have that knowledge."

In other words, the idea is that we may be out of touch with our knowledge of and witnessing of God, but we always have the ability to get back to it.

Fiṭrah as Internal Compass – Realignment

It was understood by all participants that humans all possess the natural ability and an innate pull to get back to and realign with our *fiṭrah*, to at least some degree, as if to say we have an internal compass that points back to our primordial nature of recognizing God's oneness. According to Yahya, "We are naturally inclined towards *tawḥīd* because we come from Allah". Thus we can use our intelligence and will, to draw on Muataz's point discussed earlier, to make choices that refocus our attention on God amidst the distractions and pulls towards the *dunya*. From the Islamic perspective, as conveyed by participants, aligning one's intentions and actions with the path of life that has been outlined in the Islamic tradition, one can come increasingly more aligned with their *fiṭrah*.

As Tarkki put it, "Living in some kind of-of communion with God and in line with God's commandments actually brings a deeper sense of satisfaction also in terms of actually corresponding to our-our psychological needs".

The Islamic tradition, including God's commandments in the Qur'an as well as the lessons, wisdom and advice learned from *aḥādīth* and Qur'anic *tafsīr* (exegesis) etc., was seen as the direction or map for coming back into alignment. In reference to the physical activities specifically recommended by the Prophet Muhammed (archery, swimming, horseback riding) Rahim said, "because these in particular exercises have deeper effects. You know, balance … putting things in their right order".

Structure of the Soul

Equally central to the conceptualization of the person from within an Islamic paradigm as the concept of *fiṭrah* was the discussion of the various elements that make up the soul. All 18 participants in this first phase of the study spoke extensively about the various aspects of the *nafs* when asked what the most central concepts are in an Islamic psychological understanding of the human being. The Arabic word *nafs* is sometimes translated as soul and is used to refer to the whole soul of the human being. However, in Arabic literature, as well as in the Qur'an, the same word *nafs* is also used to refer to what most closely resembles the English words self, psyche, or ego. Whereas the Islamic conception of the person is a complex one, it is important to distinguish these different meanings and their context, as it helps to illuminate the Islamic understanding of the human being.

Conception of Self, Conception of Soul

"The sort of basic models and basic ways of conceptualizing the self. That's the basis of psychology: how do we see the self" This statement by Rahim echoes most participants' view of why the concept of the *nafs* is central to Islamic psychology. However, while many of the participants often used the word 'self' in reference to the concept of *nafs*, Mustafa offered an important distinction:

> "The term *nafs* is very different from 'self' since the former is a spiritual entity and the latter is a nonspiritual concept. The term 'self' as used in modern psychology is an immaterial complex psychological concept but *nafs* in Islam refers to a real spiritual being inhabiting our physical body; it is the soul."

Mustafa went on to say that from within the Islamic paradigm, "all humans have souls that give them consciousness and motivate their good or sinful behaviour.

Materialists who do not believe in a spiritual existence have invented the construct of 'self' to describe the feelings generated by their unbelieving soul'".

Distinct Features of the Soul

It became clear through the responses from most participants that although there have been many Islamic scholars, like Ibn Sina and others, who have written and explained the concept of the soul and its make up as understood from the Islamic tradition, the famous 12th century scholar Abu Hamid al-Ghazali perhaps provided the most detailed explanation of the structure of the soul. In al-Ghazali's major work the *Iḥyāʾ ʿUlūm al-Dīn* (The Revival of the Religious Sciences), as discussed in Chapter 2, he distinguished the various features of the soul and how they relate to an understanding of human psychology. In reference to this Enas said, "He talked about what is the *nafs*, the *qalb* (heart) and the *rūḥ* (spirit) and what needs to be done when working on each of them. It is like a diagram". Here is where the distinction of the word *nafs* becomes important in that when referring to these four (sometimes three) aspects of the soul, the word *nafs* is referring to the lower self, similar to the Freudian term "ego". These different aspects represent various functions inside the human being that interact with one another in the process of the struggle within the human being to get back to or uncover the *fiṭrah* as discussed above. In reference to al-Ghazali's mapping of these features Mustafa said, "according to his model, every human being has forces of good and evil fighting in the battleground of his or her soul".

Soul as a Whole – Integral Nature of the Soul

While all of the participants described these distinct features of the soul, they all made it clear that they are integrated parts of the whole soul of the human being, and not separate entities. As Rahim described it:

> "Everything is integrated together in the self. So the body parts and the energies of the self, we don't make a division between body and mind and soul as you find in the Western thinking. They're different but they're integrated. They serve a purpose together."

It was a common understanding that while al-Ghazali did speak of these distinct aspects of the soul and used these terms to describe those different functions, he also at times used these terms interchangeably. As Tarkki said, "The *nafs*, *rūḥ*, *qalb*, *ʿaql*. So it's sort of those being equivalent expressions". And similarly, Kyle pointed out that "There's one place where al-Ghazali says these are just four different terms for the same thing". But what seemed to be the consensus among participants was that the soul is conceived as one whole entity and thus these terms ultimately are referring to that whole soul. But that it is useful for the process of mapping out and understanding the make-up and function of the soul to speak of various aspects using such distinguishing terminology, much of which is used in the Qur'an itself.

Nafs (Lower Self)

As mentioned earlier, in the case of describing the four distinct aspects of the soul, the term *nafs* is used here to refer to the lower self, similar to the id, in that it is the part of the soul that has base desires and urges. This is a central focus in any discussion of psychology because it is much of what people are struggling with and that is blocking them from their *fitrah*, as Yahya describes:

> "In Islamic psychology the key concept is the *nafs*. The *fitrah* of course defines human nature in its very essence but the *nafs* is what emerges after birth, the element of evil, psychological evil. Or you have the cosmic evil in the form of *Shaytān*. But at the psychological level we have this tendency towards greed, towards power, towards lust and so on."

While the *nafs* is often equated with the ego and/or the id, Hamit asserted that it is not quite the same and said that the Freudian concept of ego was influenced by the Christian concept that the animalistic aspect of the human being is inherently evil and thus perhaps untrainable. He said, "The *nafs* is from the Islamic perspective, not evil in and of itself. Um, rather it inclines, it's it's not trained, and in its untrained state can be hedonistic".

Most of the participants identified the *nafs* as the most problematic part of the soul in that it is the mechanism that pulls us towards *dunya* distractions and self-satisfaction and thus away from *fitrah* and awareness of God. The *nafs* then is the part of the soul that must be worked on and reformed. Cesar said:

> "The *nafs* is sort of unlike the *rūḥ* in that it's generally undesirable. It's not that, I mean you need it to live, it's you, but I'm saying it's generally like morally blameworthy. So that the *nafs* is only ... the only good *nafs* is an obedient... *nafs*."

As Cesar points out, the *nafs* is part of the soul and thus natural but from the Islamic perspective we do not want to simply allow the *nafs* to do as it pleases because this will keep us from growing to our potential and our true inner nature. As Mustafa pointed out, "It is true that sex and aggression and hostility are innate characteristics of humans, but man is not a slave of these impulses nor can these impulses explain all his noble and unearthly spiritual aspirations".

Qalb (Heart)

Qalb As Centre of the Self

The Arabic word *qalb* means 'heart'. It is generally related to the physical piece of flesh in the body that regulates the flow of blood, but that biological organ is not what is referred to when using the word *qalb* in the context of the structure of the soul. Here it is referred to the spiritual centre of the human being, which, as Rahim pointed out, is distinct from Western concepts of the self:

> "The nature of the spiritual centre of the human being. A term I prefer to use is *qalb*, which is widely understood as the inner heart. Something you could relate to Jung's understanding of the inner self, and which was not found in any major school of Western psychology or therapy. Jung is pretty marginal, and particularly Jung in its traditional school, or form."

Several participants made reference to Jungian psychology as being perhaps the closest form of Western psychology to that of an Islamic perspective, but all made the distinction that Jung's ideas were similar, but not entirely the same. The *qalb* is understood to have many dynamic aspects to it and can thus be considered the "heart" of an Islamic framework for psychology.

Participants agreed that the *qalb* becomes a central focus of the Islamic anatomy of the soul. As Muataz said, "I think if we focus on the heart as the locus of Islamic psychological attention, that is the one term that these authors usually use in any of their taxonomy". Here Muataz is referring to the fact that at times some classical authors of the Islamic religious sciences use these terms interchangeably and at times the *qalb* is used as the word to refer to the whole integrated inner soul of the person. Considering this, Muataz went on to say, "If there were to be just one way of just kind of localizing all of that is we would call it, well, the science of the heart".

In further distinguishing between Western and Islamic conceptions of the workings of the inner person, Gareth said, "In Western psychology there is a general belief that the mind is completely separate and that's what governs things, whereas in the Islamic tradition the whole idea is that it's the heart ... that thinks even". Here Gareth alludes to the notion that the heart includes more faculties than perhaps just feeling and emotion, many of which are represented in the other terms for the soul. He goes on to say, "so there's these kind of terminological things that need to be kind of sorted out".

Distinct Features of the Qalb

The *qalb* was described by many of the participants to be the intermediary between the *nafs*, as the lower part of the self, and the *rūḥ*, as the higher part of the self. Cesar explains it as such:

> "The *qalb* is that part of ... is the human entity of human self or that facet of the self that, that vacillates between *nafs* and *rūḥ*. Between you know the callings of the body and the callings of the *nafs* and on the other hand the higher light of the *rūḥ*. And it its vacillation is part of its being the *qalb* because the *qalb* you know has *taqalab*, it moves, it rotates."

Cesar is here referring to the root of the Arabic word *qalb*, which means "to turn". Other participants also used this to highlight the specific function of the *qalb* in that it can either turn towards God, via the aspect of the soul called the *rūḥ*, or turn towards *Shayṭān*, via the *nafs*. The relative direction it turns corresponds to the intentions and actions that a person makes to either remember its *fiṭrah* and the knowledge of God, or remain veiled from God and focus on self-satisfaction and worldly affairs only.

The *qalb* was also described by many participants as having an innate capacity to perceive things on a deeper level than a rational capacity. As John explained:

> "The soul, due to its fluctuations and not being in tune with the heart, and it being inclined more towards the world is preventing us from hearing that and seeing that correctly. And thus we are not seeing something as the term that al-Ghazali uses and everyone uses *kama hya*, "as they are". Just as they are in and of themselves. So the heart is that thing that can see things as they are in and of themselves."

Thus, the *qalb* was understood by participants to have the ability to regulate the human being and be an active part of the process of aligning with the *fiṭrah*.

The Cognizant Heart

As alluded to above, many of the participants specified that the *qalb* has an element to it that houses the consciousness of the human being. Abaas referenced a term that beautifully describes this aspect, "the *qalb* and the heart, or the cognisant heart – the *irada*". Muataz further illustrated the idea of consciousness being located in the heart in referring to some of the writings of early Islamic scholars:

> "What they mean by the heart, they really mean the roots of human consciousness. And that you find in every religious tradition, that same idea that there's this kind of like essential vital part of the human being in their body called the heart and it corresponds to the essential vital part of the cosmos, which is its heart, which is the root of consciousness."

He went on to explain that God is the source of that cosmic consciousness: "God is supreme consciousness and awareness and so human beings they are just manifestations of that much more primordial consciousness".

Participants made a distinction between this cosmic consciousness that is connected to God, and the faculty of rationality which is often attributed to the mind in Western thinking. The distinction was described by most as being connected to this aspect of the *qalb* that can turn. Thus while the cognition aspect of the soul sits within the heart, because of this turning nature it can either be connected to that pure God consciousness or a cognitive apparatus which utilizes sensory perception and rationality to make sense of experiences. The latter is what is usually referred to as the *'aql*, but which most participants agreed is not necessarily a distinct feature of the soul but housed within the *qalb*. As Rahim explained it, "The deeper part of *'aql*, which is the articulator of what comes into the heart. Which understands and reflects. Probably as near as you could define it, a sort of where consciousness is". So, while the *qalb* was perceived to ultimately be where cognition and consciousness happen, the importance of the distinct feature of the *'aql* is that if the person does not have *taqwā* (God consciousness), the rational faculty can lead them astray and remain caught in the separation from God, subsumed only in the realm of the material, temporal world. In this regard John remarked, "The mind can actually lead us very very very far astray from the heart". Here in referring to the mind, John is making reference to the specific distinction of the *'aql*.

'Aql (Intellect)

Lack of Distinction between Qalb and 'Aql

Almost all of the participants clarified that although they were referring to the *'aql* separately, as did scholars like al-Ghazali, in actuality it is part of the *qalb* or a function of the *qalb*. As Yahya said:

"Al-Ghazali talks about the *'aql* and the *qalb* it's almost synonymous. Whereas the *'aql* in Aristotle is mainly rationality, for al-Ghazali it's the *qalb* and the *'aql*, they are you know together. It's sort of almost like one. Right. So the *'aql* is the *qalb* and the *qalb* is the *'aql*, in that sense."

Yahya went on to provide an example from the Qur'an to illustrate this:

"Qur'an says, '*la in qulbun la aqliun*', you see, '*ya bun qulub un ya aqilun*': they have hearts by which they ... by which they ... reason. '*ya aqiluna*', from *'aql*. Qur'an doesn't use the word *'aql*. But it uses the verb *yaaqiluna*, to reason. Intellection: to apply intellect, apply reason, to apply the intellect. It uses the verb, you know, but it uses the *qalb* as a noun. You see what I mean. But the intellect is very important, because it just shows in Islam, you know, in Islamic philosophy, in Islamic mystical thought, in Islam itself. I mean, the Intellect plays an important role and I think it's emphasized by Imam al-Ghazali."

So, the identification of the *'aql* as a specific aspect of the *qalb* becomes an important distinction for participants by virtue of this nature of intellection, or cognition and its significance in the anatomy of the soul.

'Aql As Cognition Aspect of Qalb

Many participants spoke about the rational function of the *qalb* as being the *'aql* where the cognitive function of the person takes place. Hamit said, "There's an element of cognition in *'aql* and cognitive processing that exists within the Islamic tradition". That cognitive processing that Hamit refers to is not entirely about reason, as would be attributed to the mind in Western thought. In reference to the roots of this conception of the rational mind, in Greek philosophy, Tarkki explains where the Islamic conception, as interpreted by al-Ghazali, differs from a Western one:

> "What the philosophers do… they think that the highest part of our soul, what they thought first called *'aql;* intellect. Intellect is dealing with sort of figuring out the science, that sort of the rational order of the visible universe. Almost more or less into some syllogistic logical shape. Al-Ghazali thinks that the philosophers, oddly enough, aren't aiming high enough. He thinks that there is a part of our rational soul that is actually receptive to the divine attributes which are, in some ways, produce a deeper sense of satisfaction and are located higher in the actual ontological order of reality."

Here the distinction that Tarkki points out is that the rational faculty or cognitive functioning can perceive things based on experiences in the material world, which is useful and necessary, but which limits the person and can potentially lead to misconception or not perceiving the truth of a thing or circumstance, whereas the higher capacity of the *qalb*, to "intellect" the truth is a function of its ability to access the divine reality and thus the truth as known by God. While most participants used the word *'aql* to refer to both types of "intellecting", John made a further clarification and said that pure rationality without the "intellecting" of the heart as referenced in the Qur'an "would not be *'aql*, it would be a corrupted mental understanding". John then described how this ability to perceive things in their true reality is contingent on the state of the *qalb*:

> "The heart can perceive those realities when it's healthy. As the Qur'an says: "Do they not have hearts with which they see? Do they not have hearts with which they intellect?' The heart sees, the heart hears, right? Our hearing outwardly is one thing. But when that message that we hear is properly interpreted the heart is hearing, when that message that we hear is not properly interpreted the heart is not hearing in a sense."

Thus, according to John and other participants, in order to allow for the *qalb* to perceive things as they are in reality, the *'aql* must be trained.

'Aql Needs to Be Trained

Most participants asserted that the *'aql* is seen as being in need of reform, that it is not something to be left alone to reason on its own otherwise it will lead the person astray. Yahya said:

> "The *'aql* or the *qalb* has to be trained. The *qalb* must be purified, the *'aql* must be… And this is where we are different from Aristotle because the *'aql* is guided by the Qur'an and the *sunnah*. The *'aql* must be guided by divine guidance."

Most participants talked about the process of training the *'aql* as one of the main avenues that is employed in the process of reforming the soul. Essentially the point is that the *'aql* is pivotal in reforming the *nafs* and shifting the focus of the heart, utilizing its turning nature, to point towards or focus on and open to the *rūḥ* instead of the *nafs*.

Rūḥ (Spirit)

Concept of Rūḥ

Many participants agreed that perhaps what distinguishes an Islamic paradigm of the human being most clearly from Western conceptions is the concept of the *rūḥ*. *Rūḥ* is defined as 'spirit', but more poignantly it is the aspect of the soul that directly connects to and can receive knowledge from God. Abdelsalam said:

> "From Islamic perspective, you can say there is something that comes from outside this world which is the *rūḥ*, and the *rūḥ* is the part that Allah, *subhana wa t'ala* [the most glorified, the most high], is giving us to know Him back … to know him through. And that is when we say that we're hardwired with … and that's where the *fiṭrah* comes."

Most participants understood the *rūḥ* to be a divine element that is in the human soul. Abdelsalam went on to say that the *rūḥ* "comes from Allah and that is the big difference and that sets us apart from the rest of the animal world or the rest of creation. So, in this aspect, that is sort of divine or comes from the divine".

Rūḥ As Life Breath, Life Source

The *rūḥ* is also conceived as the life source, which further defines it as a direct connection to God, as in the Qur'an there is reference to the force of life within the human being coming literally directly from God, as Gareth explained:

> "So there's this other element to it as well. Which is kind of more, one might say, almost fundamental to humanity, this idea of the life source.

But then again, it's that life source that animates, which was that divine breath that was blown into Adam. [Recites Qur'an verse 15:29 in Arabic.] Before that Adam was just clay, he was an inanimate object. But when Allah breathed into him that's when he became a human being."

So according to Gareth and other participants, the *rūḥ* then becomes a fundamental aspect of what makes a human being a human being. It is perceived as being tied into the creation of humankind and thus integral to the defining of human existence. Cesar also expands on this concept:

"The *rūḥ* seems to be such an important part of Adam's existence as Adam and his...occupation of the, let's say you can call it, the status of being *khalifa tullah*, the representative of God Himself. The *rūḥ* seems to be such an important part of that, that it's kind of you see it almost in an ironic way missed by *iblis* [the devil], right. When he ... judges Adam and says you know ... *khaluktu min nar*, 'I'm made of fire and he's made of clay'. Well he's not made of just clay, right, there's the *rūḥ*. This is what's missing from the equation and it seems to be that's the secret part of it."

Divine Nature of the Rūḥ

As mentioned earlier, the *rūḥ* was described by participants as being divine in nature and, because of this, it was talked about as being different than the other elements of the soul in that it does not change. Whereas the other aspects have the ability to change and turn one direction or the other, the *rūḥ* is conceived as the pure part of the soul which is what is at the core of the *fiṭrah*. Cesar explained it by saying:

"The *rūḥ* doesn't become dirty or clean or that thing it only becomes sort of crowded or clouded really by the, by the pursuits of the *nafs*. The *nafs* has an ability to kind of cover up the *rūḥ* so that really with the *rūḥ* it's about polishing and clearing and letting the light, letting the *rūḥ* itself shine. The *rūḥ* doesn't change in nature."

Gareth made reference to the fact that when the pure nature of the soul is referenced in the Qur'an, the word *rūḥ* is used instead of *nafs*. Therefore, it was thought by many that the *rūḥ* represents the part of the soul that humans are trying to get back to, which leads back to God. As John said, "The *rūḥ* is in a sense thought to be a naturally inclined towards God".

Rūḥ As Access to Direct Connection to God

This divine nature inside the human soul was explained by many participants to be the reason that humans have the potential to know God while living in the distraction and veiling of life in the *dunya* and that the fact that the *rūḥ* is always there inside the soul allows for the possibility of connecting to God directly. John said, "The *rūḥ* is turned towards Allah, *subhanahu wataala*, at all times. But that connection can remain dormant in a sense for a lot of people". Here John is referring to the connection being dormant in the event that a person does not cleanse their *nafs* by redirecting the *qalb* to turn towards the *rūḥ*. Thus, in this sense, the potential for maximizing the divine qualities of the human being lies in the process of aligning these elements of the soul to open the channels for connecting to God. In describing what happens if a person succeeds in this process of alignment, John eloquently illustrated it in this way:

> "Then it's like the light of Allah, *subhanahu wataala*, shines into the *rūḥ* and through the *rūḥ* shines unto the heart and from the heart shines unto the soul. And then everything is in a sense, you know, lined up in accord with [Allah]."

While participants expressed that from the Islamic perspective this is ultimately the goal of the project of humanity, to strive towards this alignment in this life, it is a difficult process and one that is not linear nor sequential but that often involves cycling through stages.

Stages of the Soul

Changing Nature / Fluctuation of the Nafs

Another central idea that almost all participants referenced when asked about the central components or principles in an Islamic conceptualization of the soul was the idea that the soul has different stages of development that it goes through. Whereas participants specified that the *rūḥ* does not change, the other aspects of the soul are seen as the parts that go through stages. Sometimes in this context the *nafs* is thought to represent the whole soul. However, given this distinctive unchanging nature of the *rūḥ*, what is really meant by *nafs* in the context of the stages is the lower part of the self that was identified earlier. Yahya explains this dynamic:

> "The stages of the *nafs* indicate the constantly changing nature of the *nafs* and how they are always in a state of flux, always subject to change and that is why we need to be diligent and have things in place to keep them aligned on the right path. The *nafs* never reaches a static place and is ok in this life. It is always open to changing at any given moment. *Nafs* as dynamic."

Comparison to Freudian Model

Perhaps because of the common number of three, or perhaps just due to the fact that people tend to like to draw comparisons, several participants pointed out that often people attempt to equate the three main stage of the *nafs* to Freud's three-part conceptualization of the psyche as ego, superego, and id. But as Enas clarified, "They are similar to some extent to ego, superego and id but they are not the same". Yahya articulated where people often draw these comparisons:

> "There are three levels of the soul: an *nafs al-ammārah*, which is the animal soul or the soul that is inclined towards the ego, towards instinct, probably equivalent to the id, with Freud. Then we have the *an-nafs al-lawwāmah*, which is your conscience, your moral compass. Right. But for Freud he'll call it the superego, right. Freud doesn't have that... the higher level which is *an-nafs al-muṭma'innah*, the tranquil self".

Three Main Stages

There was quite a bit of variety of opinion among participants as to just how many stages of the soul there are. Abaas referred to there being four stages, Abdelsalam said he has read from various scholars that there are six or seven, and Shaykh Khalil asserted that there are seven:

> "The soul is divided into seven ranks, which are continuous classification for each class of the souls ending by the beginning of the next class till reaching, for example, the well pleasing soul [*nafs ar radiyya*] and well pleased soul [*nafs al mardiyyah*]... So, it is divided into classes."

Much of the reason for this discrepancy is because, as all of these participants recognized, all of the stages identified in addition to the three main ones are part of a more nuanced spiritual understanding of the soul as expanded on by the spiritual elite within the Islamic tradition. All participants however agreed that the main stages are most important and are clearly known to be *nafs al-ammārah bil su*, *nafs al-lawwāmah*, and *nafs al-muṭma'innah*. As Gareth explained:

> "Clearly in the Qur'anic paradigm there are three levels of the soul: *ammārah bil su*, which would be the soul that inclines to evil, which is in *surat* Yaqoub. And the soul which is *lawwāmah*, which is blaming itself, is self-reproaching – 'why did I do that?' Which is a different level of awareness from the first one obviously, because the first one is perceived to be completely self-obsessed. And the second one is 'Well, I know I did a mistake, but I don't know how to fix it.' And then the third one which is *nafs al-muṭma'innah*, which is I believe in *surat* Balad, which is this kind of elevated form of the soul and which is really the objective of purification because that's the one that enters paradise, enters into the pleasure of God, that is both pleased with God and God is pleased with it. And ultimately will enter into the ranks of the righteous."

Movement through the Stages

The stages were explained by all participants who mentioned them to be about the development of the soul throughout its life in the *dunya*. This seemed to exemplify an inextricable link between the make-up of the soul and the inevitable trajectory towards growth, or movement through the stages. While these stages were described as elements within the anatomy of the soul, a person does not necessarily move through them without some effort. It seems then that the Islamic paradigm posits the human condition as a trajectory towards such growth as a natural part of the soul's existence or purpose. Thus, if one accepts the challenge of working on his or her *nafs*, the lower part of the soul, to achieve increasing levels of alignment with the *fiṭrah*, the objective becomes to strive towards the highest stage of the soul. Shaykh Khalil explained this objective:

> "All these types of souls should be eradicated to reach the final stage which is the perfect soul which the Prophet got – blessings and peace from Allah be upon him, the perfect soul, the well pleasing soul and the well pleased soul."

While the expectation is not that one will actually reach the final perfected stage, the goal is set high in order to posit continual striving throughout one's life. All participants agreed that no one will reach the level of the Prophet, who was considered to have a perfected soul, but that few can get near to that state, and all can achieve increasing levels of purity relative to their particular state. However, this trajectory of the soul's growth towards purification was not seen as linear. In other words, a person is understood to cycle through these stages, not necessarily in successive progression always. John described this by saying, "You can be in that state for a minute, you can be in that state for years. And then you can go all the way back down to the soul that commands to evil. Here is the big problem".

Nafs al-ammārah bil su (Soul That Commands to Evil)

The first stage of the soul was described as being a state where a person is essentially following all of their base desires. In this stage, there is no sense of moral awareness or feeling of regret and shame. A person is simply consumed with satisfying their selfish impulses. Therefore, although it is called 'The soul that inclines to evil', it is not necessarily doing evil to others nor is it necessarily obvious evils. Yaqoub explained by saying:

> "There's another verse that says 'I did not make excuses for the *nafs*' ... *ina nafs al-ammārah bil su*, the soul that commands to *su*. *Su* is often translated as 'evil', the soul that commands to evil. So, this is now a trajectory that once you have an egoic identity this sense of me, ego literally means me. The *su*, the evilness, isn't the quite clear evilness that we'd all agreed is evilness, it's the

evilness premised on the state of individuation. Because that was a primal transgression so most humanity is in that, right, there is a natural sense of me."

Here Yaqoub is pointing out that in the Islamic paradigm there is an inherent evilness in forgetting God and becoming subsumed with the self only. People in this stage often only think of themselves and can often attribute all actions to their own will, therefore forgetting God's omnipotence and the Divine will.

Nafs al-lawwāmah (Self Reproaching Soul)

The second stage of the soul is where by a person is able to recognize their faults and bring in the awareness that allows for reform of the *nafs*. Enas said, "Allah talked about the self-reproaching soul and swore by it because this type of soul is like a guard for the human that does not allow negative issues to remain persistent". The function of the *nafs al-lawwāmah* that does not allow for those issues to persist is that the soul becomes suspicious of itself and accentuates feelings of guilt for behaviour and thoughts that go against the *fiṭrah*. Yaqoub explains how the meaning of the Arabic word *lawm* connects to this idea:

"*Lawm* actually means to stop castigating, stop pointing out there's something wrong. So what does that mean... that's indicating that this stage now is a kind of a step back to actually start seeing that self that is commanding to evil, to see how does that operate – which means that there actually the Islamic paradigm is positing the idea of self-awareness."

Many of the participants talked about the *nafs al-lawwāmah* as being the stage of the soul where the process of growth and transformation takes place. It is the middle ground between the soul being consumed by *dunya* and separation from God, in a state of *ghafla* (forgetfulness of God), and the soul being completely aware of God and living in the state of *fiṭrah*. Therefore, it is within this stage where most of the work is being done by a person to reform their soul. Yaqoub explains how this happens in this process:

"How does the *lawwāmah* get better? Allah says *kul ja al haqq wa za haqq al batin;* the truth comes and *batil*, falsehood, perishes *in al batil kana zaman* because falsehood by its nature has to perish but it will only perish when you bring truth to it. So that it's actually a gentle process, the gentle process is constantly bringing truth to your being. Bring truth... that every time you see the things, bring the truth to it, right, and the truth will naturally bring a transformative element."

Nafs al-muṭma'innah (Soul at Rest)

The third or final stage of the soul's development was conceived by participants as being one which is rare for a person to achieve but that people often can get glimpses of it, as they can cross into it for periods, if not staying there for very long. It was understood that in order for a person to achieve the state of the soul that lives in this stage, in most cases they would have to have done quite a great deal of self-struggle and psycho-spiritual work on themselves. This process of self-development would then lead to a deep sense of peace and contentment, as Muataz said, "The soul that's at peace with itself". This is why *nafs al-muṭma'innah* is called the soul that is at rest, and as John indicated, "That soul that is at rest is the one that actually turns towards the heart and serving the heart".

The *nafs al-muṭma'innah* was envisaged by many participants to be when the soul is in a constant state of having its *qalb* turned towards the *rūḥ* and no longer turning towards the *nafs*, or engaging in the animalistic drives of the lower self. It is the soul that has been purified. Yaqoub described how this process happens and the mechanisms that bring forth such contentment:

> "You start getting content because the more you spot the falsity the more contentment comes. Because you now realized the truth that you were not through yourself, you were, as the Qur'an says, *umakum aynankum*, 'He's with you wherever you are'."

Yaqoub describes this notion of God always being with one as "with-ness" and further explains:

> "That with-ness becomes more apparent gradually, right. And with that with-ness comes the contentment, *ala bi thikrillahi tat ma'ayna qulub*, 'is it not through the remembering of Allah', the remembering that He's always with you, 'that the hearts finally find rest'. So, the more of that contentment starts coming the more there is this natural *nafs al-muṭma'innah* that comes. You go from *ammārah bi su, al-lawwāmah, nafs al-muṭma'innah*. Now you're coming closer to the return, the return in what was a sense of separation and in reality you could never be separated from Allah, it's the *waham* [illusion], nothing separated you except delusion."

So, for Yaqoub and several other participants, the object of purification then is to reach closer to the stage of *muṭma'innah*, and strive for this deeper and deeper realization of God's *tawḥīd*, the divine unity which the soul comes from and will eventually return to.

Development of the Soul

The Human Project of Development

In the conception of the structure of the soul and understanding the make-up of the human being and human nature from a psychological point of view, it was almost impossible for most of the participants not to equate this knowledge directly with the process of purification of the soul. Several participants pointed out that the Islamic paradigm of understanding the human being views the purpose of human life as an opportunity to purify the soul and many described it as a project of development, to uncover the *fiṭrah* inside by purifying the *nafs*. Thus, as both Rahim and Abdelsalam specifically pointed out, any conception of an Islamic psychology would necessarily involve this purification process, and that it would be absurd to envision a study of psychology without it. Rahim said, "It's a more complete existence. It's not focused on just getting people back into the capitalist system for instance, and just defining human functioning as being productive in a material sense", pointing out that a Western approach to psychology will seldom include the state of the soul in the treatment plan.

Another idea that Abdelsalam presented was that an Islamic perspective would not have any use for the study of the soul without a direct link to treatment. He said:

> "So it is not just the study of psychology but the process of cleansing, the process of cleaning, making the mirror shine. You know the *nafs* is like a mirror and it is turbid and it needs to reflect the light of the divine, you know, and it's turbid full of dirt. So these are all benefit for the study, so it is not just like studying the *nafs* for the sake of the *nafs*."

He went on to draw the analogy of the study of anatomy versus the treatment of illness in the body, and that an Islamic perspective of psychology is inextricably linked to the process of cleansing the soul. He then pointed out that the terms *'ilm an nafs* (knowledge of the soul) or *fiqh an nafs* (deep knowledge of the soul), as Yahya said al-Ghazali used, are more about the study of the structure of the soul, while *tazkiyat an nafs* (purification of the soul) was traditionally just viewed as a practical way of living and is more about putting that knowledge into application, or the process of shining the mirror.

Tazkiyat an Nafs (Purification of the Soul)

Almost all participants used this metaphor of shining a mirror in reference to doing work on the soul to clean the heart and uncover the *fiṭrah*. The usefulness of this metaphor seemed to be that it exemplifies the idea that the purity or light that one is attempting to shine is not their own, but that an individual's soul can be a reflection of the divine light if cleaned and polished of the crust that accumulates from the illusion of separation from life in the *dunya*. In reference to this Cesar said, "The *nafs* has an ability to kind of cover up the *rūḥ* so that really with the *rūḥ* it's about polishing and clearing and letting the light, letting the *rūḥ* itself shine". One term commonly used in reference to this cleaning process is *tazkiyat an nafs*, as referenced above.

Tazkiyat an nafs can be seen as a deep process of inner work to purify and perfect the soul to allow it to shine in its highest state, the essence of that higher state being the *rūḥ*. Both Shaykh Abdalbarr and Shaykh Aziz described this process as a higher level of purification and attributed it to a person perfecting their intentions and actions by doing things like extra worship in addition to what is required at the minimal level. This can thus be seen as a more advanced form of work of polishing the mirror to be as clean as possible. This however is a higher spiritual state than most people will achieve in life, closer to the stage of *nafs al-muṭma'innah*. In reference to the writings of the 9th century Islamic philosopher al Harith al Muhasibi, who was influential in the development of an Islamic conception of psychology, Gareth explained that:

> "He focuses on the undeveloped form of the soul. So, in other words, you know, the whole idea of purification takes one to the highest level – the *nafs al-muṭma'innah*, or the tranquil, serene soul. But he doesn't really focus on that. He focuses on what your soul is like now, in its kind of general state – what most people experience. That's his main focus, I think that's important."

Several participants talked about that which is of relevance to the majority of people as they struggle to simply chip away at the crust covering the mirror, rather than polishing an already mostly uncovered reflection. This more fundamental process was commonly referred to as *jihād an nafs* (struggle of the soul).

Jihād an Nafs (Struggle of the Soul)

The main focus for most of the participants in asking them to conceive of an Islamic paradigm of the person in relation to psychology was that it primarily entails struggling against the powerful influence of the *nafs* in the process of trying to come back in alignment with *fiṭrah*. This is essentially what is at the heart of the *deen* (religion) of Islam and what much of the commentary on the Qur'an expands upon. As Yahya pointed out, in reference to the scholars who wrote those Qur'anic commentaries, "It's the *mujāhadah*, the struggle over the *nafs*, it's back to psychology. It's just that they don't call it psychology … we're calling it psychology". He then went on to say:

> "Islamic psychology is to do with those *nafs*, the *jihād*. The *mujāhadah* – the struggle over the *nafs*. Because when we struggle… because the *nafs* is this… is sort of influenced by certain contingent happenings from the environment from our instincts or from environmental influences that cause us to deviate from *fiṭrah*."

This struggle involves looking at the state of the soul and being self-reflective. Therefore, it only happens within the stage of *nafs al-lawwāmah*, when the person is able to have self-reproach. In reflecting on the self, as John said, "It's thought that one would find out where one's weaknesses lie. And one has to deal with them". The *jihād* then is not simply about fighting against the *nafs*; rather it involves a constructive response to the discovery of faults.

It was explained by many that the act of dealing with the weakness, lower impulses or bad character traits involves training the *nafs* and following the guidance from the Islamic tradition as a map to the desired outcome. Hamit said, "We believe foundationally that there's a training process, that the training process entails that one try to bring one's *nafs* or self in conformity with the Islamic tradition". Yahya said, "and that's why we need Qur'an and Sunnah – to guide us on to that path, to bring us back to our state of *fiṭrah*". Thus, the religious obligations and advice from the Qur'an and the example of the Prophet Muhammed were explained by all participants to be seen within an Islamic paradigm of psychology as being the sort of treatment for the *nafs* in the process of reform. Whereas this guidance is in the form of a holistic, all-encompassing path of life and one that is embarked upon over the course of a lifetime, it was not conceived of as an easy fix. In explaining this process of conforming to the guidance from the Islamic tradition, Hamit said, "That's not an easy process to begin and at the beginning that's not gonna feel very natural, and it's normal to allow for that discomfort ... towards the discipline of formulating the *nafs*".

Tahdhīb al-akhlāq (Reformation of Character)

Need for Moral Reform

Whereas Western psychology does not necessarily have one defined, universal set of moral guidelines to hold people to or encourage alignment with, an Islamic psychology necessarily involves the moral framework and guidance set out by the Qur'an and Sunnah as the benchmark for human ideals. In reference to the Western model, Hamit said, "It's relativistic...there's all 'small t's', there's no 'big T'. It's whatever you really feel inclined towards and that we trust that human inclination". The "t" that Hamit is referring to here is "truth". In other words, from this paradigm of secular generality, everyone's own truth (small t) is potentially equally valid, with no universal or objective truth (big T) that people are expected to be held accountable to. Many participants talked about the need for moral reform, for a person to work on improving their character, as an integral part of what must happen in the stage of *nafs al-lawwāmah*, in the path of aligning with *fiṭrah* and striving towards the stage of *nafs al-muṭma'innah*.

In talking about this need for moral reform in the Islamic conception of human psychology, Tarkki referenced the importance of some of the early classical scholars of Islamic philosophy and their "treatises in moral philosophy, with people like Yahya Ibn Ali or Miskaweh, each of whom produced a work called the reformation of morals or the ... sort of the improvement of character, *tahdhīb al-akhlāq*". *Tahdhīb al-akhlāq* literally means the reformation or refinement of character and, similar to *tazkiyat an nafs* and *jihād an nafs*, involves working on the *nafs*. The distinction with *tahdhīb al-akhlāq* however is that it is specifically about redirecting blameworthy character traits and adopting praiseworthy ones. This involves, again, redirecting away from what the *nafs* want, with the assumption that those desires are generally not what is best for the person. As Cesar put it, "With the uncontrollable, insatiable, you know, desires the human beings have can lead to tremendous moral problems". Participants specified that these inclinations are not seen as psychological deficiencies in the person but as normal characteristics of the uncontrolled *nafs*. John said, "It's understanding these as not just fissures of the psyche but inclinations of the *nafs* and treating them on that level as inclinations of the *nafs*". Similarly, Yaqoub pointed out that this view does not cause the person to identify with a diagnosis and perceive it to be static but instead to view it as a passing state that has a known treatment.

Muhlikat and Munjiyat (Vices and Virtues)

As Illness and Treatment

The Greek philosophy tradition of virtue ethics, as explored by the likes of Plato and Aristotle, and the connected field of moral psychology was influential in the development of discourse on human psychology by classical Islamic scholars. Tarkki argued that, "Al-Ghazali is far more focused than any other author I know up to that point ... in trying to figure out what the systematic bases for our various shortcomings, psychological shortcomings, would be ... so the moral psychology aspect". Many of the participants, particularly those that have an academic orientation to the study of Islamic philosophy and spirituality and the history of such thought, recognized the significant contribution that Islamic scholars like al-Ghazali offered to the field of moral psychology. Gareth pointed out that while these scholars took some ideas directly from Greek philosophy, they had a different orientation to the application and purpose of such knowledge. He said, "They're really looking at it from the paradigm of what is the method to get you out of these character traits and get into the character traits that you should have that will make you purified". So, vice and virtue, in the Islamic context, become specifically about illness and treatment in the process of purifying the soul.

Almost all of the participants who spoke in detail about the process of *tahdhīb al-akhlāq* identified al-Ghazali's contribution as being most significant in that he developed a systematic framework for the treatments of these illnesses of the soul, in his discussions on the *muhlikat* (vices) and *munjiyat* (virtues). In describing al-Ghazali's system Abdelsalam said, "The *munjiyat* are the things that help you to get to your goal, but the *muhlikat* are the things that keep you away from your goal". Often the cure for a certain *muhlikah* (vice) is its opposite in the form of a *munjiah* (virtue), as Abdelsalam went on to say, "because to rule with justice you need to get rid of *zulm* [injustice], which is the opposite to justice". Not only did al-Ghazali give an exhaustive list of illnesses, or *muhlikat*, and their treatments, or *munjiyat*, he also outlined a programme for how to go about treating each one. This is found particularly in book three of his *Iḥyā' 'Ulūm al-Dīn*.

Muhlikat

Participants described the *muhlikat* as natural tendencies within the *nafs* of the human being which pull a person towards the lower part of the self and a downward trajectory in the realm of *dunya* and the forces of *shayṭān*. Yahya said, "At the psychological level we have this tendency towards greed, towards power, towards lust and so on". Often many of these destructive character traits are conceived of as appetites of the *nafs*. Tarkki said:

> "Appetites and the spirited part of our soul in various ways have to do with our more selfish impulses … but at the same time they…don't allow for an alignment of the way we live our lives with the sort of larger order of the universe or of reality and of course that's detrimental to us ourselves."

These appetites were understood as distractions from alignment with our *fiṭrah* and as things to be systematically broken and eradicated. In discussing al-Ghazali's writing on the *muhlikat*, Kyle said that "He talks about breaking the appetite of hunger … pursuing a strategy to try to break hunger's hold on us".

In addition to base bodily desires such as hunger, al-Ghazali gives a great deal of attention to vices of the heart, where the *nafs* influence the *qalb* and infect it with things like greed, envy, or anger, a trait which gets an entire chapter of its own in al-Ghazali's *Iḥyā' 'Ulūm al-Dīn* due to its apparent centrality in the downfall of human character. Also given a great deal of focus is the general tendency for human beings to think highly of themselves and be selfish. Tarkki described the danger in this:

> "The desire for status and or whether it's sort of superiority over our neighbours or just feeling good about ourselves or sort of papering over our shortcomings, or failure to want to own up to them, and so on, that that leads to us even to sort of aim for the wrong kinds of things in life and to be reticent about going to any kind of hard work in genuinely improving ourselves."

Munjiyat

The *munjiyat* were described by participants as the Godly qualities that are a part of our birthright within our *fiṭrah* and connected to the *rūḥ* aspect of the soul. Thereby when we adopt these character traits as treatments for the illnesses of our *nafs*, we get closer to embodying that innate Godly nature within and, as Abdelsalam pointed out, this is where we can access our higher purpose as human beings as *khalifahtullah* (vice-gerent of God). In referring to what is meant by the Biblical as well as Qur'anic saying that humans were created in God's form, Abdelsalam explains that "He has made us such that we can rule over ourselves and over … you know … with the same justice and wisdom". Thus, by demonstrating these qualities sincerely and authentically, we elevate our status and move upward on the trajectory towards *nafs al-muṭma'innah*.

The *munjiyat* as set forth by al-Ghazali and others are for the most part directly taken from Platonic and Aristotelean thought and the "cardinal virtues". In reference to this, as well as the similarly adopted Platonic tripartite model of the soul, Yahya relates that "From the three faculties, you have four cardinal virtues; ... wisdom – *hikma*, justice – *adl*, temperance – *iffah*, temperance come from the control of your desire, and then you have courage which is *shuja'*, it comes from the control of your emotions". Al-Ghazali then added to these Platonic/Aristotelean virtues additional Islamic virtues, which St. Thomas Aquinas, who lived around the same time as al-Ghazali in the 12th century, adopted. Yahya explains this saying, "He saw al-Ghazali's synthesis with Aristotle and he tried to do the same thing for Christianity... and he added the additional virtues like hope and charity and so on". By pursuing these *munjiyat* it was understood by participants that this becomes a vehicle for moving "up and up and up in the ladder of development", as Abdelsalam put it, this being the focus of human existence in the *dunya* and therefore the focus of an Islamic perspective of the psychology of the person.

An Islamic Model of the Soul

The theoretical model presented in this phase of the study and illustrated in Figure 4.1 was developed from the participants' consensual understanding of the nature, structure and development of the soul as it relates to human psychology from the Islamic tradition. According to this theory, the human soul has an innately pure and good nature, *fitrah*, that comes from and is connected to God but that becomes covered over and forgotten as a natural part of life in the *dunya*. Throughout its life in the *dunya* within the soul there exists a dynamic interplay of conflicting forces that affect the psychological state of the person and determines relative levels of alignment or misalignment with *fitrah*. (This process is represented by the purple elements in the middle of the model in Figure 4.1).

The *qalb*, which is the spiritual centre of the person and where the faculty of intellect is located as the *'aql*, has the potential to turn in either of two directions which shapes the relative, transient outcome of this conflict. It can turn towards the lower impulses of the *nafs* and become further misaligned with *fitrah* by the influences of the *dunya* and *shaytān*, resulting in increased negative characteristics of the *muhlikat* and a state of *ghafla*. (This process is represented by the red elements towards the bottom half of the model in Figure 4.1). Or it can turn towards the higher, Godly nature of the *rūḥ* with the remembrance of *Allah* and the *akhirah*, resulting in increased positive characteristics of the *munjiyat* and come more in alignment with the soul's state of *fitrah*. (This process is represented by the blue elements towards the top half of the model in Figure 4.1).

The relative state of the soul in relation to either of these two poles at any one time is articulated in three distinct stages of the soul's development throughout life in the *dunya*, namely: *nafs al-ammārah bil su*, *nafs al-lawwāmah*, and *nafs al-muṭma'innah* (see Table 4.3 for a list of key terms used in Figure 4.1). This theory posits that the soul has an inherent inclination towards growth,

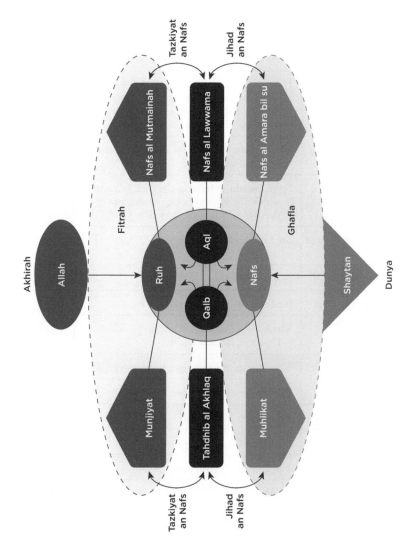

Figure 4.1 An Islamic Model of the Soul.

Table 4.3 Key Terms (English Definitions from Figure 4.1)

Transliteration	English Translation	Arabic term
Akhira	Afterlife	آخرة
Allah	God (literally "the God")	الله
Fiṭrah	Human nature/natural disposition	فطرة
Nafs	Soul (sometimes in reference to the soul in entirety, and sometimes in reference to the lower part of the soul, similar to the concept of ego)	نفس
Qalb	Heart (usually in reference to the spiritual centre of the human being, including the faculty of reason which is sometimes singularly referred to as 'aql)	قلب
'Aql	Intellect (the faculty of reason that is an aspect of the qalb)	عقل
Rūḥ	Spirit (usually in reference to the Divine spark within the human being, or the aspect of the soul which is connected to God)	روح
Nafs al-ammārah bil su	Soul that inclines to evil	نفس الامارة بالسوء
Nafs al-lawwāmah	Self-accusing soul	نفس اللّوامة
Nafs al-muṭma'innah	Soul at rest	نفس المطمئنة
Munjiyat	Virtues (for example; Wisdom, Justice, Courage, Temperance)	منجيات
Muhlikat	Vices (for example; Anger, Envy, Greed, Lust)	مهلكات
Tahdhīb al-akhlāq	Reformation of character	تهذيب الأخلاق
Tazkiyat an Nafs	Purification of the soul	النفس تزكية
Jihād an Nafs	Struggle of the soul	النفس جهاد
Ghafla	Forgetfulness/heedlessness of God	غفلة
Shayṭān	Devil	شيطان
Dunya	Temporal world	دنيا

and an upward trajectory in relation to the model illustrated in Figure 4.1, due to its primordial nature of knowing God, and that the Islamic tradition, as guided by the Qur'an and Sunnah, encourages and maps out a path for the human being to pursue this trajectory. This is demonstrated in the description of processes along the path that act as mechanisms for exerting effort in the dynamic interplay within the soul as it struggles between the two opposing forces, namely: *jihād an nafs, tahdhīb al-akhlāq,* and *tazkiyat an nafs.* These mechanisms have particular relevance to application in psychotherapy, which will be further explored in the second phase of the study reported over the course of the following two chapters. Findings will be discussed in Chapter 7 alongside the findings from the second phase, as the phases have been conceptualized as two parts of an integrated whole.

References

Ahmed, S. (2015). *What Is Islam?: The importance of being Islamic.* Princeton University Press.

Al-Attas, S. M. N. (1978). *Islam and secularism.* Muslim Youth Movement Of Malaysia.

Al-Faruqi, I. R. (1982). *Islamization of knowledge.* International Institute of Islamic Thought.

Al-Ghazali, A. H. (2014). *Imam Al-Ghazali Mukhtasar Ihya Ulum Ad-din* (2nd ed.). Spohr Publishers.

Badri, M. (1979). *The dilemma of Muslim psychologists.* MWH London.

Charmaz, K. (2014). *Constructing grounded theory: A practical guide through qualitative analysis.* Sage Publications.

Coon, D., & Mitterer, J. O. (2008). *Introduction to psychology: Gateways to mind and behavior* (12th ed.). Wadsworth Publishing.

Delaney, H. D., & DiClemente, C. C. (2005). Psychology's roots: A brief history of the influence of Judeo-Christian perspectives. In W. R. Miller & H. D. Delaney (Eds.), *Judeo-Christian perspectives on psychology: Human nature, motivation and change* (pp. 31–54). American Psychological Association.

Elmessiri, E. A. M. (2006). *Epistemological bias in the physical & social sciences* (A. M. Elmessiri, Ed.). International Institute of Islamic Thought.

El-Zein, A. H. (1977). Beyond ideology and theology: The search for the anthropology of Islam. *Annual Review of Anthropology, 6,* 227–254.

Gilchrist, V. J. (1992). Key informant interviews. In B. F. Crabtree & W. L. Miller (Eds.), *Doing qualitative research* (pp. 70–89). Sage Publications, Inc.

Glaser, B. G., & Strauss, A. L. (1967). *Discovery of grounded theory: Strategies for qualitative research.* Routledge. https://doi.org/10.4324/9780203793206

Haque, A. (2004). Psychology from Islamic perspective: Contributions of early Muslim scholars and challenges to contemporary Muslim psychologists. *Journal of Religion and Health, 4,* 357.

Mohamed, Y. (1996). *Fiṭrah: The Islamic concept of human nature.* Ta-Ha Publishers.

Mujiburrahman. (2001). The phenomenological approach in Islamic studies: An overview of a Western attempt to understand Islam. *Muslim World, 91*(3/4), 425–450. https://doi.org/10.1111/j.1478-1913.2001.tb03725.x

Payne, S. (2016). Grounded theory. In *Analysing qualitative data in psychology* (pp. 119–146). SAGE Publications Ltd.

Williams, N. P. (1927). *The ideas of the fall and of original sin: A historical and critical study.* Longmans, Green and co.

Reflection 3: In the Field: A Finite Pool of Clinicians and a Sea of Reluctant Scholars

One of the most challenging parts of my research was the fieldwork, particularly the data generation process. As per the grounded theory approach, data are generated through the dynamic interaction between the researcher and participants. This meant that my ability to generate data was dependent on the cooperation of others, who were often not as motivated as me to engage in an analytic conversation at a specified time and place while being recorded. I found that it took much longer than I expected to track people down, get them to agree to participate, and then actually follow through with scheduling a time and place to do this favour for me within their busy schedules. One thing I learned early on is that people don't like to be recorded; they seem to worry that it could get used against them or just that their words will get used out of context. I was sensitive to this because I myself have the same reaction to being recorded.

I had thought that the interviewing process would be as simple as selecting who fitted the sample criteria, contacting them and then interviewing them. While this was (relatively speaking) more how it was with the second phase (with clinicians who integrate Islamic principles into the psychotherapeutic practice), it was most challenging with participants in the first phase, that is, with scholars of Islam. Given my position as an insider to psychology and specifically to Islamically integrated psychotherapy, I in the same field as the potential participants of phase two, also, due to the nature of the emerging field and therefore the relatively small number of practitioners, I had at least some familiarity with most of the pool of potential participants for phase two. For instance, in some cases I had been a contributor to an edited volume on Islamic psychotherapy to which they had also contributed or I had spoken at a conference where they had also spoken. On the other hand, given that I am not a scholar of Islam, I had much less connection to the sample pool for phase one which meant that it took much longer to identify the appropriate people.

I think I wound up with more rejections than acceptances of my invitations to Islamic scholars. Some simply did not respond to the invitation and some declined based on unavailability. But what I found most interesting was that several scholars claimed that they could not possibly contribute something relevant or worthwhile to a discussion of psychology. Some of these scholars seemed to feel that there was no connection between Islamic studies and psychology, while others felt that they could not competently speak to the psychological aspects of Islamic principles. In one instance I even found myself trying to convince a scholar that indeed he had something valuable to contribute, assuring him that I had read his work and had specifically selected him based on this. I even quoted where he had used the term 'Islamic psychology' in one of his books! Through experiences like this, I came to ascertain that there was a range of reasons why these scholars were reluctant to speak on the topic. One was a desire to stay in their lane when it comes to their area of expertise, perhaps connected with the fear of being recorded and potentially saying something unfounded or inaccurate. One was a total lack of familiarity with the notion that there even could be a connection between Islam and psychology. Another was a presumption of the approach to the topic based in a rejection of the idea that Islam should be compared to Western notions of psychology or made to fit within narrowly defined constructs that separate psychology from the rest of Islamic knowledge.

While many of the scholars who did accept the invitation did so willingly and enthusiastically, I found that more often than not I needed to put extra effort into making them feel comfortable with me and my intentions with the research. For this reason, I did most of the interviews in the first phase in person, face to face with the participant, even if that meant traveling to another country to do so. This was very different than the second phase where, due to the already established familiarity with the topic, it was easy to build rapport and therefore not as necessary to do interviews in person if it wasn't convenient. For phase two I did a majority of the 18 interviews by video conference and found it not to be an impediment. It was the opposite with phase one where only three of the 18 interviews were done via video conference, and even in those few I felt it impacted my ability to generate rich data.

Once I was able to break through these barriers and successfully built rapport with the scholars in phase one, it allowed for the interviews to flow in a way that elicited the type of conversation that generated rich data. Making the effort to go to them and meet them in person helped, as well as having some more time in those instances to explain my research intentions, a bit about myself and my history and get the chance to let them get a sense of who I am. In reflecting on the way those interviews took shape, I am aware that the relative orientation of the scholars changed the feel of the interview as well as the type of data that were generated from/with them. Scholars whose orientation to Islamic studies was purely academic, some of whom were not Muslim, offered a great deal of information about the various philosophical perspectives and historical contexts and how the relevant Islamic knowledge fits within the history of thought in the area as well as the larger Islamic cosmology. Scholars whose orientation to Islamic studies was focused more on the nature of the soul tended to speak a lot about Sufism but from a removed stance, often reporting on what "Sufi authors" wrote about. These scholars seemed to have a deep appreciation for Sufism and a great deal of knowledge but less experiential knowledge that gave insight into how their scholarly knowledge of texts is applied in Islamic spiritual tradition from a lived perspective.

It was the Sufi shaykhs whom I interviewed that were able to draw upon the actual reality of how the philosophical concepts provide guidance for a person on a path of development. While it was clear that these men possessed an incredibly deep understanding of both the inner and outer knowledge, they tended not to articulate it in nearly as much depth and clarity as the academic scholars who studied Sufism. These shaykhs answered my questions often with very simple and straightforward remarks, seemingly without much depth. This could be due to the nature of their orientation, perhaps not being academics and thus not being accustomed to overly verbose discourse. However, given that some of them are or were professors or scholars at one time, I wondered whether there was another reason for this. Perhaps it could be because they are accustomed to preserving deeper knowledge for the initiated or only specifically for those to whom certain knowledge is applicable. Whereas academics tended to explain things in terms of what makes sense and the 'why' behind such knowledge and concepts, Sufi shaykhs tended to speak solely from within the Islamic paradigm without feeling the need to contextualize concepts as they relate to other philosophies or religious traditions. These men tended to put things in simpler terms, almost as if speaking in parables, much of which I didn't fully comprehend until later on when I was poring over the transcripts and reading them over and over again to make contextual references and linkages with other Islamic principles that the academic scholars had contributed. It was as if their accounts, as well as their presence in emulating the concepts, provided the perspective that highlighted the experiential aspect of the knowledge of the soul, and the idea that the knowledge of the soul cannot truly be known through the study of books but by sitting with those who have traversed the path of development of the soul.

5 The Nature and Structure of the Soul: Therapeutic Conceptualizations in Islamic Psychotherapy

Introduction

Within the development of the Islam and psychology movement (Kaplick & Skinner, 2017) an area that has received perhaps even less attention than the construction of theoretical foundations of an Islamic paradigm of psychology is that of uniquely Islamic therapeutic approaches to psychotherapy. In Haque, Khan, Keshavarzi, & Rothman's (2016) survey of research in the field from the previous ten years, they found that out of the five categories that studies fit into, the domain that had the least amount of contributions was what they called the "development of interventions and techniques within Islamic psychology" (Haque et al., 2016). This category had only a few studies that put forth an attempt at both proposing a basic framework and offering some suggestions on how those concepts might be translated into therapeutic interventions (Abdullah et al., 2013; Keshavarzi & Haque, 2013; Naz & Khalily, 2015). The dearth of research in this area is likely due to the fact that in order to truly conceive of and construct clinical psychotherapeutic approaches that are unique to an Islamic framework, the theoretical framework from which to conceptualize such interventions must first be more fully established.

Michie, Johnston, Francis, Hardeman, and Eccles (2008) identified three reasons why a theoretical model is needed to inform the development of psychotherapeutic interventions. The first reason they identified is that "interventions are likely to be more effective if they target causal determinants of behaviour and behaviour change" (p. 662); thus it is necessary to understand how and why change is affected from within the theoretical framework. The second reason was that "theory can be tested and developed by evaluations of interventions only if those interventions and evaluations are theoretically informed" (p. 662). The third reason Michie et al. (2008) identified was that "theory-based interventions facilitate an understanding of what works and thus are a basis for developing better theory across different contexts, populations, and behaviours" (p. 662). Therefore it is crucial for the "development of interventions and techniques within Islamic psychology" (Haque et al., 2016) to be constructed from an articulate theory of Islamic psychology and not simply through improvised attempts to adapt Western theories with

Islamic principles. The second phase of the study in this research approaches that task by building upon the theoretical model constructed from the data in the first phase and conceptualizing therapeutic techniques and interventions based on that model. This will be realized by presenting and analyzing the input of psychotherapy practitioners who integrate Islamic principles in their clinical work in the form of qualitative interview data and, through this analysis, developing a therapeutic conceptualization of Islamic psychotherapy.

The phase of the study presented in this chapter and in the next chapter offers a data-grounded, consensual model of Islamic psychotherapy based on the Islamic model of the soul presented in the previous chapter. Qualitative interviews with a range of psychotherapists from diverse backgrounds provided the necessary input with which to construct a theoretical conceptualization of Islamic psychotherapy. The research question that underpinned this phase was: "How is the Islamic model of the soul conceptualized into a psychotherapeutic approach?" The models produced in this phase, and presented in this and the subsequent chapter, constitute a theory of Islamic psychotherapy.

Method

Participants

In this phase participants were sought who integrate Islamic conceptions of human psychology into their practice of psychotherapy and who could therefore act as "key informants" (Gilchrist, 1992). Twenty five individuals were identified as practising within an Islamic orientation, relative to their own understanding of and claim to that, and were invited to take part. Most were known by the researcher to be self-identified as 'Islamic psychotherapists' but others were identified through personal recommendations and "snowballing". All were trained in some form of Western therapeutic modality (shown in Table 5.1) and some had training specific to Islamic psychology. For this phase of the study the potential pool of participants was much smaller and therefore easier to identify than in the preceding phase due to the rarity of practitioners who integrate an Islamic paradigm of psychology versus the large number of Muslim psychotherapists who practise only within a secular Western model. Four of the participants from phase one were also participants in phase two based on their meeting the inclusion criteria for both phases, namely that they were both academic scholars of Islamic psychology and practising psychotherapists who believed that they integrate Islamic principles into their work with clients. (These participants are identified by a star next to their name in the list of participants in Table 5.1).

Eighteen people agreed to participate: 12 men and six women who ranged in age from 26 to 89 years, with a mean age of 46. Participants came from six countries across four continents. The sample consisted entirely of practising Muslims. Six participants practised Western therapy in an Islamic context and integrated Islamic principles and concepts in an *ad hoc* way, based on their own interpretation and connections with secular approaches, only engaging

Table 5.1 Participant Groups, Training, and Location – Phase 2

Pseudonym	Location	Training (self-descriptions)	Participant Group
Fatima	United States of America	Relational, CBT	Improvised integration of Islamic principles into Western therapeutic approaches
Maha	United States of America	Person-centred, CBT, mindfulness	
Matthew	United States of America	Humanistic, somatic, existential	
Obaid	Qatar	Neuropsychology, clinical psych	
Safa	United States of America	Eclectic	Levels of the soul engaged: Nafs, 'Aql
Siraj	United Kingdom	CBT	
Firas	United States of America	CBT, clinical psych	Deliberate integration of the Islamic model of the soul to inform uniquely Islamic therapeutic approaches
Hind	United States of America	CBT, person-centred	
*Hamit	United States of America	EFT	
Kabir	United States of America	Humanistic, existential, CBT	
Mahmoud	United Kingdom	CBT, psychodynamic	
Rayyan	Turkey	Humanistic	Levels of the soul engaged: Nafs, 'Aql, Qalb
Samir	United Kingdom	Eclectic	
Shahid	United Kingdom	Psychoanalytic	
*Enas	Saudi Arabia	Eclectic	Active engagement of all levels of the soul guided by traditional Islamic spiritual healing practices
Harun	United States of America	Somatic	
*Mustafa	Sudan	Clinical psych	
*Rahim	United Kingdom	Psychodynamic	Levels of the soul engaged: Nafs, 'Aql, Qalb, Rūḥ

the first two (sometimes three) levels of the soul.; eight had Islamic religious education and used this in a more deliberate way to draw connections with scholarly frameworks in the context of psychotherapy within a uniquely Islamic paradigm, engaging the first three (sometimes four) levels of the soul; four practised psychotherapy in a uniquely Islamic indigenous approach and did so within the framework and guidance of traditional Islamic spiritual teachings, engaging all four levels of the soul. A list of participants identified by pseudonym, the geographic location where they practice, their relevant training in psychotherapy orientation, and the relative participant group that they fall under can be found in Table 5.1.

Participants in group one represented an approach to psychotherapy in an Islamic context which appears to be more commonly practised within the field of Muslim mental health. However these six participants represent a more pronounced intention to be working within an Islamic framework than the majority of Muslim practitioners in the field (as noted in Chapter 2). Even in this case, however, the study found that most in this category were more aspirational towards such a model without in fact actually practising in any overtly uniquely Islamic way. For many of these participants, it was not until they were engaged in the process of the interview for this phase of the study that they realized that they are not in fact operating from as fundamentally Islamic a way as they had thought. This was because many of them had not realized exactly what is involved in or what differentiates an Islamic paradigm of psychology from a Western one.

Those in group two, who had Islamic knowledge training, claimed that this is what is necessary to be able to do Islamic psychology. However they did not necessarily actively incorporate a process of *tazkiyah* into their clinical practice, either due to lack of personal experience with it themselves or lack of understanding of how or if it has a place within a psychology/psychotherapy context. Most participants within this category, although possessing more Islamic knowledge and training, were still working on their own for the most part in attempting to then stretch from the theological knowledge to psychological application. Thus to some degree participants in groups one and two remained in the territory of fusing Islamic teaching onto a generally Western framework, with the second group getting much closer to actual integration.

However those in group three, who had actual training in *tazkiyat an nafs* and were working primarily from within an Islamic spiritual framework of treating the soul, seemed to have a more explicit way of working with the Psychology from Islamic sources without having to do as much interpreting because it was already formulated within the traditional practice of Islamic spiritual healing. In these cases the participants seemed actually to be integrating the Western psychology concepts and methods to strengthen the traditional approach and make it more relevant to a Western context, where psychology is perceived as something separate from other aspects of religion and health. This group most closely resembled a uniquely indigenous approach to psychotherapy, but it was the smallest in participant numbers of any of the groups, demonstrating the rarity of such an approach and pointing to where it seems this study found the most need for development.

Data Generation

Data were generated through individual semi-structured interviews conducted by the researcher. The interview schedule featured open-ended questions that were developed to elicit participants' sharing of their personal practice and experience regarding how they integrate Islamic principles into psychotherapy in their own therapeutic practice. At this stage of the interview participants were not shown the Islamic model of the soul that was generated in phase one. The researcher asked participants to explain their approach, and their personal experience and ideas were explored without specific direction from the interviewer: for example, "What approaches do you use with your clients that are informed by Islamic principles?" Only after these open ended questions in the initial stage of the interview were participants shown the model of the soul (Figure 4.1). The interview schedule then focused on the particular principles from the model of the soul that resulted from phase one of the study, such as "How would it look to use the *muhlikat* and *munjiyat* in therapeutic interventions with clients?"

Analytic Procedure

Carrying on with the analytic procedure from phase one, transcripts in this second phase were also analysed using constructivist grounded theory (Charmaz, 2014). In this case, the categories represented similar thematic concepts to those that were generated in the first phase, as this phase was intended to build on the developing theory and model. Therefore, this phase with the additional participant sample was designed to further elucidate the emergent theory and explore other domains in which the theory holds up or changes due to new contexts, in this case that of application in psychotherapy.

The approach to quality control in grounded theory research is based on four factors: fit, work, relevance and modifiability (Glaser & Strauss, 1967). Weed (2017) explains these four factors this way:

> "Fit" relates to how closely the theory generated fits the phenomena it is proposed to represent, and is ensured by constant comparison and theoretical saturation. The ability of a theory to offer analytical explanations for processes within the context in which it is situated is the extent to which it "works". "Relevance" is the expectation that a theory will engage with the real world concerns of those involved in the processes it seeks to explain. Lastly, the theory generated should be designed to be open to development or extension as a result of new insights provided by further future empirical research, that is, it should be "modifiable".

Thus, in an attempt to assure methodological integrity with high quality results, this second phase was designed to implement these four factors, with the "relevance" being that of the applicability of the model of the soul to psychotherapeutic interventions. Furthermore, as this research is primarily concerned with the domain of psychology rather than that of theology, and more specifically with the "fit" for psychotherapy, the analysis of phase two will be divided into two chapters in order to account for the breadth of relevant data that emerged from the study as it pertains to the application of theory into practice. The argument for extending the analysis of a grounded theory study is inherent in the methodology itself as Weed (2017) says "it is constant comparison that ensures that GT [Grounded Theory] remains grounded" (p. 8). Data is compared to other data and theoretical categories and concepts are continually cross referenced with each other "to check that such concepts remain relevant given insights developed from subsequent data collection" (Weed, 2017, p. 8). For instance, a participant who is a psychotherapist referenced the way they use the concept of *nafs al al-lawwāmah* in their therapeutic practice with clients in holding themselves accountable for their behaviour. The data excerpt that captured the participant's understanding of the Islamic principle being applied here was compared with a data excerpt from the first phase of another participant who is an Islamic scholar which captured their explanation of the concept as relayed directly from religious sources. This process allowed for the constant comparison necessary in the aim of accurately translating theoretical concepts into practical application.

During this process, sampling continued by recruiting new participants who could further elucidate emerging theoretical categories through "theoretical sampling" (Glaser & Strauss, 1967). For example, when it became clear that a majority of the participants who were interviewed towards the beginning were incorporating Islamic principles into their therapy but not necessarily using a uniquely Islamic approach (falling into the first category explained above), participants with a more deliberately Islamic approach were then sought. Again later in the data generation process it was identified that there are some practitioners who are trained in traditional Islamic spiritual healing who could offer important insight into the emerging theory, so more participants with this experience were sought and invited to participate. As the data from these interviews was analysed and coded in the ongoing process, the initial set of potential theoretical categories was then refined/developed through "axial coding" (Charmaz, 2014; Payne, 2016), recording possible relationships between categories in the second phase with the categories generated in the first phase. The new themes were hypothesized and tested against data obtained in ongoing theoretical sampling until saturation (Payne, 2016) was reached just before the eighteenth participant's transcript was analysed, as data collected from interviews at this point were only producing recurring codes and categories. The further developed model of an Islamic psychological conception of the soul in therapeutic practice was then re-"grounded" by going back to the data and validating it against actual text (Payne, 2016).

In the data excerpts that are used to illustrate the findings in the next section, pseudonyms have been assigned to participants and their status is indicated in Table 5.1; dots indicate pauses in speech and empty square brackets indicate where material has been edited/excised. Data that are more self explanatory have been only minimally explained or analysed, where content of the excerpts build directly on concepts presented in the analysis of phase one. Where data bring forth new insights into some of the theoretical categories as they specifically relate to therapeutic application, more fore-grounded analysis has been given in order to contextualize the information, thus accounting for seemingly different styles of analysis throughout the presentation of findings in the next section.

Results

The analysis followed the four categories produced in the previous phase. The elaboration of these categories in the context of practical application within psychotherapy produced a model of Islamic psychotherapy, the general struc-ture of which is presented diagrammatically in Figure 5.1 later in this chapter. The concepts that make up the categories reflect the participants' expression of their therapeutic practice in their interview responses, drawing upon their own personal experience and relevant knowledge where appropriate.

Although a diversity of knowledge, training and experience existed within the sample, highlighting three distinct levels of Islamic integration in ther-apeutic approach among the participants, there was consensus about the distinct foundational elements of an Islamic conception of the soul which create the foundation for an Islamic approach. All four of the categories ex-plored in phase one were relevant to the findings in phase two. This chapter's presentation of the results will focus on the first two, namely "Nature of the soul", and "Structure of the soul" (see Table 5.2) while the remaining two, "Stages of the soul", and "Development of the soul" will be explored further in the next chapter in order to highlight the distinction between foundational clinical conceptions and the application of principles into practice. The sub-categories included in the following analysis and listed in Table 5.2 represent the most relevant themes from study one as participants in study two elabo-rated on how these themes show up in clinical practice.

Nature of the Soul

Concept of Fiṭrah

Most of the participants referred to the concept of *fiṭrah* as a guide to con-ceiving of ideal versus abnormal psychological health. There was a common acknowledgement that underneath any potential pathology or imbalance exists a core part of the human being that is pure and that a client can and should attempt to access and align with this with the guidance of the therapist. Harun said:

> "This is our nature our first nature of *hanif* [inclination toward mono-theism], being *hanif*, and *ahsanu taqweem* [best of God's creation], ... when we have that as a reference point that's what we're trying to, like, helping the person uncover and discover."

Table 5.2 Theoretical Categories and Subcategories – Phase 2a

Main Categories	Subcategories
Nature of the Soul	Concept of *fiṭrah*
Structure of the Soul	*Nafs* (lower self) *'Aql* (intellect) • Using *'aql* as a tool to choose the upward trajectory • Reframing cognitions to align with *'aqīdah* (Islamic creed) – Islamic CBT • Cognitive reframing to accept the self, distinction of *fiṭrah* and current state • Positive psychology • Where an Islamic approach diverges from Western CBT • *'Aql* as a way to the *qalb* • Emotions attached to/behind the thoughts *Qalb* (heart) *Rūḥ* (spirit)

Here Harun is alluding to what many other participants discussed – that by having this reference point as defined by the Islamic tradition and the Qur'anic paradigm of the human being, the Islamic psychotherapist has a solid framework for understanding ideal psychological functioning or an agreed "truth" of the purpose or state of human existence, which a secular framework may not be able to provide. Shahid said:

> "*Fiṭrah* is, I guess, it's a very useful concept in terms of believing that we do actually have a nature and which we can move away from. So moving away from *fiṭrah* is moving away from our true nature, so we need to reconnect."

It became apparent from participants' responses that the more knowledge they have of the *fiṭrah* state as expressed within the Islamic tradition, the better equipped they are to guide clients who may be out of alignment with that state.

All participants agreed in general with this notion that *fiṭrah* is the ideal state of the human being which exists within the core of each person. While most agreed that the relative attunement or connection with *fiṭrah* can be used as an assessment marker for a client's relative psychological health, a few felt that it was too difficult and unrealistic for therapists to faithfully determine whether or not a person was in line with *fiṭrah*, as it is too abstract a concept. However, even among those who were skeptical, there was still an agreement that if a person is experiencing a psychological imbalance not otherwise attributed to a biological factor, it is a result of being disconnected from *fiṭrah*. Harun said "You know that much so and then we can begin to work with what's other than what is the true nature", suggesting that instead of focusing on how to determine what is *fiṭrah*, which may be outside their ability, the therapist can attune to where the imbalances with *fiṭrah* are by noticing the problem areas. Harun went on to explain how to address these imbalances:

> "What we do is enable them to get on, so in terms of them discovering their true nature, when they access even one aspect I instruct them to pay attention. And again this other principle, the word 'mind' in English was more typically a verb initially, originally, to mind something – pay attention… 'Mind the gap'. And so paying attention you know – when we pay attention to something we amplify it. So they get to the state."

Here Harun is demonstrating a technique for attuning to the balances or imbalances that arise as a result of alignment or non-alignment with *fiṭrah*. Many participants talked about paying attention or being mindful of thoughts, actions, and behaviours as a way of accessing more information to help both the therapist and client determine what aspects need healing. We will discuss this more when we look at the different levels of the self where these can occur and where Islamic psychotherapists focus their treatments.

As was the majority consensus in the first phase of the study which focused on theoretical foundations, most participants in that phase said that the *fiṭrah* of the human being is pure and good. This same sentiment was reflected by most of the participants in this phase of the study of clinicians. Harun felt it was important to have that notion as a foundational concept within therapy, as a form of positive reinforcement. In reference to his own practice he said, "and always reminding people that they are good in their essence". Harun reflected many other participants' feeling that it was important to focus on the strengths and positive attributes of the client, as the Islamic paradigm of human nature posits that humans are in essence naturally good and pure.

While Enas agreed with this sentiment in general, she offered an interesting distinction with regards to the notion that *fiṭrah* in general is good and pure. The distinction she offered was in considering the different parts of levels of the soul, as distinguished in the model. Enas said:

> "*Fiṭrah*, they say it's pure goodness. For me no, it isn't pure goodness. There is the *fiṭrah* of the *rūḥ*. Yes, it's pure goodness. The *fiṭrah* of the body it's not pure goodness and the *fiṭrah* of the *nafs*, it is not pure goodness. So this is why our lord said '*hadaynah al-najayen*' there are potentialities. He can be like that, he can be like that. Because we are naturally inclined while in the *dunya* to be a certain way. *Fiṭrah* for the self, *fiṭrah* for the body."

This presents an important distinction when thinking about the actual clinical application of these concepts versus simply overarching theoretical principles. As a general concept Enas herself said she agreed that "in essence" the *fiṭrah* is pure and good. However this is when we conceive of the *fiṭrah* of the person actually being contained within the part of the soul that is the *rūḥ*, where the primordial nature was breathed in and still exists. Whereas within these other facets, or levels of the self, some participants clarified that they could be conceived of as being manifestations of the soul in different states, rather than being conceptualized as separate "parts" or "aspects" of the soul. This could suggest that when a psychotherapist uses this model in action to target these various states of the soul for the purpose of treatment, a more nuanced and subtle conception may be required.

It became clear through the accounts of all participants that there remains a gap in the specifics of how more precisely these sorts of nuanced conceptualizations can be determined for targeting treatments to engage the soul in a meaningful way. The gap appears to be in understanding how to incorporate the rich philosophical and theological knowledge of the soul, while appreciating the idea that this is an area of vast expanse of spiritual knowledge that few understand fully, as is reflected in the Qur'anic verse, "and they ask about the soul, say, little knowledge is" (Q 17:85). Some participants took this verse as an indication that people should not attempt to understand what perhaps is not understandable. Meanwhile others took it as an indication that there needs to be more effort to understand as much of this spiritual knowledge as is possible to attain from those who do have this knowledge in order to inform deeper, more nuanced treatment of the soul within the context of psychological treatments.

Nonetheless, it was agreed overall that no matter the level of intricacy of understanding just how to define what is in fact *fiṭrah* or how to determine one's alignment or misalignment with it, it remains a central factor for guiding the therapeutic treatment goals and defining exactly what it is that therapy should be aiming for. Samir said:

> "The client who might experience a disturbance in their life because they have gone away from the *fiṭrah* and veered away from that path of the *fiṭrah* and the *fiṭrah* is very important way of grounding the individual, that the client is to come back to the *fiṭrah* and the *fiṭrah* will enable that person *insha'Allah* [God willing] to start realizing what is their sense of purpose."

This reflects what others shared, that, more than simply removing or decreasing problematic symptoms in therapy, an Islamic approach should involve a direct connection with what has been set forth by God in the Qur'an as the reason for life, and that this can be defined and is established within the teachings in the Islamic tradition. Many participants said that they saw part of their goal to be helping the person to understand their tribulation and their behaviour and motivation within the context of following what God wants from Muslims as indicated in the Qur'an, and that being a source of achieving therapeutic success. Enas said, "My therapy aims to relocate this person in the same way with what Allah wants". In other words she is using the guidelines of best action and intention from the Qur'an as the framework for delineating where the client should be aiming for as a benchmark. Likewise Kabir referred to "trying to reactivate the total self", indicating a belief that this innate pure or true nature is already contained within the soul of the person but that it must be "reactivated" or "reconnected".

Structure of the Soul

Nafs (Lower Self)

Most of the participants thought of the *nafs* level of the soul or self as the aspect that is related to behaviour, motivation, and impulse. Whereas from a theoretical standpoint in the first phase the *nafs* was conceived of as the "lower self" that, from a theological standpoint, may often be thought of in terms of the self that accumulates sin or is driven to be disobedient to the commands of God and/or the natural good *fiṭrah* self, it seems to become more nuanced within the context of application in psychotherapy. While a religious scholar may be more concerned with what motivates the person to go against God's command and be in a state of religious disobedience, the therapeutic practitioners in this phase seemed to be more concerned with how to engage these different aspects of the soul for the sake of working towards change. In the case of the *nafs* several participants spoke about it as not necessarily "bad" or "evil" but seemed to try to understand its part in the broader system of the person and how it influences the symptoms or state that the client is in that is creating the presenting problem or desired change. In discussing how he engages the aspect of the *nafs* in therapy Matthew said he will introduce to clients "the idea of the self and the different levels of the self and some levels of the self that could be harmful to us if we give them free rein in a way". Matthew, among other participants, related using this conception of the *nafs* as being harmful if unchecked, and that the main utility in addressing this in therapy was to somehow work with the client to control the inclinations of the *nafs*.

In speaking of this distinction Firas said, "behavioural inclinations like *nafs*, we use that term behavioural inclinations, for *nafs*, it could be positive or negative". Here Firas illustrates a commonly shared sentiment among the participants that the goal in therapy is not necessarily to subdue or override the *nafs* but to understand and get it working with the system towards therapeutic change. To this end Enas went as far as to say that the seemingly negative inclination of the *nafs* can even in effect have a positive impact on changing the system, or whole self. She said, "the *nafs* suffer. This suffering of the *nafs* will nourish the *rūḥ*", suggesting that even when a person goes towards these so-called "evil inclinations", the trials and tribulation caused by such inclinations have the potential to motivate a person towards change, and even further, to actually cleanse the overall soul. While this could be a potential avenue for further exploration, it seemed that it was Enas's extensive experience with more advanced levels of spiritual understanding and training with traditional healers in the Islamic tradition that informed such understanding. Her insight and experience did not appear to be common among other participants and thus did not inform their way of working in therapeutic approaches.

In identifying the distinction between *nafs* level inclinations and cognitive or *'aql* level influences, Hamit described a clinical situation where a client had what in traditional Islamic conception would be termed *waswasa* (evil whispering), more commonly understood in Western psychology as Obsessive Compulsive Disorder (OCD). He explained that this client obsessively makes *wuḍū'* (ablution) thinking that he is never clean or ritually pure and therefore does not perform the Muslim prayer because of this belief. Hamit conceived of the act of not praying as an act of religious disobedience and therefore an avoidance behaviour. While it could be conceived that it is the cognition itself that is the problem, here Hamit articulates an important distinction within the context of an Islamic paradigm where the five daily prayers are an obligation. Thus he understands it as the inclination of the *nafs* that is keeping the person from praying, where the *nafs* is influenced by *shayṭān* (as depicted in Figure 4.1) and further inclined to disobedience of Allah, and that the cognition is in effect validating the behavioural inclination. In describing how he approached this case Hamit said:

> "So what we have to deal with that feeling? We have to go against it – *mukhalafah al-nafs*. So what are we going to do? I need you to come with me and I am going to start to pray *salah* [obligatory prayer] together."

The Arabic term used here *mukhalafah al-nafs* means to go against the whims of the *nafs*. So here Hamit is describing a behavioural intervention within therapy, at the *nafs* level, which is actually a prescribed act of *'ibādah* (worship) within Islam. While Hamit explained that he also worked with the person at the level of *'aql* to reframe the cognitions that were validating the behaviour, the actual behavioural remedy, as found directly in the teachings of Islam, is to override the cognition and use the will power and discipline to carry out the physical act of prayer. As Hamit explained, the belief is that this, along with other supports and methods of processing, will help to break through the pattern and the person will be strengthened by the increasing of *īmān* (faith) that is believed to be a result of establishing the *salah* prayer.

Many participants referenced the *salah* and other acts of *'ibādah* as treatment approaches, particularly at the level of *nafs* to target behaviour and impulse. Part of that, they said, was their recognizing that the function of disciplining the *nafs* through the use of will power is an aspect of the treatment that breaks through the dysfunctional pattern. Another aspect of these acts that participants recognized as having therapeutic effect was an inherent result of doing the behaviours themselves. There was a commonly shared belief among participants that these religiously prescribed acts of worship in and of themselves can have a positive impact on a person towards change. Harun said:

> "You know, I mean the *salah* is healing. You know the *wuḍū'* [ablution] is healing, the *sadaqah* [alms giving] is healing, and all that. So I try to find as many of these things and inform the people because a lot of people don't understand."

Harun is highlighting the fact that, like most of the participants reported, many clients' relationship to the prescribed acts of worship is devoid of this understanding or recognition that they have an inherent benefit. Participants related that for many Muslims these acts have become purely ritualistic and may even be considered archaic and futile as relics of a cultural heritage they inherited from their parents, but they do not have an intrinsic motivation or understanding of these behaviours as being useful, much less as healing. As Samir said, "How we make *salah*, for example, as a connection with Allah *subhanah wa ta'ala* [glory be to God] not to inform just the way we feel but the way we think and the way we behave", highlighting how *salah* can be approached as a means of treating or changing behaviour and even feelings.

For some clients, participants reported, there is an understanding of *'ibādah* as a source of healing but they may find that there are other factors within the self that are impeding their motivation to maintain the behaviour. Fatima said:

"With the individual feeling like they were not praying as often or maybe not connected, the behavioural aspect would be just to engage in *salah*, But I think first finding out what's blocking that connection. Is it just their psychological issue of being depressed or are there other things that may be blocking them from feeling connected to their religious identity or their spirituality?"

Whereas the behavioural intervention is an important part of overriding the inclinations of the *nafs* to "break" their hold on the person and trust in the prescription of *salah*, for example, as an obligation set by God within the Islamic paradigm, it was understood by most participants that there needs to be a level of self-awareness in conjunction with the behavioural intervention. Maha said:

"My goal is to get them to establish a level of self-awareness and you could call this watchfulness, you're just mindful of what's going on so like when you're in the moment, and this obviously is a thing that you improve on, you don't just arrive there and it's an evolving thing. But to be able to get to a point where you know for example when you speak that okay 'Is this coming from ego, like what was I trying to say here?' To be connected to your self is the goal here."

Matthew expressed a similar sentiment and approach in his own therapy practice:

"I think being able to start to recognize what those aspects are of the self would be, those are conversations that I would have. So like noticing the self that is addictive and just continuously has to kind of seek craving through that and trying to kind of, through a variety of different interventions, trying to kind of break through that into another, allowing them to see that there may- that there's another level to that aside from that base level."

Participants seemed to insinuate that helping clients reflect on their behaviour and motivation, and introducing some tool for self-awareness was an integral part of the therapeutic interventions that are useful within this level of the *nafs*. The popular conception among them was that bringing greater consciousness to a person's motivation and impulses can help move them from simply being a slave to these inclinations, succumbing to the drives of the *nafs*, and allowing this insight to further help fuel the will power to overcome them through changing behaviour.

The participants who were more familiar with the Islamic tradition used Arabic terminology and concepts to understand, explain and inform their approaches within the *nafs* level. Those who did not have as much of an Islamic education in this regard still seemed to talk about similar approaches, even if they used secular Western terminology. In some areas, particularly with regards to the idea of helping a client inculcate increased self-awareness, it was clear that the Islamic approach may not in fact be much different than the secular one, in which case it was merely a distinction of terminology. This seemed to be more so the case within the realm of *nafs* and *'aql*, where behavioural and cognitive techniques are appropriate and very familiar within the context of Western psychology. Firas described his approach to working with a client who had anxiety and as a result had difficulty sleeping due to racing thoughts or preoccupation with concerns of wrong doing or self judgement. He instructed his client by saying, "Why don't you take five to seven minutes to just sit down and do just kind of a *muḥāsabah* of your entire day and accountability just to kind of go through your day from morning until night?" The term *muḥāsabah* is an Arabic word meaning introspective examination and is a process of taking account of the soul or self. It is known to have been referenced in the Islamic tradition as far back as Umar ibn al Khattab, a companion of the prophet Muhammad and was made most popular by al Harith al Muhasibi, whose name became synonymous with the practice (Picken, 2011).

Firas explained that he integrates this Islamic concept of *muḥāsabah* with the popular Western psychological therapeutic approach of keeping a journal or diary of thoughts and activity throughout the day (Kazantzis & Ronan, 2006). He has a handout that he gives to clients that has sections to track their thoughts and reflections on behaviours for each section of the day. Traditionally this practice would be done in long hours of contemplation or under the direction and oversight of a shaykh. However, given the modern lifestyle and the way people have become accustomed to managing multiple things at once within their busy lives, the advent of writing down these thoughts and reflections is a useful innovation that can be incorporated from Western psychology, as it fits very well within this Islamic framework for engaging the *nafs* in reflection to counteract the base inclinations of the *nafs*. While the ontology of those inclinations may be a point of contention with a secular conception, where *shayṭān* is not necessarily considered a legitimate factor in human influence, nevertheless the effect and the treatment of such is very much aligned and a similar approach to popular Western psychotherapy.

Yet there are some aspects that both stem from an Islamic source and address factors that may be less important or off the radar of a secular therapist. Firas went on to explain that in addition to tracking thoughts and behaviours on his assigned handout for clients, there is a section for them to rate their *īmān* (faith) for the day. *Īmān* is one of the central tenets of the creed of Islam (*'aqīdah*). Here the translation of the word faith is not to indicate the religion itself but the relative degree to which a person has faith in God. This is generally understood and assessed by the person's relative state of comfort with what God has ordained and to what degree they are willing to submit to the "will of God". This indicator can help clients understand their thoughts and behaviours in light of the goal of having increased *īmān*, and thus an increased sense of submission to God's will, which is perceived to result in a sense of ease and decrease in dysfunctional symptoms. Firas said, "The night section kind of asks them to rate their *īmān* for today and their mood for today and what are some specific things I'm grateful for". Here Firas talked about how focusing on what one is grateful for can increase the state of *īmān*, as the belief is that God is the source of receiving those blessings to be grateful for, thus helping a person focus on the desired state of submission. This sounds very similar to central practices of secular therapists within the positive psychology movement (Emmons & Shelton, 2002), and indeed it is. However, as Firas mentioned, he is taking this notion not from the likes of Martin Seligman whose writings have been influential in this area in the past fifty years, but from a much older scholar from the Islamic tradition. Firas related that Abu Zaid Al Balkhi, an Islamic scholar who lived in the 9th century, specifically suggested instructing patients who were suffering from depression to focus on positive cognitions. We will return to this in the section on interventions at the level of *'aql*.

In general, there appeared to be something of a consensus among participants that the common way to address the level of the *nafs* in therapeutic application was through ways of increasing conscious awareness of potentially problematic behaviours and by prescribing behavioural modification to counteract such behaviours. Mahmoud recognized that this approach is somewhat reflective of what Muslims are instructed to do in the holy month of Ramadan and that using this familiar religious context was a useful way to introduce the idea of a programme of regimenting behaviour. Mahmoud said:

> "So one of things I do is use Ramadan as an example of you know how we can transform ourselves spiritually and through fasting and restricting food and restricting sleep and focusing on our primary purpose of creation to worship Allah."

He went further to offer the possible conception that Islamic psychotherapy can be seen as a reflection of that experience of Ramadan. His contention was that, instead of restricting the disciplined way of living and increased conscious awareness of thoughts and behaviours to one month per year, as many Muslims do, Islamic therapy can be thought of as a programme of being guided to do that more often. He also referred to the social aspect of Ramadan, how the whole global Muslim community is doing this programme together at the same time, which helps to encourage people, in effect riding the wave of critical mass. He said:

> "One of the things you try to do is to get people to socialize and think about good company and not spending time on their own and that type of stuff. So that would form a maybe some sort of behavioural stuff about avoidance behaviour."

his notion of the social aspect being another way of supporting a client's efforts at changing behaviours as intervention at the *nafs* level, was shared by other participants. Firas and Hamit referred to this as the *ijtima'i* (social) aspect, and referenced aspects of the Islamic concept of *ummah* (community) as another healing injunction within the tradition to tap into and utilize as a therapeutic intervention. Ultimately, as many participants reflected, the idea is to utilize these structures and frameworks within the Islamic tradition as therapeutic direction to bring balance and help clients to understand them in this light rather than as simply cultural or ritualistic obligations devoid of utility. These religious acts were thought of by participants to be invaluable resources to help clients maintain a level of accountability and submit to a conscious, deliberate programme of discipline in order to keep oneself in balance and manage the *nafs*.

'Aql (Intellect)

Participants collectively had the most to say about interventions that they use at the *'aql* level. This is presumably because, although most of them aspire to a genuinely Islamic model of practice, their training is in the Western schools of psychology, as that is what is available, and therefore most of the tools they have learned fall into the category of cognitive processing. The Western model of psychotherapy is dominated by a conception of psychology as being a domain mainly of the brain, as the location believed to be where all cognitive functioning happens. This is evident even in the name of the domain, as referred to as "mental health". Thus while many of the participants in theory believe an Islamic approach to be more holistic and to lean more heavily on the notion of the heart as the centre of an Islamic conception of psychology, these are people within the Western profession of psychology who have been trained in and largely adopted the tools of the trade from this Western discipline. Within their use of these cognitive interventions, however, there emerged a theme of recognizing that in fact such strategies have their roots within the classical scholarly tradition of Islamic sciences and that while the Islamic approach to cognitive intervention in many ways may not differ much from the modern approach, there were various levels apparent in the data regarding the use of these cognitive strategies which reflect varying degrees of Islamic specificity.

Using 'Aql as a Tool to Choose the Upward Trajectory

One aspect of the use of cognitive strategies in the therapeutic encounter, as relayed by participants, was the usefulness of engaging the *'aql* as a tool for influencing the dynamic interplay in the soul in an attempt to encourage an upward trajectory towards the upper, blue half of the model in Figure 4.1. In other words, the *'aql* was seen to serve as a regulating factor in helping the person make the choices that help to rein in the destructive inclinations of the *nafs* and exert control over it to lead towards more disciplined action and alignment with *fiṭrah*. Firas explained this by saying:

> "So like for thoughts, right, to be able to identify as an objective process: I'm having these thoughts, are these thoughts that are taking me towards *ghafla*, are these thoughts that I'm supposed to tackle and challenge or are these thoughts that, like for example, if I'm doing something wrong and I'm having this thought of guilt, is that supposed to be something that I'm supposed to hang onto because it's helpful, right? Because it's taking me towards the *fiṭrah*."

The word *'aql* in Arabic also has another meaning which means shackle. There is a common understanding within the Islamic tradition that the *'aql* acts as a shackle, reining in the *hawa* (desire) and the influence of *shayṭān* and acts as the reins on a horse, as in Galen's reference to the intellect being the rider of the horse, the horse being the impulses (*hawa*) (Walzer, 1954). Thus several of the participants with knowledge of the scholarly writings from the Islamic tradition referenced scholars like al-Ghazali and their conceptualization of the function of the *'aql*. Enas said:

> "So al-Ghazali, when you talk about the power of the *'aql*, it is a balancing. How to balance all this – it is a *jihad kabir* [big struggle]… So you have this and you have the *nafs*. The *nafs* have *qua aqlia* [mind power]. Islam wants from the mind power the *hikmah* [wisdom]. And not wisdom like in the West to be smart. No, you have to be smart inside the *Minhaj ilahi* (curriculum of God). Don't go out and be smart, I mean you could be a smart criminal – you may serve your impulses, you may serve your self-interest."

So here both Firas and Enas point to how the use of the *'aql*, or cognitive strategies within the context of Islamic psychotherapy, are not used simply to reframe to what the client may be more happy with on the basis of their 'impulses' but that the *'aql* can be used to direct the person towards the path that is posited by the Islamic paradigm to move along the trajectory towards the higher self, towards the *fiṭrah*.

Participants reported that, as therapists with an objective of helping their clients achieve positive change and growth towards a conception of "healthier" mental health or a perceived ideal level or state of functioning, having the framework of the Islamic paradigm was a major advantage. They believed that, without an Islamic framework, a therapist operating in a secular paradigm may not have a clearly defined end point of where the cognitive reframing should be focused on, in which case the default can become "healthy functioning" which they saw as often being defined narrowly in terms of living a comfortable life in the *dunya*. Participants pointed out that by having the Islamic religious definition of optimal functioning as defined by *fiṭrah*, this can inform the direction towards which cognitions should be reframed, to the end as defined by Islam. Enas said, "Choosing between alternatives and the freedom of will. I mean you choose in the values between good or evil, right or wrong". Enas is pointing out here that often cognitive interventions aim to restructure and make sense of maladaptive thoughts to bring them into greater congruency with what the person wants for themselves, what the client determines to be right or wrong relative to their own conception, whereas Islamic psychotherapy – one that is truly situated within the Islamic paradigm – necessarily accepts that which is right or wrong as determined by the Qur'an and Sunnah. In this regard Enas went on to say:

> "All Qur'an is about how to free this, to reach this *hikmah*. This is the wisdom, to choose between options and free will and how to choose the alternatives. There is always a characteristic and its opposite. You can choose to lie or to say the truth. You can choose to be trustworthy or to betray. So all the *tahdhīb al-akhlāq* [refinement of character] is choosing between alternatives, and the *'aql* is involved in this process."

Reframing Cognitions to Align with 'Aqīdah (Islamic Creed) – Islamic CBT

Another aspect of engaging the *'aql* in a similar regard, reported by participants, was to utilize cognitive reframing methods, in the same manner as modern Cognitive Behavioural Therapy (CBT), to align cognitive constructs with the *'aqīdah* (creed) of the Islamic religious worldview. In discussing this practice in his therapy Obaid related an example of working with a girl who had a seizure disorder and was partially paralyzed and struggling to understand and accept the notion that everything, including her situation, is the will of Allah. Obaid said:

> "We were talking about like the difference between acceptance and approval and kind of accepting certain realities in our lives doesn't necessarily mean we approve of them but accepting them helps us come to a better place where we can cope. So in that context bringing up the idea that Allah does certain things or he has designed things in certain ways, he has designed every individual in a particular way and having to accept that as kind of this decree but not necessarily that you don't still view this as a test or you know you might even deep down inside wish things were different and that's okay."

Obaid's account presents the dilemma of helping a client to simultaneously embrace and integrate the Islamic belief that everything is the decree of God with the cognition that rejects what is happening to them as the source of their tribulation. While the client's worldview would dictate what the relative congruence of thought with belief is, and in this case the client was a believer in Islam, the approach to CBT does not necessarily need to change as a technique. Hind said, "I found that I can still use the same framework of CBT or I can incorporate a lot of the techniques or interventions while also bringing in the Islamic components. So it kind of just flows you know".

Most participants seemed to agree that CBT was not at odds with an Islamic approach. Maha said "This is what I think where CBT comes in. It is very in line with the perfection of character [*tahdhīb al-akhlāq*]". Indeed some participants argued that CBT is Islamic. Siraj said "CBT, from its basis in core therapeutic principles which include empathy, active listening, is actually, that's part of the Sunnah". Siraj argued that there is no need to *adapt* CBT to fit within an Islamic context because by its nature it is Islamic just in the fact that it does not go against anything in Islam. He quoted a popular saying of the Prophet Muhammad that "All knowledge is the lost property of the believer", insinuating that there is no need to identify anything as Islamic *per se*: as long as it benefits a person towards a good end, then it is Islamic. While most if not all participants seemed to agree with this sentiment in general when it comes to the integration of Western methods in an Islamic context, with regards to CBT in particular several participants made reference to the fact that the 9th century Islamic scholar Abu Zaid Al-Balkhi wrote a manuscript which outlines a treatment of depression and other mental "disorders" which could easily be read today as a manual of what is now known as CBT. For example, Hamit said "Abu Zaid Al-Balkhi talks about like the positive opposite thoughts, and even talks about reciprocal inhibition". Thus, the argument made by some participants was that not only is CBT compatible with the Islamic framework but that CBT is fundamentally Islamic.

Cognitive Reframing to Accept the Self, Distinction of Fiṭrah and Current State

An important distinction that was raised by Hamit and Safa and a few other participants was that in the goal of using cognitive strategies, such as CBT, to help a client bring their cognitions in line with the Islamic ideal, this needs to be situated within a context of self-acceptance. They pointed out that while some religious figures may make Muslims feel ashamed or lead them to feel "bad" or inadequate for not having their thoughts and behaviours match those of the Islamic ideal, within the context of therapy it is imperative to instil a sense of self-acceptance. While some critics of religion in the context of therapy may claim that these two things are mutually exclusive and use this as an argument for religion not having a place within ethical counselling practice, many participants countered that view. Hamit said:

"One of the things that we were talking about is differentiation of personality, *shakhsiya* [personality], from character attributes. So an individual has such a heightened critic, this comes of *khawf* [fear] and he says 'I am bad, I am bad', or you know, 'I should be behaving this way. I should be behaving that way'... So there is an expectation or belief that 'I am supposed to be in a certain way'. Let's challenge that construct and move to self-acceptance of what your personality is and acceptance of that."

Here Hamit is clarifying that while an Islamic psychotherapist may be encouraging a client towards actualization of the ideal personality through working on the self, there is still a need for the client to accept where they are at and any innate obstacles or limitations that they have within their personality that they need to work on in that process. Using cognitive techniques at the level of *'aql* was a common conception among participants of how to help clients embrace this seemingly paradoxical project of balancing acceptance of where a person is at with the acceptance of the need for change towards the *fiṭrah* state. To this end Safa said:

"I do a lot of cognitive work in terms of challenging their assumptions. So if they say, you know 'I must be a bad person because God has punished me in this way' so I have to challenge that. Like 'Do you have any evidence of God's presence with you, like in your journey towards survival?' So there's a lot of challenging the cognitive distortions."

Safa also said that a big challenge in her own work as a therapist within the Muslim community is to combat the predominant condition that Muslims display of having a negative picture of themselves and a negative experience of God. She attributed that to the prevalence of Imams and other religious figures and parents using guilt and shame as a way of scaring Muslims into doing "the right thing" as delineated by Islamic religion and that this prevails due to lack of knowledge of the religion among the majority of believers in Islam.

Mustafa echoed this and expressed his great concern for this prevalence in the Muslim community, saying, "What really bothers me is the person's conception about the nature of Allah. This to me is the core that can cause psychological disorders, cause depression and a number of things". Mustafa said that he believes this wrong conception of God begins in childhood, and he went on to say:

"If he does anything, you know, 'You don't listen to your mother, then Allah will punish you'. Then he will at once with his great imagination he will make Allah as such. This picture will never disappear again. So it is to me it is something which when the person begins to feel that he has no hope for the future I at once begin to feel that he has a wrong conception about Allah."

Reframing a client's conception of God from an Islamic epistemological viewpoint may in fact be beyond the scope of many practitioners, yet the prevalence of this theme and the agreement among participants that this can be a root cause of many clinical problems, is a strong argument for therapists needing to have a solid ground in Islamic knowledge as well as to have resources to refer to for these matters. Aside from the matter of correcting the actual cognitive construct to align with Islamic '*aqīdah*, at the very least participants agreed that there is a need to reframe many clients' relationship to God and Islam in a more positive light.

Positive Psychology

In explaining his use of role play as a technique within his therapy practice Hamit described how he works with clients to insert positive statements to counteract the more negative thoughts that tend to prevail in a given situation that contribute to the client's distress. Again, he referenced the 9th century Islamic scholar Al-Balkhi as a source for this technique:

> "And so what we did is exposure based therapy in the session. We role played this and so I act as the employer and then I need you to tell me what you might typically do. That's avoidance and now let's try to do that which you would feel less comfortable with doing in the moment and then we would say 'Timeout, let's get what's going on cognitively for you. What's the positive opposite?' Abu Zaid Al-Balkhi talks about the positive opposite thoughts and even talks about reciprocal inhibition. 'Think about all other types of thoughts that can replace these thoughts. OK, so now time in, let's go back to the role play'."

Here Hamit references well known techniques within the movement of positive psychology and connects them to Islamic sources. This was a popular notion among many participants, that an Islamic approach to psychology is a positive psychology. Several participants mentioned that this stems from the positive view of human nature, that the Islamic paradigm posits the natural *fiṭrah* state of the human being as good and pure and therefore this notion is underlying all of the approaches to change. In discussing his own practice of engaging the '*aql* in therapy, Rahim said:

> "These are dysfunctional thoughts, you know sometimes you have to rephrase that way of thinking so it's positive and not negative. My sense is that negative thinking is, well it's obvious I suppose, sometimes it's more intuitive the way a person is thinking is negative. But so specifically targeting those thoughts."

Where an Islamic Approach Diverges from Western CBT

While participants acknowledged that the cognitive approach to psychotherapy certainly has its place within the Islamic framework, many shared the notion that it should really only be considered as one aspect of both the theoretical conception of the person and in turn the therapeutic approach. They all reflected a concern that their clients, as most people in general, over-identify with thoughts and that while, because of this, therapists need to work with those thoughts, they also want to be moving beyond the thoughts as the identification of self. Kabir said:

> "I always tell my Muslim clients, 'Your mind is not your identity, it's just an instrument, it's not your total identity, you need to get out of your head. Stop assuming everything is happening in your head, that's not Islamic.' Islam includes this and this and this and this [pointing to the other levels of the soul on the model in Figure 4.1]. And so that changes things even from a CBT perspective which is supposed to be all about cognition."

Thus participants indicated that while CBT and similar cognitive strategies can be useful tools within Islamic psychotherapy, it cannot be the entire therapeutic approach, as there are other important aspects of the self and the client's psyche that must be taken into consideration. Mahmoud said:

> "Like say for example working with a person with psychosis for example, and so like psychosis so understanding it from a purely CBT perspective or a Western psychology perspective, it doesn't appreciate a wide understanding of the self or for example the influence of *waswasa* [evil whispering], or even in terms of *shayṭān*, for example, in terms of understanding their thought patterns and processes or also the possibility of some external influence on the person in terms of *jinn* [unseen supernatural beings] disturbance."

As Mahmoud points out, when considering all of these other factors that are part of the Islamic framework, a purely cognitive approach would not be appropriate or equipped to address these other factors such as *shayṭān*, and the belief in the existence of *jinn* that is believed to have an effect on a person's functioning. This crosses into the realm of the spiritual and exists within the Islamic paradigm. With regards to these things, in the eyes of most partici-pants, a secular Western framework that adopted an exclusive CBT approach was thought to be insufficient in an Islamic context.

Whereas participants generally recognized the need for other tools, it was apparent that many of them, again due to their Western training, felt more comfortable with CBT, even if out of sheer familiarity. This was also reported as being a similar reality with clients – that because of the general societal preoccupation with the identification of self with thoughts, clients tend to be more comfortable and familiar with engaging primarily with cognitions. Obaid said:

"That familiarity gives CBT the edge and sometimes unfairly it gives it the edge. And people are more willing to kind of go down that route already. So you know if they don't – it's usually someone who's really like in a – they're not necessarily in a linear mindset. Those are the ones who maybe are not ready to talk about or accept CBT as their primary mode of improvement to their condition. And those people are more, in some ways, they're already on a spiritual plane, transcendent plane."

This statement by Obaid alludes to the notion shared by several participants that underneath the thoughts or cognitions lies a gateway to a more spiritual experience of the self, which is more in touch with the soul.

'Aql as a Way to the Qalb

Among the participants who were more comfortable and familiar with engaging the spiritual realm of the client's experience within the therapeutic encounter, there was an acknowledgment that the primary objective in engaging cognitions was in effect to access the deeper emotional material. Rayyan talked about engaging the *'aql* as a pathway to accessing the *qalb*:

"I'd say that one leads to the other. So like if it's a self-statement, I feel like the self-statement leads you inward to your heart, and then once you get to your heart then it goes into a spiritual context. Where some people begin with the spiritual but some people have to begin on the outside because they don't even know themselves enough…So it's kind of like a pathway."

In addition to this notion of the *'aql* as a path to the *qalb*, there was an understanding shared by most participants as well as the participants from phase one, that the *'aql* is in effect a function of the *qalb*. Specifically their belief was that, while we perceive of our intellect as being located in the head or brain, there is also an aspect of the intellect that is located in the heart and has to do with feeling. Samir said:

"I would engage the *'aql* but then I will engage the *rūḥ* in terms of the feelings and the heart … I can talk about the intellect we can talk about the *'aql* and the heart, that being where the intellect is, both the feelings of the person and … that you feel with the *qalb* as well as the intellectual kind of ability to discern."

Here Samir is pointing to a shared theoretical conception by participants which posits that the *'aql* is really the aspect of the *qalb* that perceives and discerns things. While this was a popular belief among participants, there seemed less actual or consensual understanding among them of how to engage this within a therapeutic intervention.

Emotions Attached to/Behind the Thoughts

While Hamit and Firas made reference to the engaging of emotions as a separate aspect of the structure of the soul, it was Enas, who has significant experience and training within the science of *taṣawwuf* (Islamic spirituality, Sufism), who was more articulate about how she accesses emotions at the level of the *qalb* and how the *'aql* shares a part in this process. In speaking of her work with a client in session, Enas said, "When I ask about your heart, I mean, it is your emotions or things like that ... and some emotional mind or so. When I ask them, they say from the body, the body wants". Enas explained that she conceives of the emotions as having an element of *'aql*, meaning that there are emotions stored in the body from trauma that, when accessed or uncovered, contain "cognitions" or aspects of a notion that can be perceived and expressed by the body itself. She explained that she tracks these emotions to their deeper source within the person's stored emotional material: "I reach the core, core, core of the thought that make the problem. I believe every thought is formed inside of it emotion, every thought". Enas, and similarly Harun, expressed the view that the body itself has an element of knowing and of thinking, which would be considered *'aql* as well, and that it is essential to find ways of accessing this bodily knowing as a guide to where the source of the pathology or imbalance in the whole system lies in order to heal it.

In further exploring this notion of the entire system of the person or soul in effect containing aspects of *'aql*, Enas went on to say:

> "From my experience, in the *rūḥ* there is a cognitive process. In the *qalb* there is a cognitive process. In the *nafs* there is a cognitive process. So there is no *'aql*. Because the Qur'an never mentioned *'aql*. It only says *yaqilun* ... it is only processing."

Enas is referring here to the *ayah* (verse) in the Qur'an that mentions the concept of *'aql* and where the actual word *'aql* is not used; it is not referenced as a thing in itself but as a function of the *qalb*, which John pointed out in the first phase of the study. The *ayah* says, "So have they not travelled through the earth and have hearts by which to reason and ears by which to hear? For indeed, it is not eyes that are blinded, but blinded are the hearts which are within the breasts" (Q 22:46). As did the scholars in the first phase, Enas points to the fact that the Islamic concept of *'aql* is much wider than the popular notion of the intellect as being isolated to the mental faculty. As Harun also explained, the Islamic conception involves a level of thinking that extends even to the limbs of the body. He mentioned the notion that instead of saying something like "Explain what it feels like to have your feet contact the ground", in this conception he often would say "What does the mind of your feet perceive as it contacts the ground?" In talking about accessing the emotional material by having the client concentrate on the body, Enas said:

"When I talk to any part of the body they will just respond and tell me. So their legs will testify. On the judgement day Allah will make the legs for example talk. So will all the cells in the body. It is written in [the Qur'an]."

Enas references here the *ayahs* in the Qur'an that say that on *Yom al Qiyama* (the Day of Standing), when a person is taken in to account for their actions in this world after they die, the person's own limbs will testify to what they did with them. While some may not read this literally, there are traditional *tafsīr* (exegeses) that understand this to mean that there is an aspect of memory in the body. It is this bodily memory that both Enas and Harun actively look to engage in their treatment of emotional material that creates blockages to a person being able to live within their *fiṭrah* state.

Enas said, "Every block has *'aql*". She further explained that her conception was that every memory or traumatic experience that created some imbalance and causes dysfunctional patterns within the whole system of the soul actually has a cognition. In other words, there is information behind each blockage within the psyche that, when understood and unpacked and reframed or realigned, can release the hold that it had within the person and thus alleviate the maladaptive symptoms it was causing. She explained further, saying:

> "The Qur'an is very literal and there is illustration. It says, '*wa lama sakt a'an Musa al ghadab*', the anger is talking, it has language, it has 'aql. It has a cognitive component. '*wa lama sakt a'an Musa al ghadab*', 'when the anger stopped'. There is an entity that has *'aql*, that has language. Because anger talks to you, fear talks to you, the adrenaline talks to you. … This adrenaline, this is a soldier among the soldiers of Allah. It tells you 'I can help you', your physiology. For this you feel all this so you can understand."

Enas explained that the interpretation of this *ayah* from the Qur'an is that when referring to the anger that Musa (Moses) displayed in a certain context, the Qur'an talked about it as the anger having its own consciousness or "thinking" as it were. This, she explained, is another way of conceiving of the force of anger within a person as having its own drive and reason that may not be connected directly with a person's conscious awareness but that is nonetheless connected to some other reasoning within the self. This level of *'aql* that Enas is referring to seems to be an area that is under-developed, as she was the only one who talked about it among the participants. It is reflective of the Islamic conception of the heart being the seat of consciousness, something that is shared by other spiritual traditions including Judaism (Morinis, 2014) and Buddhism (Pine, 2005) but which really does not have a correlation with anything one would learn in the field of Western psychology.

Qalb (Heart)

As with the 18 scholars interviewed in the phase one, almost all 18 clinicians interviewed in phase two emphasized the centrality of the *qalb* (heart) in an Islamic conception of psychology. This emphasis was substantiated in the first phase by the citing of primary sources, from the Qur'an, *aḥādīth* and scholarly *tafsīr* which provided clear evidence of the theological conception of the *qalb* and how theoretical constructs could consequently be drawn upon in a relatively straightforward manner. However, when it came to clinical application in the form of therapeutic intervention, the level of *qalb* within the Islamic conception of the human being seemed to be the least developed in terms of articulated strategies. Participants collectively had much less to say about how they engage the *qalb* in their practice of therapy. This was somewhat ironic given that many of them talked a great deal about how their understanding of an Islamic approach is about working with the heart as the centre of the person and their psyche. Yet, when it came to discussing how they actually access and work directly with the *qalb*, the responses were thin.

Most participants talked about how much of their work in therapy with clients initially focuses on helping them to conceptualize a different relationship to what they perceive as "mental health" by introducing this notion that the heart has a more central role and that their psychology is not simply synonymous with their thoughts. Kabir discussed this initial phase of psychoeducation with his clients and said, "Recognizing that they have you know an organ of perception as the heart and that it's not just all about your mental cognitive dimension". Here Kabir touches on the notion of the heart being an additional element of consideration in understanding our psychology. He said that he is not suggesting that it is only the heart but that, given most people's preoccupation with their thoughts and being mostly unaware of the heart as a factor in the realm of the psyche, the first stage is to bring the two into consideration together. Matthew similarly discussed doing this psychoeducation work with his clients and said, "A harmonious relationship between the mind and the heart is another concept that I often will talk about". As Matthew expressed and other participants echoed, the second step after simply getting clients to recognize and be aware of the heart as a factor is to then help them understand how these aspects correspond or interact together and an encouragement towards greater balance between the two as a therapeutic goal.

In further exploring the idea that the Islamic model of therapy involves an integration of what we generally term as the heart and mind, Samir commented on how he felt it is important to help clients understand that the two concepts are not necessarily distinct entities and that in fact, as identified in the first phase, the *qalb* actually has a part in what we call the intellect. He said:

> "It is a complete way of cognition because cognition is not just about thought. It is about the whole aspect and I think sometimes … a lot of people live in their head most of the time more than kind of live holistically."

This "living holistically" or, as other participants called it, a holistic understanding of mental health, is something that most participants alluded to as a vague goal of therapy, both for helping clients develop greater self-understanding but also as a sort of preparation for the therapeutic process. Maha said:

> "I try to tell them how we all potentially can experience symptoms by our mind and to get ourselves away from that we need to be in the here-and-now because that's the only way that our heart can actually be activated."

Maha mentions here what many other participants also described as the second step after the psychoeducation phase in which the concept of *qalb* is introduced. This second step was reported to involve, as Maha said, the therapist guiding the client to "activate" or, as others said, "connect" with the *qalb* somehow.

While participants seemed to generally agree conceptually that connecting to the heart should be a goal of therapy, they differed in how they approached initiating this connection, if they did it at all. Participants who generally adhered to their Western training seemed not to have a clear sense of how to perform this task of accessing or connecting to the *qalb* actively within a therapeutic context. Of these participants, all but two verbally acknowledged that they believe this to be important or necessary but simply did not have the training or knowledge of just how to do it, but they desired to do this. Of those who did have some form of approach to engage the *qalb* within an intervention, many indicated that cultivating a state of present awareness within the self was a key factor in this process.

Presence or *hudur*, as it is known in the Islamic tradition, is an integral part of many spiritual practices and is believed to be useful in helping a person make contact with an inner state of calm that is focused on the present moment and not preoccupied with the inner turmoil often caused by a focus on thoughts and emotions which can fluctuate. For many Muslims the practice of cultivating such a state is often a foreign concept and many do not have an experience of it being a part of the religion of Islam. However, there is a great deal of historical context to the cultivation of this practice within the Islamic tradition. While some of the participants acknowledged being aware of this fact, only very few of them, primarily those in the third participant group, had experience of training in the Islamic practices traditionally used to cultivate *hudur*, such as *tafakkur* (contemplation), *murāqabah* (meditation), *muhāsabah* (introspective examination) and breathing practices that are taught within the Sufi *tariqat* (paths/orders). Several participants mentioned that they felt this is an area that needs to be further explored and that these traditional tools and techniques can be adapted to the therapeutic context for the purpose of deepening this attempt to connect with the *qalb*.

Of those few participants who do use some form of therapeutic approach within session to engage the *qalb* in this way, most had a similar practice of working with clients to spend time physically focusing on the heart centre in the chest and quieting thoughts during this process. In this regard, Maha said, "The goal is to connect them, to get them to look inward because the problem is one where we disconnect from ourselves and look everywhere else for peace and stability". This idea of "looking inward" was shared by a few participants who referred to this as a literal act of closing the eyes and dropping into the inner world of the self, experiencing this state of presence within the body. In explaining his use of this technique, Matthew said:

> "Often these ideas of following your heart or like getting out of your head and like trusting what's here, pointing to my chest, rather than always trusting what's up there [pointing to his head]. And I think even from a mindfulness-based perspective, of which I adhere to, it's just this idea of can we get out of the rumination of the mind and of the brain and drop down into what's real for us in the body and in the heart."

Harun also described a similar process of orienting a client to the experience of the body in order to cultivate a sense of presence in the total being of the holistic notion of the self but also to access the emotional material to work with and work through in the process of therapy. He said:

> "I say; what do you notice in your body at this particular time? And the homework I give all my patients and all people I work with; I say between now and our next session notice what happens in your body the physical states in different situations and depending upon how resourced they are I may start with very positive things. when you see something beautiful, notice what happens in the body."

Whereas Harun reported being able to access deeper emotional material by guiding his clients to attune to their body, Rayyan reported a similar end point of accessing the emotional material but by following her client's thoughts and helping them connect with the feelings behind the thoughts, as a pathway to experiencing the heart. Rayyan said:

> "I would also point out feelings. So, for example, a lot of people when they start out with self-statements, the more they do it and the more they come back and talk to me about what they've done I can see they're moving closer and closer into the heart, and then we start focusing on 'OK what did you feel?. Where did you feel it?' … And then we start focusing on that and naturally I've found that with my clients they go to that spiritual trajectory themselves, especially because they're already Muslim. Even if they haven't really practised fully, but once we get to the point of reaching that place in the heart they naturally want to go towards the spiritual."

Whether approaching through the body, like that of Harun's approach, or through verbal expression of feelings, like that of Rayyan's and other participants' approaches, there was a shared conception that the emotional material stored within the *qalb* is a deeper underlying source of pathology or imbalance within the total system of the person and the human soul. Rather than simply focusing on restructuring thoughts as a way of alleviating maladaptive symptoms, the idea shared by several participants was that the *qalb* is an access point to the inner spiritual reality of the person and in effect allows the therapist to work within a more spiritual domain of the person as a soul rather than just the surface level experience of the person's reactions, impulses and thoughts in their life in the *dunya*.

Thus, the more participants were versed in Islamic knowledge of the soul and had been trained to some degree in methods of accessing the deeper aspects of the soul through techniques such as presence, body awareness, and emotional tracking, the more they were able actively to engage the level of *qalb* in their practice of psychotherapy. For those that did not possess such familiarity and proficiency, the *qalb* level remained a mysterious area of the Islamic model that seemed to intrigue them and call to them as developing practitioners in this growing field but for now appeared to be masked in uncertainty which served to bar them from fully traversing into this territory within the model of the soul. Obaid described this uncertainty in his own work, in reflecting on his approach in relation to the Islamic model of the soul:

"I do feel it must be present somehow but at the same time it's not well articulated, at least very consciously and it would be subconsciously there. And it might just come up in glimmers here and there, like where I'll be, you know, thinking about a particular client or having a second session and something will occur to me about, you know, maybe what this person's *nafs* is doing to them at this moment or what is the struggle they're having with *nafs* right now or the *nafs* of someone else in their family. And so it definitely pops up. I feel like it definitely has its kind of-it's kind of interwoven in the experience but yeah I'm definitely not, you know, trying to call that up purposely. And so I feel you know the way you've been asking me, conducting the interview, you have made me think about, you know, challenge some of these boundaries and that's good. I think it's a good thing because maybe I should try to be more purposeful when I sort of call up these concepts from my spiritual understanding and try to use it more actively."

For those participants in group one, almost everything below the *'aql* level remained a relatively unexplored or unarticulated aspect of their identification with what they perceived as "Islamic psychology". They seemed to have a vague sense of the concepts but lacked an overt sense of how to implement them in practice. This became even more pronounced and included most of the participants in group two when it came to the level of the *rūḥ*.

Rūḥ (Spirit)

Similar to the *qalb* level of the soul, the *rūḥ* was an area that most participants seemed to be vague about when it came to discussing just how they engage this aspect with clients in therapy. For some this was just due to the abstract reality of the spirit, where the way *rūḥ* is engaged is difficult to articulate in a linear, concrete fashion and for others it was because they simply do not have a grasp of how to do this or even a belief that it is possible. Maha expressed this skepticism of the possibility of engaging the soul in therapeutic intervention as she said:

> "I think with that just is more about again psychoeducation because I mean you can't really – how do you engage the soul in session, I mean you do but like how do you ... it's not something that you would just know, like a concrete intervention."

While this view was shared by most of the participants who had less formal training in the Islamic religious sciences or *taṣawwuf* because of a general lack of knowledge and understanding, there seemed to be an apprehension in fully embracing and engaging with the *rūḥ* in terms of clinical treatment even among many of those who were more learned in this respect. Participants reported a central factor that contributed to this apprehension: that in general the *rūḥ* is perceived as something only truly known by God and therefore should be regarded with reverence and caution. As mentioned above, several participants referenced an *ayah* in the Qur'an that says "And they ask you, [O Muhammad], about the *rūḥ*. Say, 'The *rūḥ* is of the affair of my Lord. And mankind have not been given of knowledge except a little.'" (Q 17:85). This *ayah* was interpreted to mean that the *rūḥ* is a sort of secret of God's and that even among the learned there can never be full understanding of it. Leading from this interpretation, all but one of the participants seemed to act as if there were "red tape" around the issue of knowing and understanding the *rūḥ* and therefore for the most part appeared to keep clear of attempting to involve this aspect in any clinical treatment plan.

Even though participants felt the *rūḥ* had a sort of untouchable aspect to it, in some ways they had more to say about it then the *qalb* in terms of what they actively do as interventions that address or are directed towards the *rūḥ*. This was due primarily to the fact that most of them considered the involvement of religious practices of worship, as prescribed in the Qur'an, as being nourishing for the *rūḥ*. So whereas they may not necessarily understand how to assess the state of the *rūḥ* or a person's connection to it, they could involve it in the treatment plan simply by recommending that which is recommended or even obligatory from the religion. Hind said:

> "I really feel like they have this thirst for 'I just want to know more about' and you know I'm like I can connect you to a scholar. So I feel like a lot of

them want that. They really look forward to those tidbits that I give them in sessions. So it really shows you that the *rūḥ* is like starving for that. Sometimes it's so deprived for so long because it's so closer to this direction [pointing to the bottom half of the model in Figure 4.1]."

Hind went on to say that often she will bring acts of worship into the session and do it with the client, for example making *dua* (supplication), and if the client is female, even praying the *salah* together in session, a practice common in other spiritually integrated psychotherapy such as Christian counselling (Tan, 2011).

In discussing the assignment or suggestion of *'ibādat* (acts of worship) to clients, Hamit said "They are going to help you gain spiritual strength so you're sort of essentially feeding to the *rūḥ*, the spirit, there". He went on to say that he sometimes will do what he called a "spiritual inventory" where he helps the client assess how much acts of worship are a part of their daily routine and then make suggestions about how to increase those, maybe recommending reading Qur'an or doing *dhikr* (a practice of remembrance), for the sake of nourishing the *rūḥ*. Speaking about the same practice within his own work with clients, Mahmoud said, "Ideally the first one of the things you try to put down is the five daily *salah* for example, but it's all dependent on that person and where they are in their journey". Similarily Rahim reported doing the same. However he added the caveat that he is still cautious about doing this to the degree with which he feels is within his expertise. Rahim said:

"As a specific area I would occasionally recommend certain spiritual practices like listening to Qur'an. Within my knowledge reciting certain names or a certain *ayah*, like *surat al khaf*, before sleeping for bad sleep. But I know the limitations of my knowledge in this. I would be prepared to say 'Go and see somebody that knows more about these things' for something that is more specific."

Rahim spoke here to a sentiment that was shared by many, that participants were generally wary about being conscious of where their knowledge and expertise lie and where they might cross the line into another domain of religious guidance. While some of the participants responded to this by stressing the need to refer to religious leaders, like Rahim noted, or to have ongoing relationships with Imams within their practice, others stressed the need for the therapist him or herself to have substantial education in Islamic religious knowledge. Several of the more learned participants even went as far as to say that they should be dual-trained, in both Islamic sciences and psychology.

Enas, who herself had extensive training and tutelage in Islamic sciences and had a considerable mastery over many branches of Islamic knowledge, was actually the only participant who expressly said that she purposely stays away from prescribing or suggesting religious acts of worship or even Islamic knowledge to some clients, at least at the beginning. Enas indicated that in her experience the timing for introducing Islam into sessions was of crucial importance. Enas said:

> "Sometimes I don't mention Allah in the beginning because they are annoyed by Allah, they are angry with Allah. I mean, they said that, 'Oh Allah forgive me, Allah is unfair because this …'. They say He didn't help them. So I don't say Allah in the beginning, if you say Allah in the beginning you are just like any *murshid* (religious guide). [The client may say] 'It isn't different, what is new? I hear this on the television, they say Allah guide you.' But after you solve all these problems, you put Allah in a beautiful way."

Enas points here to a concept that most other participants did not mention, the idea of timing as a key factor in when certain interventions are used in therapy with clients. Enas reported that this knowledge of the right time to use a given approach is something that she learned from studying Sufi shaykhs. She said that they did not treat each individual the same, so there was no formula for implementing a given treatment approach, that the approach would be different for each individual based on their relative state and what they were ready for in order to have them be most receptive. She felt that the key factor in having this type of knowledge of timing comes from intuitively perceiving the state of a person's heart. She believed that this comes from the practitioner's own work of *tazkiyat an nafs*, where they have "polished their mirror" to the point of being a clear reflection and thus able to respond to the needs of the client in a more nuanced way, directly giving to the soul what it needs for development, rather than merely interacting with the person's cognitive constructs or the outward persona that the client projects. In further explaining what is important about the timing of interventions, Enas said, "because if he is stuck in one block, if I didn't remove this, I couldn't put anything else in its place, neither cognitive nor religion or anything else. It will not work".

Among the few participants who discussed actively engaging the *rūḥ* in clinical treatment, some conceived of it simply as the act of the therapist always keeping the *rūḥ* in consideration within the treatment. Mustafa said:

> "The spirit [*rūḥ*] is good, and this spirit is the one which is blown by Allah *subhana wa ta'ala* [glory be to God] into Adam and his offspring, his children. Now if you understand this spirit as such, then the spirit will be angry and unhappy with the soul when the soul is behaving in an evil manner but it is compelled to continue in this body to continue in this condition. As the person becomes better, a better *abid* [servant of God], he will gradually reach a point where the spirit will be in harmony with the soul."

Mustafa expressed the view that while both the client and therapist may not know much about the *rūḥ* as it is a deep secret, it plays a central role in the Islamic conception of the soul and thus must be accounted for within any treatment plan. Other participants also spoke about the understanding that the *rūḥ* is affected by whatever imbalance that has resulted in a person living out of accord with their *fiṭrah* and that it will respond or contribute to symptoms that will show up as presenting problems, even if the root is not as obvious, because it is part of this spiritual reality of the soul in relation to its connection to God or lack thereof. In reference to this, Firas explained how a client might be tormented with a thought or feeling that something is 'off' or have anxiety, the root of which may not be obvious. He said:

> "You know that's more like a *rūḥani* [pertaining to *rūḥ*] thing that's telling you that you know there's something that you did that you've left out that you need to take care of and it [the *rūḥ*] can't sit with that, you know that causes that anxiety."

Both Mustafa and Firas seem to be suggesting that the relative state of the person, based on the blockage or imbalance at all the other levels of the soul, has a direct effect on the *rūḥ*, as it responds to the larger system being out of *fiṭrah*, and that this can be a central aspect of the root of the pathology. Thus these few participants who were more comfortable with the level of *rūḥ* within the treatment conception appeared to be making the argument that whether or not someone understands the nuances of the *rūḥ* on a spiritual level, within this Islamic framework the *rūḥ* must be taken into consideration in any appropriate or effective treatment plan. These participants asserted that only by engaging the *rūḥ* can the therapist truly effect change towards the objective of helping to bring the client in closer relationship with God, as this seems to define optimal psychological health within this paradigm.

A Theory of Islamic Psychology in Practice: The Iceberg Model of Islamic Psychotherapy

Figure 5.1 shows the Islamic model of psychotherapy, including the four levels of the soul, as an iceberg. The *nafs* level is what participants reported generally appears "above the water line" or where most of the clients' presenting problems manifest. This can show up in cases as explicitly behaviour-oriented patterns or even somewhat more subtly as personality patterns, where a person might be struggling with either the stage of *nafs al al-ammārah* or *nafs al al-lawwāmah*, or vacillating between the two. Thus what is "visible" within the client's presentation was generally considered by participants to mostly be symptomatic of imbalances or blockages at one of the other levels of the soul, further down the iceberg, beneath the "waterline".

Just underneath the waterline is where the level of *'aql* resides, where cognitions that are attached to the behaviour or personality pattern reinforce

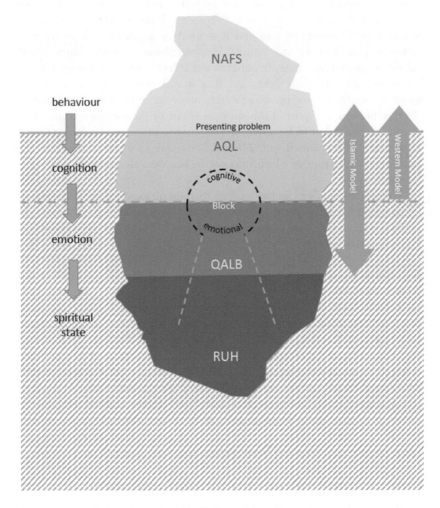

Figure 5.1 The Iceberg Model of Islamic Psychotherapy.

or keep in place the maladaptive function or symptom. Here is where Cognitive Behavioural Therapy reaches to help reframe and reprogram the dysfunctional cognition that is causing or keeping the problem in place. For most secular models of psychotherapy within the Western paradigm of psychology the treatment only goes as far as the level of *ʿaql*, without delving further into the depths of the psyche or soul of the individual. In some cases, the lack of attention to these deeper parts may be a lack of understanding of how to deal with them, as with both non-Muslim Western-trained psychotherapists as well as Muslim therapists who have the intention of practising within an Islamic framework but without having the knowledge or frameworks to do so, as represented by the participants in group 1.

Where therapeutic interventions as deep as the *'aql* level may touch on the cognitive aspects of blocks to the *fiṭrah* or higher spiritual self that lies beneath the surface in the depths of the psyche, they largely do not engage the deeper emotional material connected to or causing the block, which would be within the level of the *qalb*. Those participants who had an understanding of how to engage the *qalb* in therapeutic interventions, represented by a few of those in group 2 and all in group 3, did so by accessing the emotions and unlocking the block to the *fiṭrah* self. This removal or opening of the block happens only at the level of the *qalb* and, as this phase of the study found, is where the key to an Islamic psychotherapy approach lies, represented by the keyhole shape in the centre of Figure 5.1. The bottom part of the keyhole represents the opening to the *rūḥ*, which happens as a result of removing the emotional block that was keeping the person from living closer to their *fiṭrah* state, in remembrance of God and their primordial state.

The deepest part of the iceberg, which is the one further into the darkness of the depths and shrouded in mystery and the unknown, is that of the *rūḥ*: the pure soul which reflects the truth of God. Only those participants from group 3 truly engaged this level of the soul in their therapeutic process, and even then it was agreed that there was a limit to how much can be delved into at that depth within the context of psychotherapy. Further exploration of this level of the iceberg was assumed to be left to the domain of a spiritual master, or shaykh, who has charted such deep waters and has attained a rare, higher spiritual state with which comes greater knowledge of the soul. This is the point where participants considered that the continuation of the journey of *jihad an nafs* departs from the realm of psychology, which is mostly concerned with bringing one's *nafs* into equilibrium or more optimal functioning, and crosses into a purely spiritual pursuit, which is more concerned with perfecting the *nafs*. These distinctions and the relative scope of Islamic psychotherapy versus the realm of Islamic spirituality will be further explored in the presentation of findings in the following chapter. Findings from this and the following chapter will be discussed in Chapter 7 alongside the findings from the previous phase, as the phases have been conceptualized as two parts of an integrated whole.

References

Abdullah, C. H. B., Abidin, Z. B. Z., Hissan, W. S. M., Kechil, R., Razali, W. N., & Zin, M. Z. M. (2013). The effectiveness of generalized anxiety disorder intervention through Islamic psychotherapy: The preliminary study. *Asian Social Science, 9*(13), 157.

Al-Karam, C. Y. (Ed.). (2018). *Islamically integrated psychotherapy: Uniting faith and professional practice.* Templeton Press.

Charmaz, K. (2014). *Constructing grounded theory: A practical guide through qualitative analysis.* Sage Publications.

Emmons, R. A., & Shelton, C. M. (2002). Gratitude and the science of positive psychology. In C. R. Snyder & S. J. Lopez (Eds.), *Handbook of positive psychology* (pp. 459–471). Oxford University Press.

Gilchrist, V. J. (1992). Key informant interviews. In B. F. Crabtree & W. L. Miller (Eds.), *Doing qualitative research* (pp. 70–89). Sage Publications, Inc.

Glaser, B. G., & Strauss, A. L. (1967). *Discovery of grounded theory: Strategies for qualitative research.* Routledge. https://doi.org/10.4324/9780203793206

Haque, A., Khan, F., Keshavarzi, H., & Rothman, A. E. (2016). Integrating Islamic traditions in modern psychology: Research trends in last ten years. *Journal of Muslim Mental Health, 10*(1), 75–100.

Kaplick, P., & Skinner, R. (2017). The evolving Islam and psychology movement. *European Psychologist, 22*(3), 198–204.

Kazantzis, N., & Ronan, K. R. (2006). Can between-session (homework) activities be considered a common factor in psychotherapy? *Journal of Psychotherapy Integration, 16*(2), 115–127. https://doi.org/10.1037/1053-0479.16.2.115

Keshavarzi, H., & Haque, A. (2013). Outlining a psychotherapy model for enhancing Muslim mental health within an Islamic context. *International Journal for the Psychology of Religion, 23*(3), 230–249. https://doi.org/10.1080/10508619.2012.712000

Michie, S., Johnston, M., Francis, J., Hardeman, W., & Eccles, M. (2008). From theory to intervention: Mapping theoretically derived behavioural determinants to behaviour change techniques. *Applied Psychology, 57*(4), 660–680. https://doi.org/10.1111/j.1464-0597.2008.00341.x

Morinis, A. (2014). *With heart in mind: Mussar teachings to transform your life.* Shambhala Publications.

Naz, S., & Khalily, M. T. (2015). Indigenous adoption of Novaco's model of anger management among individuals with psychiatric problems in Pakistan. *Journal of Religion and Health, 55*(2), 439–447. https://doi.org/10.1007/s10943-015-0012-y

Payne, S. (2016). Grounded theory. In E. Lyons & A. Coyle (Eds.), *Analysing qualitative data in psychology* (pp. 119–146). SAGE Publications Ltd.

Picken, G. (2011). *Spiritual purification in Islam: The life and works of al-Muhasibi.* Routledge. https://doi.org/10.4324/9780203835043

Pine, R. (2005). *The heart sutra.* Counterpoint.

Tan, S.-Y. (2011). *Counseling and psychotherapy: A Christian perspective.* Baker Academic.

Walzer, R. (1954). A diatribe of Galen. *Harvard Theological Review, 47*(4), 243–254. https://doi.org/10.1017/S0017816000024974

Weed, M. (2017). Capturing the essence of grounded theory: The importance of understanding commonalities and variants. *Qualitative Research in Sport, Exercise and Health, 9*(1), 149–156. https://doi.org/10.1080/2159676X.2016.1251701

Reflection 4: The Analytic Process: A Symphony of Voices with One Conductor

As described in the discussion on methodology, in grounded theory the analytic process proceeds alongside the fieldwork, as the coding of transcripts can reveal aspects of the emerging theory that inform decisions on where to sample in order to further develop the emergent theory. I found the initial stages of this process a challenge, as not only was this my first time doing grounded theory, the task at hand: distilling the theoretical framework of human psychology from the cosmology of a major world religion, was a lot to try and take on. It was difficult to know where and how to start. I knew that the technical answer was just to start with the first interview transcript and begin open coding anything and everything of relevance, which I did. However, all that did was open up a world of seemingly endless permutations and possibilities of where this could go. It wasn't until about three interviews in that I actually started to understand the grounded theory process.

Over the course of those first three interviews I was pretty much looking at each one separately as I was just coding what was there, or so I thought. As I began to conduct more interviews, have more data and more codes, I noticed that my perspective of what to code and how began to change and be influenced by the other data and the codes that I produced from other interviews. So that now what was on my radar as a potential idea, category or code, based on let's say a recent interview, I was starting to realize hadn't been on my radar when I was coding earlier transcripts. Whereas I may have been perceiving certain data as a "new idea" I came to realize that this idea may very well have been expressed in earlier interviews but I had not been keyed into it because at the time of coming across it earlier in the process it hadn't yet proved to be a relevant piece of the puzzle. This led to me having to go back to those earlier transcripts and re-code them in light of the new and emerging developments. The more data I had, the more the analytic process unfolded and the more the pieces that could potentially be constructed into theory began to present themselves.

Once I had other data to compare data to and make connections with, I started to see where the linkages are and how the data could be strung together and cross referenced to construct concepts and categories. It was as if the analytic process was a dialogue or discussion between various viewpoints on the same topic. However, in reality each instance that involved actual people involved only dyads – me and a single participant. And yet when it was just me sitting at my computer in the Nvivo software interface, it was as if I was facilitating a dialogue using the snippets of voices represented in the data set. As I write that, it sounds like I'm some sort of sinister puppeteer manipulating a world according to my vision. And while my intentions were neither sinister nor autocratic, there was a reality to the idea that I was conducting and therefore heavily influencing this dialogue of data and fashioning it in a way that made sense to me. And still all of the voices used in the construction of this dialogue were not my own – but the choices of how to construct them into a cohesive theoretical framework were.

An example of the types of choices I made is one instance where a participant was talking at length about how Western psychology focuses on the mind and doesn't necessarily deal with the soul. I could have created a whole category on the distinction between the Western concept of mind and the Islamic concept of soul, the nature of the difference between the two paradigms and where that difference lies. Certainly this is an important consideration that warrants investigation due to the fact that the concept of the self as mind is so influential and dominant in contemporary society and contemporary psychology. But instead I chose to code this data excerpt more generally under "Western psychology paradigm differs from Islamic paradigm" because my focus and the question underlying my research was "What are the core principles and concepts regarding the conceptualization of the person from within an Islamic paradigm?" I chose not to focus on the comparison of the Islamic paradigm with that of a Western paradigm as my main concern in developing the theory. This inquiry comes up in the discussion of the findings and it could be reasonably argued to be an important consideration in the development of such a theory in terms of its applicability in the contemporary world. Certainly an important aspect of defining something is in comparing it to other similar things to determine what it is and what it is not. But it was my contention that trying to understand Islamic psychology as a unique paradigm from within the already accepted paradigm of Western psychology could potentially colour the way in which the content is viewed and understood, which seemed to be antithetical to the whole project. Since the research aim was to elucidate a uniquely Islamic paradigm of psychology, I wanted to be as unencumbered as possible, if that is even possible, by preconceived notions of psychology as have been understood in contemporary times. These and other choices that I made influenced the analytic process and in turn the theory that was produced as a result, as I single-handedly conducted a symphony of voices.

6   Stages and Development of the Soul: The Clinical Scope of Islamic Psychotherapy

Introduction

Given the lack of development of and therefore research into indigenous approaches to Islamic psychotherapy, it has been unclear until now what the scope of such therapy might be. It may be assumed that a religious orientation to psychotherapy is focused primarily on the spiritual beliefs of clients and that the range of what such approaches can address is limited to aligning with religious teachings rather than addressing serious mental health issues. The question can also arise as to just how far religiously oriented psychotherapy can or should delve into matters of spiritual development and where the line should be drawn in terms of addressing one's psychological state for the purpose of mental health versus acting as a spiritual guide. This presents the need to define the clinical scope of Islamic psychotherapy in an attempt both to construct appropriate parameters for professional capacity and to distinguish it from other traditional religious guidance within the context of the Islamic tradition.

Perhaps the most poignant and relevant direction for understanding the role of the therapist within the Islamic tradition and the paradigm it is situated in is found in the writings of Abu Hamid al-Ghazali's *Iḥyā' 'Ulūm al-Dīn*. In a passage from the third quarter of that seminal volume al-Ghazali proposes that there are two ways of acquiring self-awareness. The first and more desirable of the two pathways, albeit the most uncommon, is that a person would "be in the hands of one of his shaykhs" (al-Ghazali, 2014, p. 256) and be guided and instructed on an intimate level with a disciplined commitment to advanced study and development. This path that al-Ghazali refers to is that of traditional Islamic spirituality (*taṣawwuf*) where a practising Muslim would adopt a spiritual mentor (shaykh or murshid) to guide them in this process of self-awareness (Ernst, 2017). The second pathway is that one should set out "to seek a sound companion, knowledgeable in the secrets of this matter, and appoint him as an observer of his self, to note his states and alert him to his faults. Thus did the great leaders of the religion" (al-Ghazali, 2014, pp. 257). By this he means that while this 'sound companion' may not be at the level of a shaykh who is versed in the intricate secrets of the soul, this alternative role can be filled by one who has trodden the path of self introspection with some effort and success and has thus achieved somewhat of an elevated psycho-spiritual state. This opens the doors to defining the scope for the Islamic psychotherapist.

Whereas some models of care within the health sciences rely heavily, if not entirely, on the practitioner's knowledge and mastery of technique in the process of "administering" treatment to clients or patients, within the realm of Islamic psychotherapy, as with other spiritually integrative approaches, it is perhaps less plausible that such professional proficiency is solely sufficient for effective treatment (Shafranske & Malony, 1990). In models of care that acknowledge and incorporate the sacred and spiritual realms, the scope of therapy can be greatly affected by the therapist's capacity for competently traversing such non-conventional territory within a professional therapeutic relationship. Indeed it would seem that, in addition to conventional professional training, the role of the therapist within an Islamic context and their relative spiritual state become equally important factors due to the religious nature of the milieu. This is evident in the accounts of the participants and highlighted in the analysis that follows, and it is also reflected in classical sources from the Islamic tradition.

Given the proposed role of the therapist being one that could achieve some of the utility of a spiritual guide, the relative spiritual state of the therapist becomes a relevant factor. It is recognized in many schools of Western therapy, particularly in Jungian and the Humanistic schools of theoretical thought (Rowan, 2014), that the competent therapist must continually be engaged in doing their own work on themselves. Baldwin (2000) talks of the conception of the therapist's "self as instrument" and others expound upon the merit of continued therapeutic growth of the therapist (McWilliams, 2004; Orlinsky & Rønnestad, 2005). Indeed it has been said that a therapist can only get their client to stages of growth that the therapist him or herself has achieved. Thus from within the Islamic model of development of the soul, it could be suggested that the Islamic psychotherapist should have personal experience and active commitment to working toward the advancement through the stages of the soul in the struggle against the *nafs* (*jihād an nafs*).

This chapter presents a continuation of the analysis of the data from phase two in order to further elaborate on the emerging theory, specifically as it relates to the stages and development of the soul and how these inform the scope of Islamic psychotherapy within this theoretical framework. The same set of qualitative interviews with the same range of psychotherapists from diverse backgrounds provided the input with which to develop the theoretical conceptualization of Islamic psychotherapy. The models produced in this phase, and presented in this and the previous chapter, constitute a theory of Islamic psychotherapy.

Results

The first two of the four categories generated by the analysis (Nature of the Soul and Structure of the Soul) were presented in the previous chapter. Here the focus is on the remaining two categories: Stages of the Soul and Development of the Soul. While the first two categories represented the foundational constructs that participants used in conceiving of their theoretical orientation to approaching psychotherapy within an Islamic paradigm, the latter two categories represent a further exploration of the development of those principles into practice. Thus the analysis presented in this chapter demonstrates a development of the theory into practical applications and helps to construct a model of the clinical scope of Islamic psychotherapy. Table 6.1 lists the two theoretical categories and new insights related to them based on the participants' input from phase two which help to develop the theory in light of their clinical experience.

Stages of the Soul

Participants seemed to agree that most of their work, at least initially or with short term clients, is focused on the level of *nafs*, as that is where most of the visible manifestation of psychological and/or spiritual imbalance appears. When it came to talking about the stages of the soul (*nafs al-ammārah bil su, nafs al-lawwāmah,* and *nafs al-muṭma'innah*), those participants with more familiarity with the Islamic teachings of these stages conceived of

Table 6.1 Theoretical Categories and Subcategories – Phase 2b

Main categories	Subcategories
Stages of the Soul	Majority of psychotherapy is between *nafs al-ammārah bil su* and *nafs al-lawwāmah* Movement through the stages as treatment goal *Nafs al-muṭma'innah* and beyond – scope of Islamic psychotherapy
Development of the Soul	Development of the soul of the client – treatment approach • *Jihād an Nafs* (struggle of the soul) • *Tahdhīb al-akhlāq* (reformation of character) • Using the *Muhlikat* and *Munjiyat* in assessment and treatment Development of the soul of the therapist – training approach • Role of the therapist • Therapist's own *Jihād / Tazkiyat an Nafs* • State of the therapist • Differentiating between Islamic psychotherapy and *taṣawwuf*

them not as different stages that one achieves but more as qualities that the *nafs* takes on based on the person's degree of *jihād an nafs*. Participants said that when a person is not exerting much effort in their *jihād an nafs*, then the *nafs* is more in the stage or state of *ammārah bil su*, where the person is following base inclinations which pull them further away from *fiṭrah* and tend to result in psychological imbalance, dysfunction or *ghafla*. However, they believed that when the *nafs* is in a state of struggling to control itself, then it has the quality of *lawwāmah*, where it is attempting to regulate itself and find equilibrium. Participants emphasized that this change in the state of the *nafs* is very volatile and subject to change based on the will and self-control on the part of the client. Maha said, "Every day we go out and we have the potential to come back home with *nafs al amara bil su* or to come back home with the *nafs al-muṭma'innah* … It's literally a daily thing and it's a fact that it's a moment to moment thing".

Majority of Psychotherapy Is between Nafs al-ammārah bil su and Nafs al-lawwāmah

Due to the volatile nature of the *nafs* and the idea that this is where a client's presenting problem will most likely surface and be identified as the problem they are seeking help with, participants expressed the view that the client and thus the therapy process is often dominated by work at this level of the soul. Rayyan said, "For people who generally come to me we're stuck in this *nafs*, identifying of the *nafs* process. And usually they're between the *nafs al-ammārah* and the *nafs al-lawwāmah*". Rayyan was not alone in recognizing that much of this *nafs* level work is a back-and-forth process between the two lower stages, with only very brief glimpses into or periods when a person is crossing into *nafs al-muṭma'innah*. Rayyan went on to describe how she works to identify the stage of the *nafs* that her clients are in and that a large part of her job, echoed by other participants, is to help the client learn how to be aware of and respond to this dynamic process within the work of *jihād an nafs* and *tahdhīb al-akhlāq*. Rayyan said:

"It's about teaching them that feelings are soldiers. And they're trying to get us to do something. And if I feel guilt then the immediate reaction is that I need to do something to remove the guilt which is to act in a just way. If my guilt is coming at times which when I haven't done anything wrong and it's just taking over my life then my guilt is what needs to be calmed down, not my actions. That I feel is just right there in the *nafs*. And if they stay too long in the *nafs al-lawwāmah*, they'll fall back into the *nafs al-ammārah* because they get tired. You know they get tired of this constant inner battle. And so a lot of the talking I do is really on the level of the *nafs*."

It was a notion shared by many participants that movement between the stages of the soul is not only natural and healthy but is what the therapist should encourage in the therapeutic process as it is the dynamic that activates and fuels the balancing process and thus moves toward equilibrium and healing.

This idea was developed further by four participants who said that if a person stays in either of the two lower stages too long, it becomes pathological. It was a shared belief among them that if a person stays in *nafs al-ammārah* they can become pathologically hedonistic or even narcissistic, feeding into the ego and being overtaken by a constant preoccupation with fulfilling one's every desire to enact selfish tendencies. It became apparent through the account of many of the participants that narcissism – a pathological preoccupation with aggrandizing the self – is considered one of the worst psychological disorders from an Islamic perspective. This comes from a central tenet in Islam that a Muslim is a servant of his or her lord and that anything good that comes from him or herself in fact is a blessing from God and not due to the person's own greatness. The state of rejecting this idea and adopting a belief that one is self-directed, not subject to the will of God, and thus individually deserving of praise is likened to that of *shayṭān* or *iblīs* (Satan), whom several of the participants referenced as the ultimate narcissist. These participants explained that there is a healthy amount of narcissism that is needed for self-preservation, self-love and self-motivation but that it needs to be tempered and brought into balance with self-regulation, that of the domain of *nafs al-lawwāmah*. In this vein Hamit said:

> "Your impulses might be healthy. There are biological drives and there are healthy routes for that. But then there is unhealthy and that's where your *nafs al-lawwāmah* comes in. It is not just a critic that's trying to get you to socially comply. It's for your own good."

The idea expressed here and by the others who talked about this dynamic is that *nafs al-lawwāmah* is a necessary stage that the soul must move into, by exerting the will in the processes of *jihād an nafs* and *tahdhīb al-akhlāq*, in order to regulate those natural tendencies and keep them from becoming pathological or creating imbalance in the whole system. While the *nafs al-lawwāmah* in an imbalanced state can become an overly critical voice within the person, as Hamit alluded to, with the right balance it can act as a regulating factor within the person's psyche.

Similar to the idea of *nafs al-ammārah bil su* potentially becoming pathological if one stays there, Enas discussed the dangers of staying in the stage of *nafs al-lawwāmah*. In describing the effort one exerts in the *jihād an nafs* and striving toward the development of the *munjiyat*, she said:

> "You use here *al-lawwāmah* – the self-reproaching soul. You can make benefit of the self-reproaching soul. It is a device. *Nafs al-lawwāmah* is a device. For this, I think the self-reproaching soul is very positive unless you are stuck here. If you settled in the reproaching soul it is pathological and you will get a serious illness, like neurotic guilt, maybe psychotic. You may punish yourself."

These four participants described the danger of staying in *lawwāmah* as being one where the natural function of this stage becomes unhealthy and detrimental, causing psychological imbalance and emotional blocks. Rayyan describes it like this:

"The *nafs al-lawwāmah* that has been hijacked, which I see a lot, which is you know the low self-esteem and self-deprecation and always hating yourself and always thinking of yourself as wrong and "I can't do anything right". So I see that as, you know, *nafs al-lawwāmah* is healthy, and which you know when you've done something wrong you reproach yourself. However, because of the culture in which most of my clients are coming from, which is built on guilt and shame, and often religion and family structures are built on fear and guilt. And then a lot of them come with this *nafs al-lawwāmah* that comes with a lot of negative thoughts and oppressive thoughts to themselves. And so here we work on trying to get them to not remove the *nafs al-lawwāmah*, right then because they're going to fall into *nafs al-ammārah*. But to go past the *nafs al-lawwāmah* and into the *nafs al-muṭma'innah*, where I can hear a thought and I will process it. I will see, ok if I'm wrong then what can I do to do better?"

Movement through the Stages as Treatment Goal

It was articulated by participants that much of the work on the *nafs* level was finding ways to help move the client from one stage of the soul to the next. They saw part of their role as therapists as being a catalyst for movement to help their clients not be stuck in either of the two lower stages of the soul. Hamit describes one way that he engages his clients in this process in a therapy session:

"So that's the self-critic, *nafs al-lawwāmah* is extreme here. So what will I do? I might use chair techniques which I illustrate. I say I am going to put your *nafs al-lawwāmah* in the other chair. And I want your *nafs al-lawwāmah* to make you feel bad. 'Oh, you are so useless, you don't pray *salah*, you don't do this, you don't do that' and then I want you to come back in this chair, how does that feel?' Feeling-wise... and what happens is ... the change occurs when there is a negotiation between the two sides such that the *nafs*, the *nafs al-lawwāmah* trusts that it is not going to ... going to hedonism and therefore can lighten the reins a little bit."

In this account Hamit is using a well-known technique from his training in Western psychotherapy methods but is implementing the conception of the Islamic model of the soul to help the client understand their relationship to their own inner process. Where this technique might normally be used by asking someone to imagine a person with whom they are in conflict in the other chair, this approach, from the Islamic paradigm of psychology, engages the notion of the soul in session and involves these conceptions in the therapeutic process.

Another example of participants' accounts of how they encourage movement through the stages of the soul was Kabir's explanation of how he works with a client to bring conscious awareness of the dynamic interplay that happens within the soul. He employs a directive within the session to help his client see the bigger picture at play, as he describes:

> "One technique is to do a personal checklist with yourself. If I do what I want, you know, either way you're going to suffer. For example, I sat at this point with the *nafs al-lawwāmah*, your *nafs* is vacillating because it wants something, but it also knows there's consequences to either pathway. You know, pros and cons, and for example with the addicts I'll point out that if you do decide to follow you know the red [referencing the lower half of Figure 4.1], you're going to experience short term pleasure but you're also going to have the *haram* [forbidden] hang over or the after effect of lowness and depression. If you decide to go towards Allah, you're going to have short term pain but you'll have longer or more sustained sweetness and tranquillity and connection."

Here Kabir describes how he helps clients do what many participants expressed in different ways, which is to help clients understand that what they experience as struggle within their self may have more to it underneath the surface of their perception. Participants said that they help clients to engage with their struggle from within this larger Islamic perspective of the soul, taking into account the drives and motivations and consequences within this framework.

In the same way, participants described that they help a client to work toward recognizing these different states or stages of the soul and to understand what they look and feel like so as to be able to know not only how to strive toward the next stage but what they are actually striving toward in the process of *jihād an nafs*. Harun said, "The practical dynamic the clinician can meet that, and in understanding the broad principles of what we're working toward – their actions, you know, what is *nafs al-muṭma'innah*? What does it look like, what does it feel like?" Harun brought up an important point here as participants agreed that it is hard to help clients understand these stages of the soul, given that they are abstract concepts and many clients do not have a clear understanding of what they mean in a practical sense. This did not only apply clients: only a few participants, primarily those from group three, shared a clear idea of how to introduce clients to what the stage of *nafs al-muṭma'innah* feels like.

Similar to the accounts of participants in the previous chapter, most of whom had less of a clear idea of how to engage the *rūḥ* level of the soul in therapy, participants in groups one and two offered less in terms of how to engage clients in moving into *nafs al-muṭma'innah*. It was primarily only Harun, Enas and Mustafa who shared practical tools that they use within the context of therapy to encourage movement towards or at least 'tastes' of this stage of the soul. This was primarily done through the use of Islamic contemplation practices such as *murāqabah* (meditation) or *tafakkur* (contemplation). Mustafa described *tafakkur* in an Islamic context and how he uses guided imagery in sessions with clients:

> "In Islam contemplation is appreciation first, that is to cross from the beauty of the things to its creator. *Tafakkur* I think it has its steps to me, there is the way, just get to appreciate creation. Then you move from the appreciation to the creator of this thing that you have appreciated because I think that people who are not Muslim, who don't believe in God, also appreciate the beauty of nature. Once you get to appreciate, then this will move you gradually to close your eyes, take a deep breath and imagine yourself in the ocean and you can hear the waves coming onto the shore, making this noise. You can see far away, you can hear children playing, you can hear them. Until he really imagines this very well, now if from this you go to the creator, Allah is overlooking all this"

Mustafa went on to explain that by guiding a person to experience this serene state of calmness within, while witnessing the power or glory of God, this gives clients a taste of what *nafs al-muṭma'innah* feels like, so that they know what they are striving for and can work toward coming back to that place more often.

Enas described a very similar practice of guided imagery that she does with her clients in session. Here she shares what some of her clients have shared with her after experiencing this:

> "They feel that there is a divine existence. When one of the patients said 'When you told me about that I see the universe I saw the stars and planets. I saw that I am big but because of Allah's support not big by myself. Not high self-esteem. Not ego. The *rūḥ*. I felt that Allah is protecting me. I felt that everything can harm me before is very small. And was completely protected by light.'"

The cognitive conception of a theological notion of God can be an impractical thing to expect clients to connect with while being occupied with a difficult life situation or psychological problem. Participants reported these types of guided experiences to be very useful and very powerful in achieving a similar aim of connecting with God. It was understood by all participants that living in the stage of *nafs al-muṭma'innah* is very difficult and not practical nor within the scope of psychotherapy treatment for most clients. However these practices, shared by the few participants who use them, appeared to be aimed at helping clients at least to cross into this more advanced stage, with the expectation that they would vacillate back and forth. Mustafa explained that his aim in using *tafakkur* in therapy was to build on experiences that clients may already have in glimpses and to help strengthen or elongate those experiences to use as tools going forward. He said:

"It is rare not to find a patient who has had such a feeling in his own place, the palm trees in the desert he sat down for a time, when were you most happy when you are watching nature, he will mention then I come to make him relive this again."

Nafs al-muṭma'innah and Beyond – Scope of Islamic Psychotherapy

While participants talked about the *nafs al-muṭma'innah* as being a crucial factor for motivation and having a goal to move out of *nafs al-lawwāmah*, they all agreed that it is much less likely that a person is able to dwell there, and if they were to then they would essentially have graduated from what Islamic psychotherapy can offer. In this regard Enas said, "The serene soul needs a lot of *jihād* [struggle] to reach and settle". Several participants said that they see their work being within *al-ammārah* and *lawwāmah* and the goal being to get the client to the door of *muṭma'innah* but beyond that point they mostly agreed that it was more appropriate for the therapist to then refer the person to a shaykh who can guide them on a more explicitly religious path of spiritual development. Commenting on this, Rayyan said:

"So obviously for me to get them to be stationed in *nafs al-muṭma'innah* is hard because you would need someone very powerful for that, like a shaykh. But they get flashes of it, glimpses of it. And when they get those glimpses it feels so natural. Like 'Finally I'm functioning.' And when they feel that on their own they are the ones who then strive and work hard to get themselves to the *nafs al-muṭma'innah*. Then they will work on their own to get there or they'll seek a person outside of me who is more specialized in that to help them in that way."

Whereas in the previous chapter participants' accounts suggested the need to rely on Islamic scholars for issues pertaining to religious knowledge, here what Rayyan is referring to in reference to a shaykh is somewhat different. Whereas a religious scholar may be able to offer knowledge that can be limited to the memorization of texts within Islamic law, a shaykh of *taṣawwuf* (Sufism) was seen by most participants to be someone who, in addition to book knowledge, has experiential knowledge or *ma'rifah* of the soul due to their own elevated spiritual state. Many participants said they perceive a line where their work within psychotherapy reaches a point beyond which the further development of the soul would lie in the realm of work of a shaykh of *taṣawwuf*. This will be explored further later in this chapter in the discussion of the role of the therapist.

As it pertains to the stages of the soul, the reason why a shaykh may be better equipped to work with a person within the realm of the soul's development in and beyond *nafs al-muṭma'innah* is based on the conception that there are higher and higher stages of spiritual attainment. In the first phase the data showed that the scholars who were interviewed mentioned additional stages of the soul beyond the three that were identified. The reason why the findings of that phase focused on the three main stages is that, in addition to being the ones most frequently referenced in the Qur'an and in scholarly writings and *tafsīr*, they were also thought of by participants in that phase as being most applicable for something like psychotherapy. This notion seemed to resonate with the clinician participants in this second phase who agreed that, as their primary objective is to help clients achieve a state of equilibrium within their soul, the highest stage they would be working with would be *nafs al-muṭma'innah*. Enas referenced the additional stages of the soul from the primary religious source saying, "The Quran says, *arg'y illa Rabika radiyyatan mardiyyah*. It is just an emotional status, something like this – 'Return to your lord well-pleased and well pleasing'. Still there is more definition, more and more". She explains that there are indeed additional stages beyond *nafs al-muṭma'innah* and that, from her point of view, these additional stages are higher states of the soul as it progresses, which most people do not achieve. Thus participants understood their role as Islamic psychotherapists to involve only minimal engagement with the stage of *muṭma'innah*, as their main focus is working with clients in the struggle between the two lower stages.

Development of the Soul

Development of the Soul of the Client – Treatment Approach

Most of the participants conceived of their role as an Islamic psychotherapist as being to help their clients grow and develop, not just in life and the pursuit of happiness but in the development of the soul for the sake of God. It was generally agreed by all 18 participants that simply removing symptoms or helping a person to achieve a more functional life in the *dunya* was not what their primary objective was. Hamit said:

> "So the human health and pathology is, essentially from an Islamic standpoint, ultimate health is salvation in the afterlife and at minimum, you know, being free of the fire of hell and entering into paradise and at maximum it is *ma'rifato Allah* [experiential knowledge of God] so that meaning at higher state is that, you know, we reach a state where we truly kind of regain the love of God and we have this sort of special relationship with Allah *subhana wa ta'ala* and that is sort of the ultimate kind of indicator of health. And *al-shariah* [Islamic religious instructions] is *al-tareeq* [the path], it is literally a pathway to get us there. So anything that gets us off of that pathway is worthy of intervention."

The thing that participants seemed to agree on as defining the therapeutic process as Islamic was that a central motivating factor in the treatment goal was to get closer to God. This was further defined by many participants as fundamentally being about struggling with or even against the *nafs* or self in order to attain greater closeness to God. Imbalance or psychological "problems" were not primarily seen as problems in and of themselves but were seen as symptoms, signals or signs of the real problem being a disconnection from God or disconnection from the awareness and remembrance of God.

Jihād an Nafs (Struggle of the Soul)

The most common defining aspect of where participants saw the focus of their work in relation to the model of the soul was in the process of *jihād an nafs*. Many participants remarked that they did not necessarily make a distinction between *jihād an nafs*, *tazkiyat an nafs* and *tahdhīb al-akhlāq*, agreeing that while *tazkiyah* and *tahdhīb al-akhlāq* may be more advanced or refined stages of the *jihād*, the term or concept of *jihād an nafs* encompasses both. Essentially what they came to articulate collectively is that in order for one to make advancement on the path of submission to God and thus toward equilibrium in the self, one must come up against or face their *nafs* and struggle (*jihād*) against the tendencies that serve to distance them from their *fiṭrah* state of submission to God. Firas said, "For you to do *jihād an nafs*, you have to face the *nafs*", meaning that there is a necessity to discover within the self what is blocking someone from submitting to and/or remembering God. Thus participants often distinguished an Islamic model from many Western models which lack a paradigm where pursuit of closeness to God plays any direct role and where the treatment goal may simply be to get a person to a point of functioning in their life where they are not being made to feel uncomfortable by the dysfunction. Participants believed that in an Islamic model that is only a secondary part of the treatment goal. Instead treatment was seen as more primarily concerned with the development of the soul, which may include or necessitate some struggle, dysfunction and discomfort. Enas said, "The *nafs* suffer. This suffering of the *nafs* will nourish the *rūḥ*", pointing out that in an Islamic model suffering is often understood as a cleansing or purification of the *nafs* in order to reveal the true eternal self that exists beneath the suffering of the self in the *dunya*.

Participants represented the goal of Islamic psychotherapy as including the removal or tempering of symptoms of suffering, dysfunction or discomfort but also as helping a client at the same time to understand the potential that exists within the suffering and that within it lies the capability to grow on a deeper level in the soul. This soul growth appeared to be an aspiration of all 18 participants regardless of which of the three groups they belonged to. For some it remained more of an aspiration while for others it was a conscious and active part of their approach to psychotherapy. Therefore, all had in common an understanding that the Islamic approach aims to uncover the true self that exists underneath the psychological problems and imbalances and to connect the client to this deeper level of their identity in relation to God and their primordial truth beyond just this *dunya* existence, where these presenting problems manifest. Problems and psychological issues were seen not only as symptoms of a deeper issue but as signposts along the path of uncovering what lies beneath, in the *fiṭrah* state, the *rūḥ* aspect of the soul (as depicted in Figure 5.1).

Participants described the development of the soul as being an active engagement in the *jihād an nafs* to fight against the pull downward toward the red elements in the model in Figure 4.1, and actively striving toward the upper blue parts of the model or higher self. Kabir said:

"In the moment of *jihād an nafs* you are literally experiencing this dialogue. You are presented with options which will take you closer to the *rūḥ* and Allah and options which will continue to pull you down into the *shayṭān* and into your lower desires."

Similar to al-Ghazali's reference to the soul as a battleground, many participants described the work on the self as being a dynamic struggle much like a fight. Safa said:

"People are torn, they want, like so when it comes to forgiving – forgiveness right which is a part of the process, there has to be a process of like well first connecting to yourself and Allah *subhanah wa ta'ala* [glory be to God] to be able to get to that process of forgiveness. But to me that whole process is *jihād an nafs* because you maybe want to be angry, maybe you want to take revenge, maybe you want to just jump off a cliff. So all of the battle that people are going through, for me, it's manifestations of *jihād an nafs*."

Tahdhīb al-akhlāq (Reformation of Character)

Part of this process of *jihād* that participants described at a certain point takes on the quality of refinement, so that it moves from a battle against the self to a refinement of the self. This is where participants said they use the concept of *tahdhīb al-akhlāq* within the process of assisting clients in their *jihād an nafs*. From what participants described, it could be thought that *tahdhīb al-akhlāq* is something that a person can employ once they have gone out of *nafs al-ammārah* and are in the stage of *nafs al-lawwāmah* and beyond. In reference to further dynamics of refining the character, Rayyan offered some useful distinguishing terms, saying "*takhliyah* is like removing those negative qualities and then *tahliyah* is beautifying yourself with the beautiful qualities". Here Rayyan was commenting on the functions of the *munjiyat* and *mukhlikat* in helping a client to refine their character (*tahdhīb al-akhlāq*). She said that she often will have to work with people to maintain a balance by not only focusing on the negative traits they wish to get rid of but the positive ones that are often opposite to the negative traits and that should replace them. She went on to say, "I feel like where a lot of, at least the people that I've worked with, struggle is they can do *takhliyah* and then they don't do *tahliyah* so they can slip right back into where they were". Rayyan reflected a sentiment shared by a few participants who recognized that there is a subtle interplay of how and when these qualities are applied in order for them to be most effective.

Using the Munjiyat and Muhlikat in Assessment and Treatment

Both Rayyan and Mustafa said that they identify the *mukhlikat* that present themselves in the character of the client when they first come in as a way of assessing what are the character traits that need addressing. From their perspective and experience, this dictates the treatment and where to approach the client from. Enas said, "A lot of the psychological disease categories are based on *al muhlikat*", implying that much of what is listed in the *Diagnostic Statistical Manual of Mental Disorders* matches with what is conceived of as *muhlikat* within the Islamic teachings. Mustafa explained how he assesses his clients in this way, identifying the *muhlikat* to know where to focus his treatment. In the following excerpt he references the "lion and the pig". Here Mustafa is referring to the language used by al-Ghazali to describe the *muhlikat*, the lion representing pride and arrogance and the pig representing greed and self-indulgence; both are personifications of certain types of *muhlikat* that work in conjunction with the *shayṭān*:

> "In psychotherapy you all the time, first of all when the patient comes to speak about his complaint, you will look for the lion and the pig and you look for where the *shayṭān* is using them in this particular patient. If he comes to speak to you about people that are against me and 'My boss is so and so this is so and so', then you begin to think about the lion is at work. If he comes to say, 'I want to enjoy life and so and so but I cannot get it and my siblings actually put their hand on the money that our father has left and I'm not being given any', then you can see the pig at work."

They then use the *munjiyat* as the treatment for those traits. Rayyan related, "Whatever is keeping them in that cycle would be a *mukhlikah*, and the *munjiyah* would be what helps them transcend that situation". Both Rayyan and Mustafa discussed this as an internal process they do only within their self without sharing with clients, while Enas talked more specifically about using these concepts with clients in session. Enas was the most articulate about the specifics of how and when to bring in the *muhlikat* and *munjiyat* and that the timing of these things can directly affect their effectiveness. She said, "When you are doing like more of the conceptualization you focus more on the *munjiyat* than the *muhlikat*. So it is like positive psychology". Enas described that in the initial stages of this process she will take something similar to a strength-based approach in that she is trying to build up the person's sense of self-worth and confidence by focusing on the positive and not on the negative qualities of the *mukhlikat*. She explained that later, after she has worked to build the client up, she then uses the *mukhlikat* to reinforce the *munjiyat*:

> "*mukhlikat* themselves are high quality. It isn't pure negative thinking. So it helps me a lot the *mukhlikat*, after the *munjiyat*, to prevent relapse. I educate them: if you do this, this will happen. Because he is a believer now. He is strong. Before they are weak. When you tell them they just flip their heart, they can't tolerate. If you want to tell them about *mukhlikat*, it is after *munjiyat*, It prevents relapse. It is important, very important, the sequence."

The use of *tahdhīb al-akhlāq* as an aspect of the greater *jihād an nafs* was regarded by participants as one framework that they use to help clients fight against their *muhlikat*, or lions and pigs, the lower impulses which they perceived as the causes of most psychological problems. Thus the heart of the development of the soul was thought to be this inner work on the self.

Development of the Soul of the Therapist – Training Approach

All participants saw their role as Islamic psychotherapists, helping clients in this soul development, as necessarily involving their own work on themselves as part of the journey and part of what they consider their training for their work. Unlike some secular Western schools of therapy that may focus on technique or the implementation of a therapeutic model as the driving factor in treatment success, from the collective accounts of the participants in this phase of the study it appeared that Islamic psychotherapy requires more of a personal commitment from the therapist, more akin to Humanistic psychotherapy approaches (Rowan, 2014). Thus while all participants had extensive training in various methods of therapy, there was another factor that was felt to be of central importance in their training for their role: the role of the therapist not only as a professional providing a service but as one with a sensitive position both in the context of Islam and with regards to their own state of psycho-spiritual development was given a great deal of consideration by all participants.

Role of the Therapist

Given that the approach that participants take in integrating Islamic principles into psychotherapy or, as some of them would claim, even in operating within an Islamic paradigm, there was a pronounced awareness among participants that their role can come close to crossing from a professional practitioner of psychology into the realm of religious guide, as was mentioned earlier but further made relevant in the specific context of understanding the therapist's role. Many participants discussed the need to make this distinction both for clients and seemingly for themselves as well. Enas said:

"I mean, you are not a religious guide. You are not a religious guide, you are a therapist. 'Therapist' means that you know the rules of the human being, the psychological laws. So, you apply or implement according to what you know about the human being."

This was reflected in most participants' views, that an Islamic psychotherapist's role is not to help them be a better Muslim or understand the religion of Islam better as the primary goal. Participants stressed that the goal still needs to remain what it would for any psychotherapist, namely to alleviate dysfunctional symptoms and encourage healthy growth. However, it was clear that participants understood the potential lack of clarity when indeed they are engaging in aspects of spiritual matters with regards to the development of the soul.

Enas went on to say that while she does not see herself as a guide to the religion itself, she does recognize the role that God plays in her work. Her conception, which was shared by many participants, was that God is the one who helps a client heal and, given their integration of Islamic principles and tools, that any success in therapy is attributed to God. Interestingly, Enas pointed out that while she believes this, she does not bring the client's attention to this notion at first. She said, "The client thinks that you indeed have superpowers. I mean he must not understand that Allah helped you, for transference will not happen if you told him it's Allah". Here she highlights the subtlety that while involving God in the process of psychological growth within psychotherapy is a unique feature of a spiritual orientation, she still abides by the concept of transference, known best within the psychoanalytic framework.

Similarly, Samir mentioned his conception of his role as an Islamic psychotherapist having resonance with Western models of counselling. He identified an aspect of his approach to counselling which could easily be seen as person-centred but which he attributes to his Islamic framework:

"I'm always trying to ground my counselling and my counselling relationship that I use as a cornerstone regardless of the theoretical underpinning of my work because I feel that if we establish the trust and the ability for the client to relate to me I think that's, that's really important. From an Islamic prospective in terms of how the prophet *salalahu alayhi wa salam* [peace and blessings upon him] used to deal with people and make people, regardless of their background, the most important person. He would pay full attention and *subhan Allah* [glory to God] research in modern times says that's really important – the relationship is the core for positive outcomes of counselling."

In describing his role as an Islamic psychotherapist, Shahid also referenced a teaching from the Prophet Muhammad. He said:

"When I meet a new client I often describe this as how I see my role. I'll say that one aspect of my role I see very much as that of acting as a mirror. And isn't it interesting that the Prophet *salalahu a*layhi wa salam said words to the effect that the believer is a mirror to his brother. So again, it's a highly Islamic activity to do and the hope is that through our knowledge and experience that we can be in some ways a more accurate mirror than perhaps our clients experience in the reflections from their own parents or their own environments."

This metaphor of the mirror is one that was brought up in the phase one, where the scholar participants referenced the notion of the soul of the person being a mirror that can reflect the light of God. The metaphor was used both in the sense of the potential for a person to 'polish their mirror' by doing *jihād an nafs* and thus reflecting the light of the *rūḥ* in their soul, as well as the potential for a person to reflect back to a companion their own state of their soul. Rayyan also made this reference in describing her role:

"I am doing a lot of being their mirror. And kind of just pointing out in a clinical sense what I see of who they are. And it's nothing that I'm adding to them. It's like they're giving it to me but they're unable to see it. And again that goes back to Islamic psychology or Islam in general because the Prophet *salalahu alayhi wa salam* said 'We're mirrors of one another.' And so it's as if I'm a professional mirror."

Therapists' Own Jihād / Tazkiyat an Nafs

Given participants' conception of their role as being, as Rayyan put it, "a professional mirror", it was understood by most that it is of great importance for the therapist to make sure that they are able to be a clear reflection for their clients by polishing their mirror. As revealed in the first phase, the notion of one doing the work of polishing their mirror, to be free from the turbidity of the crust from the *nafs*, is expressly connected to the notion of *tazkiyat an nafs* (purification of the soul). It was generally agreed upon by all participants in phase two that in order for a person to truly be able to do the work of an Islamic psychotherapist, they need to be engaged in this process of purifying their own soul. Firas explained it this way:

"I do feel that as a Muslim therapist because you're considered a *murrabi* [mentor], because you're considered that guide somebody might consider you as a shaykh that you're supposed to also continuously work on reforming your own self, right. So if you're having these issues and you're just kind of ignoring them, so if you have to go see a therapist or someone you should but ideally this process of *tazkiyat an nafs* for your client is also happening within you. And every client that comes in, you could almost see some level of problem within you that they're having. Part of that healing process is going to be like you also work on yourself while you work with them."

What Firas describes is very similar to what many schools of Western psychotherapy encourage in terms of the therapist being in therapy themselves or, as in the case of Freudian and Jungian analysis, that being a primary aspect of the training to become an analyst. This notion of being a living model of the work on the self was expressed across all participants as being a key factor to effectiveness, as Hind said:

> "So I think being able to integrate that and being able to live it myself first and foremost. If I'm not living it clients see through it and they can tell. I really feel like if they see that you strongly believe in it and truly mean it and you're able to get results that that's really powerful for clients."

Hind's statement could easily be true for many schools of Western psychotherapy and indeed participants even referenced this notion from their Western training as being one of the things they integrated from that training. As Rahim said, "Jung certainly expressed that when he said for instance the only qualification for a therapist is knowing themselves therefore in effect they were an analyst, that the training was irrelevant beyond that". However, it appeared that in the views of most participants this was even more important within an Islamic context given the nature of the work on the soul.

The role of the therapist in this Islamic context was conceived of as needing to be more about a personal commitment on the journey of the development of their own soul rather than simply training for the job. Harun referred to some of the teachings from his teachers in traditional Islamic healing methods saying, "My teacher used to say 'This is for you, don't think you're out there helping other people, you know, you're helping yourself.'" He went on to say, "This principle of working on oneself and seeing what we do in the proper light and staying on the journey for our own transformation in a really full way is an important part of what this is about". This point of it being central to Islamic psychotherapy and the *tazkiyat an nafs* of the therapist being more than just training was further brought home by Shahid who again referenced the mirror analogy saying, "It's not just to get an understanding of the process or whatever, it's also to get some healing, you see. Again, if we use the mirror analogy, how can we hold up a mirror which is truly reflective if we haven't got somewhere ourselves because then our distortions come into the mirror". Here Shahid reflected a shared belief by most if not all participants that perhaps one of the most important and central aspects of effective Islamic psychotherapy is the state of the therapist.

State of the Therapist

All 18 participants were clear that the state of the therapist was, in their opinion, one of the most defining features of an Islamic model of psychotherapy. Many expressed the view that, while they recognized the importance of the theoretical framework as guided by the Islamic paradigm, none of that is useful or effective unless the therapist has not only understood it cognitively but has also lived it and is experientially engaged in the process themselves. Some of the participants in group one were just vaguely aware of this principle, demonstrated in Obaid's statement, "I feel like maybe when I'm in a better spiritual state I think I'm more effective". Others, from the second and third groups, were more explicit and specific in their stance on this principle, as expressed by Harun:

> "I believe personally in the state of the therapist. In relation to the person. I mean we believe as Muslims, for example, this is another one of those principles of Islam, we believe in transmission. And we believe in the transmission of states. And we believe in learning in the glance of an eye, and things that we cannot measure"

Here Harun illustrates his confidence in this as a fundamental principle within Islam. He demonstrates that while this concept of 'states' – the relative spiritual condition of a person's inner heart or inner self – is an abstract, unmeasurable thing, his faith in it is fuelled by his belief in the tenets of Islam.

Rahim expressed a similar experience of confidence in this inner experience and his use of it as a therapist when he said, "For me the crucial thing is my own inner state when I'm seeing a client. And the insights come from that and my confidence in relaying those insights". His confidence seemed to come from the trust in knowing that there was some source of insight or clarity with regards to what the client needs that may be beyond his own conception or insight but that comes to him from being receptive or in a 'state'. Rahim went on to say:

> "I seldom find I need to do more than point it out to somebody. You know I don't need to draw up charts and get people to keep diaries to track their thinking and so on. I think if there's that connection going on between you and the patient, there's very little sort of touching the rudder takes things in a different direction."

Here Rahim touched on a concept that seemed to be shared by all participants from group three and a few from group two – that they do not rely so much on any framework or technique as much as they rely on their connection both to God and to the client in front of them. It appeared that among these participants, the confidence they have in being able to work in this more spontaneous way with the needs of the client was due to a more developed state of their heart, from polishing their own mirror. Once these participants had a relatively clearer reflection in the mirror, they were able to work from this place where their own state was thought of as the therapeutic tool or technique in a sense.

Rayyan shared a very poignant description of what she feels it is like for the therapist to essentially use the state of their own heart as a therapeutic tool for connecting with the client and allowing for greater insights to come for the client's healing process. She said:

"And you have to really be willing to be vulnerable with yourself. Not sharing who you are, but as in allowing your heart to be very open while you're in the session with the person. So that you can feel where the person is. And I think that's another thing that's like very essential in this, where my feeling of Islamic psychology is that the base is *suhba*, like companionship. And in companionship you are not just physically with the person and not just emotionally with the person, but your heart is literally like on the table with the person. And when it's like that it's... I've found that when I've been able to open my heart to the person, and when the person has been willing to accept that openness, then this criteria, or like figuring this out [gesturing to the model in Figure 4.1] is very easy. Because then it's almost like a veil is lifted between us and these problems are just so clear. So even they'll tell me like, you know, I've been sitting here and I say things and I'm so amazed at what I'm figuring out about myself even though you've said nothing. But that only happens when I'm in a state, where I'm able to be open. But if I'm having a difficult time in life or if there's something in the person that's triggering something in me and I'm self-protecting internally, even though my words are the same, my actions are the same, that interaction doesn't happen. And this [pointing at model] becomes very difficult."

This description exemplifies what all the participants in group three pointed to as the key element in truly enacting the Islamic model of psychology. What they pointed to here was that the framework and the theory were only part of the formula, that if the therapist is not intimately engaged in their own psycho-spiritual work, they will not be able to uncover or access these deeper layers of the soul with the client. It is as if the lower two stratifications on the iceberg in Figure 5.1 are accessible by the therapist to engage the client only when the therapist is in the right state.

Rahim further expanded on how his way of working in an Islamic model is not primarily about technique or theoretical case formulation. He asserted just how important this state is in relation to theoretical orientation by quantifying it as a percentage:

"More than 50% is simply my own state. I can sometimes complete a session, even a difficult case, or maybe more sessions dealt with a typical case and I've thought, 'Well what on earth have I done?' You know, I've sort of sat there and it seemed to have hit the person in such a way that produced change and they come back with a new set of dreams or their dreams for the first time are clearly showing they've given up to their own guidance and you know, sort of, problem is over. Whereas if I was working as a Freudian or a CBT therapist I'd have very definite techniques. I'd be going through them, I'd be expecting certain goals to be reached in certain stages of therapy and that doesn't apply to me at all."

Rahim and Rayyan both commented on them not actually having to do much when they are in the right inner state themselves. Rahim went on to explain how he moves into such a state:

"It's almost like a default position. So it's about me going quiet. And I'm focusing, I suppose in my *niyyat* [intentions], on the needs of the person in front of me. I don't do a special *dhikr* [mantra], it just comes naturally. It all has to do with intention and I think love is always a part of it, we go into that state and you have a concern for that human being in front of you. There's that element of where love comes into it."

This love that Rahim mentions was not talked about as being a romantic love for the client in any way but rather a love that is predicated upon the connection of humanity and seeing God's love reflected in one another. This is a popular principle in Islam, that love between people is fundamental to being a Muslim or a believer in God. The Prophet Muhammad was reported to have said "None of you is a true believer until he loves for his brother what he loves for himself" (Sahih Bukhari No. 13, Sahih Muslim No. 45). Scholars in the classical Islamic tradition have indicated that the use of the word 'love' in this statement was significant because it points to the notion of love being a central factor in what connects people to each other.

It was apparent through the accounts of participants mainly in group three, and most articulated by Rahim and Rayyan, that the state of the therapist's heart was in direct correlation with the ability of the therapist to connect with the client. This connection was explained not simply as good therapeutic rapport but as the ability to connect to the soul of the client in a way that allows for the transmission that Harun referred to to occur. Rayyan explained what that connection is about and made a distinction with a Western notion of the client-therapist relationship:

"I mean even in Western psychology they say, I think it was like 85% of the result comes from your relationship with the person. But I think relationship isn't about how well you get along or how much the other person opens up even. I don't think that's about the relationship. I really think it's about where are you internally in your heart in that moment. I mean before a session, I prepare Islamically. So I go and I'll do *wuḍū* [ablution]. I'll do my *adhkar* [mantras]. And then I'll try to be in a state where I'm not thinking about other things. I'm not thinking about my problems. So if I can pray two *rakas* [cycles of prayer] I will pray because then I come and I am present. So definitely it would be a technique or a tool and it's a big part of my preparation for my session."

This idea of the state of the therapist being a tool used in Islamic psychotherapy was a prominent theme among groups two and three. The acts of worship (*'ibādat*) that Rayyan mentions that she does before sessions with clients was also something that others mentioned as preparations for therapy and to enter into this state that was spoken of. For those participants who see their work as integrally involving a spiritual role rather than merely a professional position, it seemed that they had a sense of gravity to what their role entailed in this regard to the point that they treated it with reverence. It was noticeable throughout the sample that as participants got closer to the higher levels of the soul or deeper into the iceberg where they were engaging the *rūḥ*, they perceived themselves as coming close to the boundaries of their work as psychotherapists and conscious of where their work ends and the realm of that of a shaykh of *taṣawwuf* may take over.

Differentiating between Islamic Psychotherapy and Taṣawwuf

This invisible line that appeared to be present in the participants' accounts of the role of the Islamic psychotherapist within the Islamic tradition was defined as both a shared sense of reverence within the larger Muslim community for the role of a shaykh, as well as participants' own apprehension to delve into territories of the soul that they may not be equipped to navigate. There seemed to be an expressed sentiment of needing to make that line clear for themselves as representing their role within an Islamic context. Harun expressed this saying:

> "Really I mean what I do is under the guise of *Hakim* [traditional Islamic medicine practitioner] but it saves me because it saves me from these other things that can become charged with these ideas that people carry, like 'shaykh', you know, or Sufi shaykh, or Sufism, or *taṣawwuf*. Half of what I'm doing is *taṣawwuf* or part of *taṣawwuf*. Half of it is healing with traditional models of healing in general and a lot of this just being like I said the comforts of just being a professional human being, you know, just being a good counsellor."

Harun clarified that what he meant by 'being a good counsellor' was akin to this notion of being in a good state in the heart, as discussed above. It was interesting to note that his use of the phrase 'professional human being' resonated with Rayyan's use of the phrase 'professional mirror' to describe the role of the Islamic psychotherapist. Both expressions reflect the notion that the idea of the therapist's role as a profession is not something attained by a degree or a license to practice but that they are making a profession out of cultivating their own state for the sake of helping others to reach a similar state. This is very much like the role of a traditional shaykh of *taṣawwuf* given that they occupy a 'position' within the Islamic tradition and not a professional position as a shaykh, their worth as a spiritual guide is predicated on the spiritual development they have been able to achieve.

There seemed to be a delicate balancing act for many participants in occupying a position between these two worlds of 'professional psychotherapist' and 'Islamic spiritual guide'. Yet many of them felt that it was important to do just that, to find a balance rather than completely go to one side or the other. Again, it was articulated that the role of the Islamic psychotherapist serves a distinct purpose of helping the client to reach a state of equilibrium, removing or equipping clients to remove the psychological impediments to further spiritual growth, but that further spiritual growth is perhaps not within the scope of psychotherapy. Hamit articulated this concept in this way:

> "Now, once we get them to normal functioning – meaning they are free of *amrad al-qulub* [diseases of the heart] and they are free of clinical dysfunction – well, our job is done but it doesn't have to be, meaning we can still help them, you know, internalize *makarem al-akhlaq*, like beautification of their character."

What Hamit is indicating here is that in his perception, the role of the Islamic psychotherapist is specifically situated within what would normally be considered the realm of psychotherapy, aiming to help clients achieve better psychological health, even if such health is defined somewhat differently in an Islamic model. His belief was that any continued work in therapy beyond that point is in a sense extra, to help further clients' growth and spiritual development. However, Hamit went on to say:

> "But the thing is my job as a clinician ends with one and two, with *inkishaf* and *i'tidaal*. Job three, I can help and assist slightly but we are not going to make the claim that as modern psychologists we replace *taṣawwuf*."

In mentioning jobs "one, two, and three" here, Hamit is referencing the TIIP model proposed by Keshavarzi and Khan (2018), with 'job three' being *ittihaad* (unity of being). Thus, what is being expressed here is that the role of the Islamic psychotherapist is situated within the Islamic tradition similar to that of a doctor from whom one seeks treatment for a specific concern that is inhibiting normal healthy functioning. In other words, the Islamic psychotherapist helps the client reach a state of equilibrium or *i'tidaal*, whereas the further development of the soul, with the goal of reaching *ittihaad*, is more appropriately left to the shayukh (Shaykhs) of *taṣawwuf* as they are believed to possess the necessary experiential knowledge of the soul to reach such heights of soul development.

Thus it seems that it is a requirement of the Islamic psychotherapist to know their limitations and to refer to the appropriate spiritual guide within the Islamic tradition for cases that reach or go beyond the point of achieving equilibrium. Mahmoud said:

> "I think that depending on your context you might, and depending on people's, you know, practices you would encourage them to go to their shaykh as well and that is in some ways a more of a longer-term relationship compared to a therapy relationship."

Almost all participants said that they would refer to a shaykh in this case but very few of them seemed to actually have the resources or familiarity with such people to do so. As Mahmoud indicated in the above quotation, the relationship of a shaykh to one who is being guided is traditionally within *taṣawwuf* considered to be a long-term or even life-long commitment. While many shayukh are in fact also equipped to help people with their development even at the lower stages of the soul and not just limited to higher spiritual attainment, it was reported by participants that these type of shayukh are perhaps few and far between. Participants also expressed the opinion that most people are only ever going to be struggling between the three main stages of the soul, with very few going very far into the stage of *nafs al-muṭma'innah*, and it is because of this that the role of the Islamic psychotherapist has such a clear position to fill within the Islamic tradition and the greater global Muslim community.

The Clinical Scope of Islamic Psychotherapy: A Theoretical Model

The model presented in Figure 6.1 illustrates the clinical scope of Islamic psychotherapy based on the input of participants in phase two of the study. In the centre of the Figure are the three main stages of the soul that were identified in phase one and illustrated in Figure 4.1 (*nafs al-ammārah bil su, nafs al-lawwāmah*, and *nafs al-muṭma'innah*), with the addition of a fourth box at the top representing the additional stages of the soul as referenced in both studies but with specific significance in phase two. This additional box lists the two additional stages of the soul that were identified in this phase, *nafs al radiyyah* and *nafs al mardiyyah*, with ellipsis signifying the mention of additional stages of the soul which were unnamed by participants. The circle encompassing all of the lower two stages of the soul and a bottom portion of the third stage represents the scope of the psychotherapist in the Islamic psychology model that was constructed as a result of the data from participants in this phase of the study.

Within the scope of the Islamic psychotherapist working in a clinical setting, the goal of therapy is to assist the client in moving through the stages of the soul in a non-linear fashion with a focus on progression upward in the model towards the higher stages of the soul. This clinical psychotherapeutic work is mostly confined to the lower two stages of the soul, with movement between *nafs al-ammārah bil su* and *nafs al-lawwāmah* in a back-and-forth fashion as clients struggle against their *nafs*, using their 'aql to access the *qalb* and remove blockages to their *fiṭrah* self (as depicted in Figure 5.1). This process is referred to as *jihād an nafs*, which encompasses all struggling against the soul at any point from the lower to the highest stages of the soul. Within the *jihād an nafs*, *tahdhīb al-akhlāq* is a process in which the therapist engages the client only when they have progressed out of the stage of *nafs al ammarah* and have entered into *nafs al-lawwāmah*, which allows for self-accountability. Here therapists use the *muhlikat* and *munjiyat* both as indicators of pathology and devices of treatment to target the balance of relevant character traits in the client

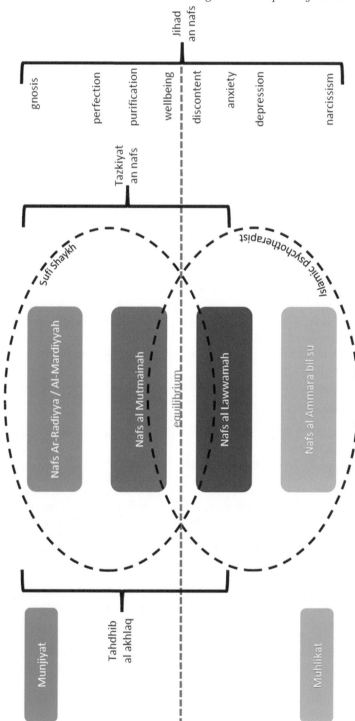

Figure 6.1 A Model of Islamic Psychotherapy Clinical Scope.

according to their treatment needs. The primary objective of treatment in this model is for the client to reach equilibrium in their soul, which is defined as the removal of psychological dysfunction that causes the client to become stuck in one of the lower two stages of the soul and thus to become stationed in between *lawwāmah* and *muṭma'innah*.

Also within the stage of *nafs al-lawwāmah* and higher, and as a part of the therapeutic application of *jihād an nafs*, the client is encouraged to engage in *tazkiyat an nafs* through the therapist's directive use of Islamic practices such as *muḥāsabah*, *murāqabah* and *tafakkur*. Once a client has progressed further into the stage of *nafs al-lawwāmah*, the therapist uses techniques such as guided imagery to direct the client toward experiencing moments of the stage of *nafs al-muṭma'innah* as a motivating factor to progress further along the upward trajectory of the soul. At the point that a client reaches into the stage of *nafs al-muṭma'innah* and is able to progress further into that stage, the client moves out of the scope of Islamic psychotherapy and into the scope of the shaykh of *taṣawwuf* who can continue working with the client to progress further into the higher stages of the soul if desired, potentially beyond *nafs al-muṭma'innah* to *nafs al radiyyah*, *nafs al mardiyyah*, and, albeit rarely, to even higher stages. This is represented by the upper circle in the centre of the figure which encompasses an upper portion of *nafs al-lawwāmah* and all of the higher stages of the soul. Findings reported in this chapter will be discussed in the following chapter alongside the findings reported in the previous two chapters, in a discussion of the theory as a whole.

References

Al-Ghazali, A. H. (2014). *Imam Al-Ghazali Mukhtasar Ihya Ulum Ad-din*. 2nd edition. Spohr Publishers.

Baldwin, M. (2000). *The use of self in therapy*. Haworth Press, Inc.

Ernst, C. W. (2017). *Sufism: An introduction to the mystical tradition of Islam*. Shambhala.

Keshavarzi, H., & Khan, F. (2018). Outlining a case illustration of traditional islamically integrated psychotherapy. In C. Y. Al-Karam (Ed.), *Islamically integrated psychotherapy: Uniting faith and professional practice* (pp. 175–207). Templeton Press.

McWilliams, N. (2004). *Psychoanalytic psychotherapy: A practitioner's guide*. Guilford Press.

Orlinsky, D. E., & Rønnestad, M. H. (2005). *How psychotherapists develop: A study of therapeutic work and professional growth*. American Psychological Association. https://doi.org/10.1037/11157-000

Rowan, J. (2014). Existential, humanistic, and transpersonal therapies and the relational approach. In D. Charura (Ed.), *The therapeutic relationship handbook: Theory and practice* (pp. 40–50). McGraw-Hill Education (UK).

Shafranske, E. P., & Malony, H. N. (1990). Clinical psychologists' religious and spiritual orientations and their practice of psychotherapy. *Psychotherapy: Theory, Research, Practice, Training, 27*(1), 72–78. https://doi.org/10.1037/0033-3204.27.1.72

7 Reflections Upon a Framework for an Islamic Psychology and Psychotherapy: An Agenda for Research and Practice

Overview

This final chapter of this book brings together the findings presented in the preceding chapters and discusses them in light of the research questions that underpinned the project. Here we discuss these findings in relation to the existing literature and illuminate where the developed grounded theory supports and builds upon previous work, where it challenges previous research and what original contributions of knowledge it makes to the literature and to the development of the field. Perspectives are offered on how the findings can inform and advance practical applications and new questions that the study raised are discussed in relation to implications for further research.

The aim of the research was to delineate a theory of psychology, grounded in an Islamic paradigm, that outlines a uniquely Islamic ontological understanding of the human being and a framework for practical applications of such a model in psychotherapy. This overarching aim was explored through two studies each driven by a question that guided the research. Phase one asked "What are the core principles and concepts regarding the conceptualization of the person from within an Islamic paradigm?" Phase two asked "How is the Islamic model of the soul conceptualized into a psychotherapeutic approach?"

The findings suggest that an Islamic conception of human psychology is fundamentally distinct from that of the dominant Western conception as represented in the literature. This was indicated in the model of the soul that was developed from the findings and suggests a departure from conventional conceptions of the self as being centralized in the mind, the Islamic conception instead involving a more heart-centred notion of self and the identification of the eternal soul as the core identity of the person. These distinctions were found to inform a unique approach to psychotherapy among practitioners who attempt to integrate the Islamic model of the soul into their clinical practice. The therapeutic approaches that were found to be unique to clinical practice informed by this model were the intentional efforts to access and release psychological blocks at increasingly deeper levels of the soul, namely in the *qalb* (heart) and *rūḥ* (spirit) levels of the soul. Additionally, the findings were used to construct a conceptualization of the clinical scope of Islamic psychotherapy, indicating that it can serve to bring clients to a state of psycho-spiritual equilibrium at which point clients may continue on in their personal spiritual development through other potential avenues within the Islamic tradition and the larger landscape of the cosmological paradigm.

Discussion of Findings: Elucidating the Clinical Relevance of the Islamic Model of the Soul

Phase One: Theoretical Foundations

In the first phase of the study, the question that underpinned the research was, "What are the core principles and concepts regarding the con-ceptualization of the person from within an Islamic paradigm?" It was found that although there exist a wide range of possible interpretations and viewpoints on what the Qur'an says about the human being and how this can be applied to formulate a structure or map of the human being, indeed many common foundational factors emerged as having primary importance to the conceptualization of a general framework of Islamic psychology. Whereas it has been argued in the literature that there could and perhaps should be multiple versions of Islamic psychology proposed (Al-Karam, 2018), the overwhelming agreement of some very fundamental principles among all 18 scholars who were interviewed showed a strong argument for the possibility of an overarching general framework for Islamic psychology, rather than simply "an" Islamic psychology. This was demonstrated in the agreement across almost all participants on the general structure of the model of the soul, as clearly represented in the Qur'an and elaborated by scholars throughout the history of Islamic thought. It may be important in the domain of Islamic Studies to highlight such differences of interpretation and the numerous permutations of details of how smaller specifics might be elaborated and conceived of. However, for the purposes of understanding the structure of the soul for application in psychotherapy, which was the primary focus of this phase, there is an arguable utility in presenting a basic consensual model. This is not as an act of reductionism, as the theory presented clearly recognizes the integral nature of the human soul and ac-knowledges that the Islamic paradigm is one of holism. It is instead an effort to make the theory most relevant for its intended purpose.

One of the criteria used to evaluate grounded theory studies is the concept of "relevance" (Glaser & Strauss, 1967; Glaser, 1978), which is similar to Elliott, Fischer, & Rennie's (1999) criterion of 'Resonating with readers' and Lucy Yardley's (2000) criterion of 'Impact and importance'. Relevance is evaluated based on the extent to which a theory engages with "the real world concerns of those involved in the processes it seeks to explain" (Weed, 2017, p. 9). While scholars of theology and philosophy concern themselves with articulating the depths of nuanced meanings contained within the epistemological framework of a religious cosmological paradigm, the domain of applied psychology is centred more specifically on the aspects of such a paradigm which affect the lived experience of a human being. Thus, for our purposes in understanding how a model of the soul can be used to help guide the therapeutic process, the theory development focused on those aspects that are most essential to understanding the basic principles of psychological anatomy in relation to personal development in order for the theory to have a higher level of relevance. For example, given that the *'aql* can be conceived as not being distinct from the *qalb*, we could have not included it in the model illustrated in Figure 4.1, and instead only represent the *qalb*, with the assumption that *'aql* is included within it. The choice was made to visually represent *'aql* because of the strong identification with cognition or thinking as a real world factor of people's concept and experience of the psychology of the self.

The aims of this phase of the grounded theory study were to distil the most essential factors, attributes and principles that underpin a foundational mapping of the human being from the ontological and epistemological framework that is delineated in the Qur'an and Sunnah and which can be understood through the *tafsīr* of scholars trained in the tradition. This was achieved by focusing the analysis on those theoretical categories which had the most agreement among participants in an effort to ensure that the theory has the appropriate "fit" for the intended phenomena it aims to represent (Glaser, 1978; Glaser & Strauss, 1967). According to Glaser and Strauss (1967, 1978), fit is ensured by constant comparison and theoretical saturation. Thus, the data excerpts that were chosen to highlight the direction of the analysis were ones that represented such agreement among participants demonstrated by the high level of theoretical saturation in these categories. This rigorous process of systematic comparisons across categories and linkages between data and analysis resulted in the construction of the model of the soul and is reflective of Charmaz's (2014) criterion of "credibility" in grounded theory evaluation. These data represented only a portion of the total number of themes and categories produced from the coding of the transcripts. It is therefore not to be understood that the participants were in such alignment and agreement in all they offered in the conceptualization of an Islamic paradigm of psychology, but that the categories chosen represent those areas where the participants' contributions were in fact in agreement, thereby representing the most uncontested and fundamental aspects of the knowledge of the soul derived from the Qur'an and Sunnah.

The findings reflect and support those reported by Abu-Raiya (2012) and Keshavarzi and Haque (2013), particularly in the centrality of the elements of the soul (*nafs, qalb, 'aql, rūḥ*). However, the specific dynamics of how these aspects interrelate and interact with each other were under-developed in Keshavarzi and Haque's (2013) work. Those dynamics are a key feature of the model developed in the present study which, in its consistently Islamic grounding, diverges more significantly from the work of Abu-Raiya (2012).

His Qur'anic theory of personality follows some of the *a priori* assumptions of Freudian theory and "holds a largely negative view of human nature" (p. 231), which more closely resembles a Christian paradigm of human nature (Niebuhr, 2004).

In addition to the positive view of human nature, the Islamic model of the soul presented in this study possesses several features that distinguish it from most secular Western models and thus reinforces the necessity of establishing such a unique model for the practice of Islamic psychology. The notion that the spiritual centre of the human being is the heart is a significant distinction, together with the contention that the intellect and consciousness are located in this heart centre rather than in the mind, as most psychological theories posit (Hatfield, 1995; Jackendoff, 1987; Penfield, 2015). It is important to note that while there does exist within the Islamic tradition a conception of the intellect being a function of the brain, it is a minority position (Kaplick, Chaudhary, Hasan, Yusuf, & Keshavarzi, 2019) and one that was not reflected in the data, as all of the scholars who were interviewed took the position of the majority of scholars throughout the history of Islamic thought in this regard, identifying the centre of conscious cognition in the heart.

Furthermore, the idea that this centre of consciousness within the human being is inherently connected and can be consciously connected to a primordial, divine consciousness is absent from Western, secular theories of human nature. The concept of the *rūḥ* as a point of access within the person which can directly receive guidance and/or healing from God and the utilization or lack of acknowledgement of this aspect within psychotherapy could have a significant impact on therapeutic guidance and treatment goals for Muslim clients. These, along with other crucial conceptual differences highlighted in the findings, suggest the need for more than just Islamically adapted or integrated approaches to psychotherapy. They substantiate the necessity of a unique framework grounded in an Islamic paradigm, as represented by this model and any theory of Islamic psychology of which it is a foundational constituent and they highlight the originality of this research and the contribution it stands to make to the field.

Phase Two: Clinical Applications

In the second phase, the question that underpinned the research was, "How is the Islamic model of the soul conceptualized into a psychotherapeutic approach?" As this was the primary objective of the research project and the driving motivation behind the development of the model in the first phase, this second phase was elaborated over the course of two chapters in order to develop a framework for the clinical application of the model. Chapter 5 presented findings focused on the nature and structure of the soul, as reflected in the categories from the first phase, in order to build upon the developing theory and understand it in the context of therapeutic application. Given the content of these two theoretical categories, the findings of this portion of the study were oriented towards the development of the theory as it relates to the concept of *fiṭrah*, and moreover the development of ways of approaching psychotherapy by addressing the various levels of the soul (*nafs, 'aql, qalb, rūḥ*) as target or entry points to therapeutic approaches.

The iceberg model that was constructed to illustrate the results of this phase of the study (Figure 5.1) visually represents a distinct demarcation between the four levels of the structure of the soul. However, it is important to clarify that this visual representation, much like the theoretical organization of these levels of the soul, are only utilitarian constructs to organize the conceptualization of abstract concepts. In reality, from the Islamic perspective, these 'levels' of the soul are in fact conceived of not as separate entities which operate in isolation from each other but as one integral system: the human soul. They are perhaps best thought of as qualities or states of the one soul and signify various functions or essences of the inner life of the human being. Al-Attas (2001) explains it in this way:

> The faculties of the soul are not separate entities, each acting differently apart from the soul itself. They appear to be so and perform different functions-some of them prior in time to others not because they are essentially different from each other, but because of the localisation of functions through different organs, and whose functions become actualised at different times, as well as due to the different states in which the soul is involved. In this respect, the faculties of the soul are in reality the soul itself as it manifests itself in accordance with its various modes. (p. 155)

As mentioned in the first phase of the study which focused on an Islamic model of the soul, within the classical Islamic literature which expounds on these concepts, the terms *nafs, 'aql, qalb,* and *rūḥ* are often interchanged and any one of them can be used to reference the soul of the human being. In addition to the differences of opinion in Islamic thought regarding what is termed in philosophy "the mind-body problem", as explained in Chapter 2, there is also a difference of opinion of whether the soul is in fact one entity, as represented in the writings of al-Ghazali (2014), or if the *rūḥ* is a separate spiritual entity from the *nafs*, as represented in the writings of Ibn Qayyim Al-Jawziyah (2001). While these differing viewpoints can be confusing and complicate matters when simply trying to understand the philosophical or theoretical ideas, for the purpose of practical application in psychotherapeutic treatment these conceptual distinctions of the terms *nafs, 'aql, qalb, rūḥ* are clinically useful and the focus on them again represents "relevance" (Glaser & Strauss, 1967) in the construction of the theory for clinical application. As the above analysis and resulting model demonstrate, practitioners of Islamic psychotherapy can use these levels or conceptualizations of the structure of the soul in assessment to identify which level might be affected by what and for treatment, to formulate interventions that target the respective quality or level of the soul in relation to the client's symptoms.

The centrality of the four levels of the soul as being indicators of certain factors in psychotherapeutic assessment which can serve as avenues for addressing corresponding presenting problems is directly reflective of Keshavarzi and Haque's (2013) delineation of examples of "markers" and "interventions" for each level of the soul. Keshavarzi and Haque (2013) articulated each level as a potential entry point to target imbalances in the psyche and devise relevant treatments for each of these levels, as did many of the participants in this phase. However, Keshavarzi and Haque (2013) were simply reporting on their ideas of how a clinician could potentially go about applying the model in therapy and did not have any sample of participants or insights from clinical experience. This phase of the study builds upon their ideas and expands not only the range of possibility represented, but develops an actual picture of what these interventions look like in the therapeutic encounter through the accounts of the participants who were actual clinicians applying these concepts in various therapeutic settings.

In analysing the data from the participants' reflections of how they apply these theoretical concepts it became apparent that participants in general had much more to say about the *nafs* and *'aql* levels as those seem to be the most closely aligned with and pertinent to the secular Western models in which all participants had been trained. Most of the tools, therapeutic resources and practical training and experience within the field of psychology are within these two realms of behavioural and cognitive approaches (Cuijpers et al., 2014; Hans & Hiller, 2013; Stewart & Chambless, 2009) and indeed most of the literature is representative of Islamic adaptations of cognitive behaviour therapy (Beshai, Clark, & Dobson, 2013; Naeem, Gobbi, Ayub, & Kingdon, 2009; Vasegh, 2009, 2014). Thus, it appeared to be much easier for participants to conceive of Islamic versions of behavioural and cognitive interventions, as there are ample models to choose from to integrate or adapt within an Islamic framework. This was particularly pronounced among the participants who were not as rooted in an Islamic paradigm and had less experience and training in Islamic sciences or familiarity with the knowledge of the soul.

Abdullah et al. (2013) outlined in their model of Islamic psychotherapy four elements of treatment. While none of these elements were discussed in detail, nor was there sufficient data presented to understand how they work in clinical application, two of the elements they identified, *tafakkur* (contemplation) and *dhikr* (remembrance of God) matched what seemed to be central techniques or approaches utilized by participants of this phase and thus are reflected in the constructed theory. This phase found that these two therapeutic directives were useful tools to help clients become aware of the subtler inner awareness of the *qalb* and are used to invoke experiences, if only temporary ones, of what it feels like to be in the stage of *nafs al-muṭma'innah*, towards which therapy is held to aim, according to the theory.

Participants who had training in somatic healing and *ṭibb* (traditional Islamic medicine) were found to be equipped with an enormous range of tools for assessing imbalance in the body and recognizing the connection between physical and psychological symptoms, as traditional Islamic healing was a holistic science (Ragab, 2015). The participant who had the most training in traditional Islamic medicine also had the least training in Western methods of psychotherapy. This did not seem to be a disadvantage for him as the implementation of the Islamic model of psychotherapy seems to require a method of understanding and accessing the whole person as a holistic system, rather than just the cognitive techniques that psychotherapists are trained in within the Western model.

Whereas it seemed that interventions that target the *rūḥ* were more easily conceivable and participants could relate aspects of religious devotion fitting into this realm, even among those participants who were more versed in Islamic spirituality there was less of a structure or framework as to how to approach intervention at this level. This could partly be due to the lack of resources or obvious carry-over from traditional Islamic spiritual healing to the context of clinical psychological practice without crossing too much into the territory of religious guidance, but it seems there is another factor. Even in the case where there could potentially be more articulation of Islamic interventions that target the *rūḥ*, there was an apparent tendency for people to remain vague in this area. This is no doubt due in part to the innate nature of the spirit itself, as literally being defined as the unseen or unknown aspect of the human being. However, in addition to or perhaps because of that, many of the participants shared the notion that we simply do not know much about the *rūḥ* aspect of the soul, and that perhaps it is meant to be kept that way. Participants generally referenced shayukh or Islamic spiritual healers, most of whom would be considered to be pious religious figures with a command of both theological knowledge and experiential knowledge, as being the ones whose domain this aspect of the *rūḥ* is, and shared a sentiment that seemed to suggest that this is a line that most therapists should not attempt to cross. Given that spiritual guidance and the soul is an area of inquiry in only a minority of domains of psychology, such as Transpersonal psychology (Friedman & Hartelius, 2015), there is little that is reflected in the literature to this extent, thus both offering originality in the research findings as well as opening new areas of exploration for further research.

More needs to be done to help clearly define this distinction and to delineate just where the line should be drawn between Islamic spiritual guidance and psychological guidance from an Islamic model. Almost all of the participants interviewed seemed to believe that this perhaps blurred line should indeed be entertained because to completely avoid the spiritual would be in effect to render Islamic psychology simply as psychology with Muslims. Nonetheless, in the effort to articulate this Islamically integrated approach, caution is required, particularly when it comes to engaging and understanding the *rūḥ* as the deeper connection with the reality of the soul in relation to God. In regard to this, several participants discussed the need to include and partner with religious scholars, thus validating the inclusion of the 18 scholars' input in the first phase on theoretical foundations as the basis upon which any

Islamic psychotherapy approaches are conceived. The focus of the second part of this phase, among other things, addresses the notion of where the line can be drawn in terms of Islamic psychotherapy and spiritual guidance for further development of the soul, culminating in a picture of the clinical scope of Islamic psychotherapy within this theory.

The insights afforded by the analysis of the second two categories in this phase help to further illuminate a practical application of the entire model of the soul. Whereas the analysis of data from the first part of phase two constructed a theoretical conception of the structural elements of the soul as they pertain to techniques and interventions that target the relative levels (*nafs, 'aql, qalb, rūḥ*), the analysis of the latter two theoretical categories, namely 'stages of the soul' and 'development of the soul', served to construct a model of effecting change within those levels and outlined the capacity within which the Islamic psychotherapist is positioned to do so.

Much of the limited research in the domain of Islamic psychology and psychotherapy has made mention of the three main stages of the soul as in the Islamic model of the soul (Abu-Raiya, 2012; Keshavarzi & Haque, 2013; Keshavarzi & Khan, 2018; Skinner, 2010). Yet none specify the clinical application of such concepts nor do they identify which stage or stages signify the focus of the majority of clinical problems. As these concepts have remained in the realm of abstract theoretical notions until now, it has been difficult to get a concrete sense of how these are applicable in working with clients to address psychological symptoms. The clinical scope of Islamic psychotherapy, as illustrated in the theory here and presented visually in Figure 6.1 (see Chapter 6), offers a new perspective that locates the majority of the therapeutic focus between the stages of *nafs al-ammārah bil su* and *nafs al-lawwāmah*. In addition, this theory posits that the stage of *nafs al-lawwāmah* is where the Islamic psychotherapist concentrates his or her clinical approach, with the aim of moving the client further into this stage as it is here that the goal of psycho-spiritual equilibrium can be reached. While Keshavarzi and Khan (2018) articulate this notion that the goal of the Islamic psychotherapist is to help a client reach equilibrium or as they term it *i'tidaal*, there has previously been no clear delineation of how or where this happens in relation to the model. In this respect, the second phase offers an original insight into a fundamental principle for the domain.

Additionally, in regards to the *nafs al-lawwāmah*, it was illuminated through the development of the theory that an imbalance in this stage or a person being stuck there can result in a pathological state of self-loathing and clinical depression. This was identified as an unhealthy relationship to the self-reproaching nature of this stage which can be an otherwise healthy and necessary trait of the human soul to self-regulate. These findings have twofold significance for clinical implications in Islamic psychology. The first is that this gives insight into understanding and demystifying a common issue identified in the Muslim community within the domain of mental health. As a result of cultural influences, in many Muslim communities the Islamic principle of self-reproach has been misinterpreted as a validation for a culture of guilt and shame (Moghissi, 2007). It is not therefore surprising that in these communities there is often a disproportionate number of clients who suffer from neuroses in the form of severe self-loathing and shame (Sadek, 2017). The second clinically significant finding is a connection between what was perhaps previously thought of only as a spiritual concept within a religious framework, that is, the stages of the soul, is here understood as a link to the etiology of clinical neuroses the symptoms of which would be recognized by practitioners in the context of conventional clinical psychology.

Another aspect of the stages of the soul that has only briefly been alluded to in the literature but has not been significantly dealt with or understood is how to engage the stage of *nafs al-muṭma'innah*. As identified by Keshavarzi and Khan (2018) and others, this stage is generally thought of as being outside the scope of psychotherapy or even out of reach for most people in general. While that notion was validated by many of the participants in phase two, it was also found that there is a usefulness in invoking this stage and indeed a way of doing so, if only in particular instances. Moreover it is a fundamental aspect of how the developed theory posits transformation in the model depicted in Figure 4.1, in terms of the progression of the soul. As the findings elucidate, the introduction of traditional Islamic practices of *tafakkur* (contemplation) and *dhikr* (remembrance) as therapeutic directives can help train clients to cultivate a familiarity with this higher stage of the soul which is defined and experienced as "the soul at rest". Whereas Buddhism has made major contributions to the domain of psychology with the incorporation of mindfulness practices into some forms of the therapeutic encounter (Germer, Siegel, & Fulton, 2016; Rubin, 2013; Young-Eisendrath & Muramoto, 2003), as the study presents here, the possibility of new contributions in this area from the Islamic perspective stands to offer something significant in this area. As the study found, not only do these practices have their roots in the spiritual tradition but there is also an articulated understanding of how these practices can open up a person to removing the blocks in the psyche that can impede an individual's development. Thus, an Islamic notion of contemplation and meditation, like the Buddhist form (Germer, Siegel, & Fulton, 2016), helps to create a sense of inner peace but, perhaps more distinctly, these Islamic practices are positioned also to invoke psycho-spiritual transformation in their application towards advancement in the development of the soul. These findings represent an original contribution in terms of identifying new horizons of research for psychology. They also provide a set of tools that are useful for clinical application across the broader domain of psychotherapy and not just in an Islamic context (Charmaz, 2014).

A further contribution that the study makes regarding the stage of *nafs al-muṭma'innah* is in the distinction of where the parameters exist in distinguishing between the traditional role of the shaykh of *taṣawwuf* and that of the Islamic psychotherapist. Whereas Al-Ghazali's (2014) early work described the distinction, as discussed in Chapter 6, it did not give a very clear picture of how to differentiate the guidance from a shaykh and the 'sound companion' who is "knowledgeable in the secrets of this matter" (p. 257). The findings presented here identify that this invisible line (represented by the dotted line in Figure 6.1 in Chapter 6) is at the very beginning of the stage of *muṭma'innah*, when the person has reached a point of development that allows for more sustained experiences of being stationed in this higher stage of the *nafs*. Keshavarzi and Khan (2018) attest to the idea that the eventual goal is to reach what they call *ittiḥaad* (integrative unity), and which they attribute to the stage of *muṭma'innah*, but that the realization of that goal is beyond the scope of the Islamic psychotherapist; they indicate that this continued development is best referred to a shaykh. This aspect of the theory presented in this study corroborates that contention and adds to it a marker for determining more specifically when a client may be better suited to working with a shaykh, when they have established themselves more firmly on the other side of the line of equilibrium.

The state of the therapist is a defining feature of this theory as it appeared in the data across many categories and in the accounts of all participants. As noted, this concept is similar to that from conventional Western psychotherapy of the therapist doing their own self-reflective work (McWilliams, 2004; Orlinsky & Rønnestad, 2005), and more specifically in the Humanistic approaches with regards to the inner state of the therapist (Rowan, 2014), which arguably drew such notions from Eastern traditions including Sufism (Taylor, 1999). Where this theory expands on the notion of the personal inner work of the therapist is in the circumstance that a therapist engages in *tazkiyat an nafs* (purification of the soul). To the extent that their heart becomes a clear reflection or "mirror" of the divine, there is a potential for transformational psycho-spiritual advances that are beyond being attributable to the therapist's own skill or technique and are understood as an opening for such a therapist to act as a conduit for God's healing. This validates what al-Ghazali (2014) contended and could be understood to be a definition of what he meant by the sound companion being "knowledgeable in the secrets of this matter" (p. 257). While few can attain such a state consistently, it is posited that some can reflect moments of such states in their work with clients, the goal of which inspired the coining of the term "professional mirror" as the ultimate aspiration of the Islamic psychotherapist.

Finally, perhaps the most overarching and defining feature of the theory is what amounts to a definition of the aim of Islamic psychotherapy and what most distinguishes it from secular Western theories. This is the contention that the therapeutic process within this model is aimed not primarily at the removal of psychological symptoms but that its primary concern and treatment goal is in effect to help the client get closer to God. This aim is shared by the practice of 'spiritual direction', usually practiced in a Christian context, which Tisdale (2003) defines as "the interaction between one person, trained to listen for the movement of God, and another who desires to develop and cultivate an intimate, personal relationship with God" (p. 53). However, practitioners of spiritual direction generally distinguish themselves from practitioners of counselling and psychotherapy (Tisdale, 2003). The theory constructed as a result of this research envisions an integration of spiritual direction with counselling and psychotherapy, perhaps more closely resembling that of 'pastoral counselling' (Hathaway, 2009; Strunk, 1993; Tan, 2011), as discussed in Chapter 1. The present theory posits that it is not sufficient to simply reorient the language of therapy to include Islamic concepts and principles, keeping the definition of psychological health as the absence of problematic symptoms. Instead what is required is a complete reorientation of the definition of treatment goals. This amounts to a paradigm shift rather than a religious adaptation.

In this spiritual context, as in other religious based psychotherapy models, the removal of problematic psychological symptoms is secondary as the theory posits that it is plausible that some psychological suffering actually could be good for the soul's development in that it could be helping the client get closer to God. The notion that suffering can result in psychological growth parallels recent work in what Tedeschi and Calhoun (1996) call 'post traumatic growth' (Calhoun & Tedeschi, 2014; Tedeschi & Calhoun, 1995, 2004) which they define as "positive psychological change experienced as a result of the struggle with highly challenging life circumstances" (p. 1, Tedeschi & Calhoun, 2004). Linking this work with religion and spirituality Shaw Joseph and Linley (2005) found that trauma can induce greater spirituality which they define as "more appreciation for each new day, reviewed life priorities, and an understanding that life is precious" (p. 2). In both secular and religious cases of post traumatic growth the traumatic experience itself is seen as a catalyst for the individual to gain a new perspective, not necessarily that the growth is achieved through self reflection or an inner struggle with the person's relative psychological imbalances. Shaw et al. (2005) reported that "spirituality helped all sixteen participants to transform their trauma into a growth experience" (p.4). In this respect the suffering itself becomes a catalyst for making new meaning about their experience, not necessarily that the content of the suffering within the person's soul is seen as an avenue for growth as a result of the person actively working through psychological blocks, like was found in the present research in the Islamic approach.

Similarly in other religious paradigms suffering is seen to give forth to a new perspective or even salvation, without there necessarily being any active role of responsibility that the person needs to play in order to achieve such transformation. Participants in Castella and Simmonds (2013) study of Christian women's accounts of suffering reported that suffering connected them to Jesus and that they believed God would purify them through the suffering alone, regardless of any inner changes earned through self reflective practice. One of the participants said, in reference to Isaiah 53 in the New Testament, "through his [Jesus] stripes you are healed" (p. 544, Castella & Simmonds, 2013). Thus from a Christian spiritual paradigm Jesus' suffering is viewed as having the power to transform others (Bowker, 1975) whereas the Islamic paradigm posits that there is no vicarious salvation.

Whereas the Christian perspective of suffering can be seen as a result of sin, either of the person's individually or the collective sin of humanity, in Hinduism suffering is not seen as a punishment but as a natural consequence of existence. Whitman (2007) says "Hindu traditions promote coping with suffering by accepting it as a just consequence and understanding that suffering is not random" (p. 609). Indeed many spiritual traditions promote simply accepting suffering as transformative without a notion that the individual has a role to play in the transformation brought forth through such experiences. Sanders (2017) says, "that sufferings are inexplicable and their solution rests with God alone is common to Wisdom Literature" (p. 1). In his study of the concept of suffering in the Jewish tradition Sanders (2017) identifies the concept represented in the Hebrew word *yasar* as central in that it signifies the notion that because of sin or transgression "God disciplines His people, wholly and individually, to bring them closer to Him" (p. 1). This concept can be found in both the old and new testament and Sanders (2017) identified three main ways in which it is expressed, namely "a lesson effected by the direct harsh action of God", "a lesson effected by God upon the nation in a less harsh manner" and a "lesson effected through observation" (p. 21). All of these forms appear not to involve an active role on the part of people in unlocking something within the lesson in order to bring forth transformation. In these spiritual traditions as well as in post traumatic growth, the utility of suffering is recognized and its potential for transformation, but they do not necessarily include responsibility of the individual in working through the psychological blocks and/or removing destructive character traits.

The transformative growth that comes from suffering as posited by the theory presented here differs from the above accounts of growth through suffering and presents a unique contribution to this dynamic in psychotherapy. As Enas said in the second phase of the study as reported in Chapter 6, "the *nafs* suffer". This suffering of the *nafs* will nourish the *rūḥ*', elucidating that in an Islamic model suffering is often understood as a cleansing or purification of the *nafs* in order to reveal the true eternal self/soul that exists as a force in potentia, beneath the suffering of the perceived self in its experiences in the life of the *dunya*. And as Firas said, "for you to do *jihad an nafs*, you have to face the *nafs*", meaning that there is a necessity to discover within the self what is blocking someone from submitting to and/or remembering God and that this inner work on the self is the responsibility of the individual and is the meaning of the *jihad*, the struggle within the self. This is based upon one interpretation of the *ayah* in the Qur'an that says "God does not change a people until they change what is in themselves" (Q 13:11). Indeed within this theoretical framework the individual has not only some responsibility in effecting change within the self, but that through this work on the self the individual has the ability to truly transform through the suffering experienced in the trials of life, not being solely at the Mercy of God or through another means of vicarious salvation.

Participants represented the goal of Islamic psychotherapy as including the removal or tempering of symptoms of suffering, dysfunction or discomfort but as having a more central focus or purpose of helping a client to understand the potential that exists within the suffering and that within it lies the capability to grow on a deeper level in the development of the soul. Enas said "the Muslim has a complete science; *fiqh al-bala'*. If you don't know *fiqh al-bala'*, you can't help a patient". *Fiqh al-bala'* is the laws or rules of trials, difficulty or suffering and is a body of knowledge within the Islamic sciences that details how one is to understand difficulty as a test from God. The notion is that there are lessons and wisdom within each trial and, if understood correctly, the person can unlock the potential in the trial by actively working through the pain and suffering to ultimately become closer to God. It was found that from this Islamic model, it is often through the embracing of the suffering that a person is best positioned to turn to God in remembrance of God's omnipotent power and ability to grant healing to the person through their submission to God through their trials.

Where the Islamic model, as illuminated in this theory, differs from other models of secular and religious psychotherapy is in the capacity for the human being to achieve purification in this life through his or her own direct intention and action to uncover and actualize the true self and witness the oneness of God within the perceived separation and fragmentation of the suffering of the life in the *dunya*. The model of Islamic psychotherapy presented here embraces this theoretical paradigm and elucidates a pragmatic pathway for rectifying the imbalance of the self/soul that is the inevitable outcome of the experience of the human condition. The Qur'an is not seen only as an explanation of human existence and is not meant to be taken as a doctrine of belief which alone brings forth salvation, it is thought to offer to the believer a corrective trajectory to rectify humanity's view of the self as a reflection of God and provide a pathway within which to achieve this realization through personal transformation. Thus the methods of therapeutic intervention are informed by the prescriptions from the Qur'an and Sunnah as they present the conditions, actions and parameters with which the human being can persist on the path of struggling within the self, bringing into balance what is out of balance and striving to uncover and actualize the potential in the true *fitrah* state of the soul.

Due to the heavy reliance on the knowledge of the soul from the Islamic tradition in the construction of this theory, it was evident in the analysis of the data from phase two that the participants in group three, those that were operating from a more uniquely Islamic approach due to their advanced training in the Islamic spiritual tradition, had significantly more to contribute to the development of the theory with regards to aspects that involved more Islamic spirituality oriented realities. It was the impression of this researcher from the interactions in the interviews during the data generation process that the participants in group one were aware of their lack of knowledge in this area and desired to increase this knowledge for the benefit of their work in this field. Several of the participants in that group reported to the researcher that through the interview process and being exposed to the Islamic Model of the

Soul, they realized that there is a great deal more they could be doing to develop their Islamically integrative approach to psychotherapy. As Obaid said:

> "And so I feel you know the way you've been asking me, conducting the interview, you have made me think about, you know, challenge some of these boundaries and that's good. I think it's a good thing because maybe I should try to be more purposeful when I sort of call up these concepts from my spiritual understanding and try to use it more actively."

This seemed to be the case not for lack of desire but for lack of opportunity to learn to adopt such a model without one having previously been articulated in such a formal way. Similarly, the participants from group two seemed to desire more insight and experiential knowledge regarding Islamic spirituality healing practices and how they could inform more developed interventions at higher levels of the soul. This points to the evident need for therapists working within this model to have a significant level of both theoretical and experiential knowledge in matters pertaining to the soul and Islamic spirituality and the void that exists in there not being an articulated model of Islamic psychotherapy.

Limitations of the Study

In the way used in this book, a theory, as defined by Reynolds (2015), is an attempt to explain a phenomenon by organizing "an interrelated set of definitions, axioms, and propositions" (p.8) into a coherent form. The theory presented as a result of this study is an effort to infer from Islamic religious knowledge what is most useful in providing a framework upon which to develop treatment approaches in the context of psychotherapy. Thus it is reflective of Glaser and Strauss's (1967) concept of "work" in that it offers analytical explanations for processes within the specific context of psychotherapy. Referring to an "Islamic theory" is not meant to claim that it has the same infallibility that Islam is believed by Muslims to have as a revealed religion. Unlike some secular theories of psychology and human nature, developing an Islamic theory poses a number of difficulties including but not limited to the spiritual and ethical constraints as defined by Islam, which are subject to a broad diversity of interpretations by its followers (Ahmed, 2015; Mujiburrahman, 2001).

It is likely, given the focus of the study on practical applications, that phase one participants' viewpoints on such foundational principles represent only some of those to be found among scholars of Islamic knowledge. Participants in that phase were selected based on their area of research or experience as it pertains to the knowledge of the soul within the Islamic tradition. This type of knowledge tends primarily to be dealt with in the domains of the religious tradition that are concerned with more phenomenological or experiential knowledge rather than or in addition to more materialist or *ẓāhir* (external or manifest) approaches to such knowledge. If the sample had featured a greater representation of scholars whose orientation to Islamic principles were from this perspective, it may have produced different findings. This is certainly a potential limitation of the research that should be taken into consideration. At the same time it would be hard to imagine how one might gain a depth of insight into the inner workings of the soul from such a perspective when this inner domain, or *bāṭin* (inner or hidden) aspect, is largely not entertained or focused on by such scholars.

Whereas the core elements of the model of the soul constructed as a result of the data analysis in phase one would presumably be acceptable to both a *ẓāhiri* (externally focused) and *bāṭini* (internally focused) reading of the Qur'an, the aspects that represent the processes of the development of the soul may indeed be more favourable to those inclined to the *bāṭin* or more spiritual orientation to the Islamic teachings, often associated with *taṣawwuf,* otherwise known as Sufism. This could be attributed to the fact that relatively recently in Islamic history the branch of Islamic knowledge known as *taṣawwuf* has come to be understood as being separate from the Islamic tradition (Sedgwick, 2016). Whereas only hundred years ago *taṣawwuf* would have been considered an integral part of any traditional education in Islamic teachings, it is now possible that one could study traditional Islamic knowledge almost entirely from a *ẓāhiri* perspective without any education in the branch of knowledge that details the inner or *bāṭini* understanding of the human being and the experiential, developmental trajectory of the soul (Ernst, 2017).

Thus, in relation to the model represented in Figure 4.1 (see Chapter 4), the elements that would likely be widely accepted by the majority of scholars of Islam are those that represent the structural elements of the soul. These include the paradigmatic assumptions such as Allah, *shayṭān, dunya, akhira,* and the concept of *fiṭrah* as the nature of the soul; *nafs, qalb, 'aql, rūḥ* as the structure of the soul; and *nafs al-ammārah bil su, nafs al-lawwāmah, nafs al-muṭma'innah* as the stages of the soul. However, the other elements included in the model in Figure 4.1, namely, *jihad an nafs, tazkiyat an nafs, tahdhīb al-akhlāq,* as the development of the soul, represent processes which allude to the inner dimension of the soul. While these terms and the processes that they represent would most certainly be familiar with all scholars of Islam, the way in which they are understood and the amount of attention paid to them may differ greatly between scholars based on their relative orientation to the Islamic tradition as noted above.

The concept of *jihad an nafs* is one that is well understood and often referenced across the broad range of orientations to Islamic knowledge. Given that this term was used by the Prophet Muhammad in a sound *ḥādīth,* it is considered as a central aspect with which a Muslim should concern themselves in the practice of Islam. Yet a *ẓāhiri* orientation to this concept could conceivably be limited to the encouragement of one to simply follow the outward prescriptions of the religious way of life as the sole struggle which is referred to in this concept. From a mental health perspective, this would be a problematic position as it could lead to spiritual bypassing (Welwood, 1984) at least and unaddressed serious clinical issues or mental illness at worst. This could give rise to notions that if one is faced with difficulty or psychological suffering, the answer is simply to concern oneself with abiding by and aligning one's behaviour with the outward religious obligations and prescriptions as the cure for any inner psychological struggle. Such *ẓāhirī* interpretations, like that of the Salafi school of thought, have the potential of triggering OCD and anxiety in that these approaches tend to be overly focused on following a detailed, prescriptive specification of ritual behaviours such as *wuḍū'* (ablution) and *salat* (prayer) which could lead to obsessiveness.

Whereas a *bāṭinī* or perhaps "Sufi" orientation would also accept the adherence to the outward prescriptions, there would also be an understanding that there is an inner struggle with which one must exert some experiential, inward awareness within the depths of one's soul that is above and beyond simply aligning one's outward behaviour with the prescribed acts of faith. This concentration on emotion and the idea of movement between the stages of the soul could cause guilt or anxiety for individuals as they move back and forth between a 'higher' stage and a 'lower' stage, with implications of failure or falling away from a 'better' stage that had been achieved. However, even considering this potential concern it appears that this perspective is more useful and opens the doors to further exploration of the development of the soul. In addition, such a perspective takes a position that a person must be self-reflective and take responsibility for their inner states, which is a more favourable position for the promotion of mental health and encouragement towards seeking psychological treatment. The prevalence of input like this within the data set further solidifies the relevance of the theory for the context in which it aims to operate within psychotherapy.

Another limitation of the study is that while the results of phase two posit equilibrium as the point where Islamic psychotherapy can end and the domain of a shaykh may take over, it is worth noting that the second phase did not include any shayukh of *taṣawwuf* to include the input of the possible range within this domain. This was due to the specific focus on clinical psychotherapy which informed the sample selection and influenced the determination of participants' clinical qualifications as inclusion criteria. Thus, a potential weakness in the study is in the tendency to create a binary perspective of the distinction between the two roles of shaykh and Islamic psychotherapist. It may be that what is within the scope of the guidance of a shaykh also could include that which has been identified here as the scope of the Islamic psychotherapist. Similarly, the role identified as that of a shaykh, in traversing beyond the stage of *nas al-muṭma'innah*, could potentially be within the scope of an Islamic psychotherapist. These two determinations would depend on the state of the practitioner and their own individual capacity in regard to the scope of the two domains. It is entirely plausible that a shaykh could be equipped to engage with the work of helping a person deal with struggling through the lower two stages, as often they do. However, from a mental health perspective, it would be favourable for that individual to have some understanding of aspects of psychotherapy or at least counselling skills, if they do not already possess such characteristics and understanding, as many traditional shaykh do. And at the same time, it is possible that an Islamic psychotherapist could have the traditional and experiential knowledge required to guide people further in the trajectory of the soul's development into what has been identified as lying within the scope of the shaykh. This latter circumstance would be dependent on the state of the therapist.

Recommendations for Further Research

Situating a uniquely Islamic theory of psychology as a paradigm within which a psychotherapist can operate has the potential to open numerous doors for innovating new techniques. While there has been recent research into the development of specific interventions with Muslim service users, most if not all of those studies and developments have been *ad hoc*, without first establishing a standard of practice or acknowledging an Islamic psychological framework beforehand. With an established theoretical foundation from which the research community can work, there is a larger potential for research development to maximize such efforts. The framework established as a result of this research, with its unique paradigmatic psychological orientation, can give rise to specific Islamic psychotherapeutic approaches and techniques that can be more fully developed and situated within a unique context. Without such efforts there runs a risk of simply offering Islamized versions of already established techniques from within a Western paradigm of the understanding of the person.

From such a situated standpoint of an Islamic paradigm for psychology, numerous approaches could then come forward such as an Islamic Cognitive Behavioural Therapy that is rooted in the early teaching of scholars such as Al Balkhi (Awaad & Ali, 2015; Badri, 2013). Also possible is an Islamic version of emotional focused therapy which targets blockages within the *qalb*, opening to the *rūḥ*, as alluded to in this theory, a Qur'anic based personality inventory and even Islamic descriptions of psychopathology in the form of something like an Islamic *Diagnostic and Statistical Manual (DSM)*. These types of manuals for this context would perhaps be better thought of as tools for understanding pathology from the Islamic model rather than as labels or 'disorders' as they are framed in the DSM. Furthermore, in defining psychopathology from this Islamic psychology framework, it could be further explored how the *muhlikat*, defined as the diseases of the heart, could be mapped onto and understood as diagnostic criteria. A useful area of focus in this respect would be to do an in-depth analysis of al-Ghazali's treatment of the diseases and cures, creating a treatment guide and diagnostic manual for the domain. This is not to suggest categories and labels of pathology that clients then identify with, but as an informative set of possibilities for further discovery. This approach is indicative of the theory produced as noted earlier that participants viewed 'pathology' not as psychological deficiencies in the person but as normal characteristics of the uncontrolled *nafs*. As reported in Chapter 4, John said, "It's understanding these as not just fissures of the psyche but inclinations of the *nafs* and treating them on that level as inclinations of the *nafs*".

Further research could expand on the grounded theory by including studies with service users as participants sharing their experience in Islamic psychotherapy. This would build on the theory and provide deeper insight into case examples of application for specific psychological issues. In addition, the theory could be expanded by developing studies based around each one of the four levels of the soul to further explicate an advisory treatment handbook for various techniques and approaches to addressing a variety of presenting problems that arise specific to each of the four domains. This would not be a scripted manual but rather a useful tool for clinicians to learn about possible approaches and ways of working in Islamic psychotherapy. This would further give rise to the ability to develop articulated modalities of Islamic therapy that can then be taught in the process of training clinicians to use such techniques as part of their Islamic theoretical orientation to psychotherapy.

Some new questions arose out of this research which would be useful avenues of questioning for further research. One is around the specific mechanism of the cognitive function within the human being. Is there a distinction between the consciousness of the heart's perception and logical reasoning? Considering the unique Islamic treatment of the 'mind body problem' as discussed in Chapter 2, is there room within the Islamic framework for conceptualizing some aspects of the intellect as originating in the brain? Where does neuropsychology fit into the Islamic framework? Another area of questioning is around the issue of mental illness. Can all psychological states and experiences be understood as having spiritual significance, or is there a place for treating some diagnoses with medical treatments alone? Can a person's genetic predisposition to mental illness be seen as purely physical, or is there an Islamic perspective of epigenetics?

The foundation set out within the theory that resulted from this research stands to lay important groundwork for the exploration of a whole host of new research. This can potentially give rise to the establishment of a recognized field of Islamic psychology within which all of these and future potential avenues of inquiry can be housed. In order to properly support efforts towards the establishment of a recognized professional field of Islamic Psychology, the theory presented here can serve as an agreed upon standard for recognizing best practice in Islamic psychology and psychotherapy. This could involve a process of engaging the intended audience of psychologists, checking the extent to which the theory is recognized and assented to, and identifying and incorporating new insights that call for further theoretical development, using the same grounded theory methods as the present research. As a model of such a process, Elliott Fischer and Rennie (1999) describe how they checked and developed their criteria for the evaluation of qualitative research. They first assembled a list of quality standards from relevant resources, adjusted them to their specific context, narrowed the list of 40 down to 11 relevant principles, and then subjected the list to review and critique by a number of different groups of professionals in the field at conferences, symposiums and discussion groups (Elliott, Fischer, & Rennie, 1999). This sort of process to establish professional standards would fit well within the grounded theory methodology and would be an appropriate development of the research into a more robust theory. Once such a theory is firmly established and accepted by practitioners in the field then institutions could follow that support, developing and expanding the theory into wider application. For example, the types of endeavours that would further establish and advance the status of the discipline potentially include the establishment of an Islamic Psychology research centre, a post Masters-level certificate in Islamic Psychology, mental health training programs for Imams and religious leaders, establishing more recognized, accredited academic programs in Islamic psychology, and establishing peer reviewed journals.

Implications for Practice

Amidst the socio-political landscape where frequent reports of acts of terror that are committed in the name of Islam dominate the imagery and discussion with regards to the religion, misrepresentation and misunderstanding of Muslims and Islam is rampant (Appiah, 2012). This not only negatively affects views of Islam from outsiders, it has also caused a significant crisis within the Muslim community as those who are not properly educated about their religion, particular young people, are influenced by popular uninformed rhetoric and are leaving the religion, losing faith in it, or adopting extremist views from radical organizations who wish to use them as pawns in terrorist plots (Bizina & Gray, 2014; Lynch, 2013). Recent research conducted by the Tabah Foundation (2017) across ten countries in the Middle East region has shown a significant rise in miseducation on Islam among Muslim millennials. While this is a common experience in cultures that embrace modernity (Taylor, 2007) and can be attributed to a number of social-cultural factors, it was also found in the Tabah Foundation (2017) study that Muslim youth feel that the way Islamic religious guidance is presented is not relevant to young people living in modern times. This crisis has led to a surge of debate and discussion among the Muslim *'ulamā* to try and find remedies that foster increased access to theologically sound religious knowledge and Islamically oriented guidance to help keep these young people within the fold of their religious communities (Tabah Foundation, 2017) while at the same time getting the support and assistance they need for mental health and general social development.

For many Muslims who have become accustomed to Western ways of life in a fast-paced cosmopolitan world, the traditional ways of religious learning and guidance are not necessarily relevant, attractive or compatible with their modern lifestyle (Mandaville, 2007). A framework for an Islamic model of psychology that utilizes the modern format of solution-focused counselling to orient Muslims towards Islamic principles that are relevant to their daily concerns and personal problems can be a pragmatic intervention for re-connecting or connecting Muslims to the meanings and potential utility of their religious tradition. The format of 50-minute psychotherapy sessions that are oriented towards focusing on current stressors or presenting problems is likely to be more accessible for the average Muslim in modern society than traditional avenues for obtaining religious knowledge or seeking spiritual guidance. Many Muslims may not be interested in becoming scholars of Islam and some may not even consider themselves particularly religious (Tabah Foundation, 2017). However many may still want to align their lives with Islamic values and principles but lack a practical way of accessing such Islamically oriented guidance (Hefner & Zaman, 2010; Mandaville, 1999). A framework for an Islamic psychotherapy model, as this research produced, could allow for such access and bridge a gap within the Muslim community. While certainly psychotherapists should not be expected to be religious au-thorities, many interpersonal issues have remedies in Islamic wisdom (Haque, 2004). Thus, if the presented model for Islamic psychotherapy, with its theological integrity and academic rigour, were taken up both by psy-chotherapy practitioners and Imams and religious leaders alike, who were able to be trained in such theory and practice, it would allow for a greater number of Muslim service users to access both mental health services as well as helpful religious knowledge and guidance in a pragmatic way.

Going forward the results of this study can serve as a general indication of how to improve therapeutic methods to fit within an Islamic framework, as well as offering a specific application of approaches in psychotherapeutic practice. For example, in a CBT approach, the terminology that came out of the study and the resulting model of the soul can be utilized in adapting cognitive strategies that fit an Islamic worldview. Using terms such as *nafs*, *qalb*, *'aql*, and *rūḥ* in cognitive strategies from within a spiritual framework can help a Muslim client to identify with conceptions of the self from within an Islamic paradigm rather than using conventional secular terminology. This has the potential not only to be more culturally relevant but also to enable cognitive reframing strategies to align with the religious framework and its spiritual assumptions, thus having a deeper impact, greater resonance and potentially increased treatment effectiveness. Also, reframing maladaptive cognitions that stem from a misguided interpretation of Islamic religious as-sumptions can be corrected with informed spiritual guidance that aligns with the paradigmatic framework set forth in the Islamic model of the soul.

Additionally, the findings from this research can serve to improve therapeutic approaches by providing a framework within which clinicians can work holi-stically. As exemplified in the accounts of participants in phase two, their Western secular training equipped them predominantly with therapeutic tools centred in cognitive approaches. The model presented in the findings from Chapter 5 provide a therapeutic framework that can serve to broaden the scope of inter-ventions to include the heart (*qalb*) and spirit (*rūḥ*) in addition to cognition (*'aql*).

Using the iceberg model (see Figure 5.1 in Chapter 5) to orient clients to go beyond cognitions and get in touch with the emotional content of the heart can be an effective tool in accessing more deeply-seated psychological material that can be useful to both Muslim and non-Muslim psychotherapists alike.

As described by some participants, by helping the client to identify the centre of the self in the heart, using techniques such as somatic tracking of sensations in the body and visualization to locate a client's awareness in the heart centre, a therapist can guide a client to a state of presence and acceptance of the psychological blocks and moreover the self. This process of accessing the deeper parts of the iceberg in an attempt to "unlock" or "unblock" the emotional blockages that have covered over the heart's innate connection to God has the potential to orient the therapeutic encounter towards a holistic form of treatment rather than just "mental" health. This can be practised in session through the use of guided imagery as well as breathing exercises and Islamic versions of meditative practice such as *tafakkur* (contemplation), *murāqabah* (meditation) and the use of *dhikr* (remembrance) in the heart rather than just the mind. Thus, the therapeutic approach informed by the theoretical framework outlined here can improve upon the existing practices which are dominated by a cognitive approach to psychotherapy. This approach adds to the cognitive one with the implementation of physical directives that help clients locate themselves in their bodies and identify the centre of the self in the heart. It shifts from an over-emphasis on talk therapy to one that integrates spiritual states of being into the therapeutic process.

Such an established approach could potentially be used both by Muslim psychologists and non-Muslim psychologists alike, as indicated or appropriate for a given service user or population. It could create numerous possibilities for training and education in situations like Syria and Palestine where often there are not as many Muslim service providers as the overwhelming need requires (Watters, 2001). An indigenous model of psychology and psychotherapy such as this, which stands to be more relatable to the worldview of Muslims and thus presumably more accessible, presents enormous potential for advancements in the success of mental health treatment with Muslim populations. This can directly impact some of the most pressing social concerns of our time, including support for humanitarian crises in treating Post Traumatic Stress Disorder (PTSD) among Muslim refugees in war torn countries and deradicalization efforts in the West and across the globe. Some practitioners may wish to interact more directly and overtly with the Islamic knowledge based aspects of the theory, either dependent on their clients' orientation or the religious orientation of the therapist. It could be therefore that only certain elements of the model be used to help clinicians better understand their Muslim clients' religious paradigm and how it affects views of psychological wellbeing and treatment goals. While other clinicians may want to go deeper into the religious aspects of the model and thus would likely benefit being trained in Islamic religious knowledge at the same time as being trained to apply the theoretical model in their own therapeutic approach.

Depending on these various pathways to implementation of the model, the appropriate context for such implementation is something that will need to be considered. For example, practitioners will likely have more freedom to overtly reference and integrate the religious aspects of the model in countries where Islam is the majority religion and is woven into the public sector than in countries where the public sector is a secular space and the overt incorporation of religion can be seen as an ethical violation (McLemore & Court, 1977; Plante, 2007). In such countries where psychotherapy is regulated by secular professional governing bodies it may be that the model presented here would not be embraced in publicly funded settings due to strict regulations that prohibit the incorporation of religion in treatment approaches (Plante, 2007). Contexts where the model may be less problematic in these countries could be in privately funded or volunteer based settings, or within the context of Islamic religious community centres (Worthington, Dupont, Berry, & Duncan, 1988).

Regardless of the context within which the results of this research may be implemented it is hoped that its implications for practice are relevant and useful not only to potential Muslim service users and communities but to the wider fields of psychology, psychotherapy and mental health. The insights and perspectives explored and elucidated through the accounts of the participants and the review of literature pertaining to psychology in the Islamic tradition stands to make an important contribution to the collective understanding of the self. Throughout the development of the field of psychology we have seen the thought from various religious traditions be embraced by the academic community in efforts to enhance our understanding of the human psyche. In a time when Islam is frequently attributed with fear and destruction, this research represents a hopeful and positive potential for the world to benefit from the resources of health and healing which exist in the Islamic tradition.

Conclusion

The aim of this research was to build a framework for an Islamic psychology and its application in psychotherapy. The findings suggest that the Islamic model that was constructed as a result of this research is distinct from conventional Western psychology and psychotherapy. While some aspects of the model are re-descriptions of one or more standard aspects of Western secular therapeutic models, some aspects depart from those models in terms of taking the concept of God seriously. Some of the ways in which the model presented here understands and incorporates God and spirituality into the therapeutic process are analogous to Christian, Jewish and/or Buddhist models of therapy. However there are uniquely Islamic aspects of this model that have no analogous aspects in Western secular, Christian, Jewish or Buddhist models of therapy and thus constitute an original contribution to the research and present a justification for a new theory of Islamic psychology and psychotherapy.

Unique to the model presented in this research is the Islamic conception of the centre of the conscious self being located in the heart rather than the mind. In this model the function of "mind", usually attributed to cognitive processes in the brain in Western secular psychology, is conceived of as an aspect of the self that perceives with the heart. This heart centre is understood as the core identity of the person, rather than the conscious self, and is thought to be the true identity of the person, as an eternal soul. In this model the human soul contains within it an access point to God directly (the *rūḥ*). The therapeutic approaches that were found to be unique to clinical practice informed by this model were the intentional efforts to access and release psychological blocks at increasingly deeper levels of the soul, namely in the *qalb* (heart) and *rūḥ* (spirit) levels of the soul. The Islamic psychotherapeutic approach presented here aims to uncover the true self that exists underneath the psychological problems and imbalances and to connect the client to this deeper level of their identity in relation to God and their primordial truth beyond just this temporal existence, where these presenting problems manifest. Problems and psychological issues are seen not only as symptoms of a deeper issue but as signposts along the path of uncovering what lies beneath, in the *fiṭrah* state, the *rūḥ* aspect of the soul.

In Malik Badri's (1979) book *The Dilemma of Muslim Psychologists* he used a metaphor of a building to illustrate the difference between adapting secular Western psychology with Islamic concepts versus approaching psychology from an entirely different framework; that of an Islamic paradigm. He said that simply integrating Islamic principles into the Western concept of psychology is akin to painting a deteriorating building with a fresh coat of paint in an attempt to make it look new. What Badri was calling for all those years ago was the need to construct a new building from the ground up with an Islamic foundation in order to truly have an Islamic paradigm of psychology. This research provides a solid foundation for that new construction, offering new insights into the understanding of human psychology not just for Muslims but for the broader field of psychology. It is hoped that this contribution of new knowledge can be further developed and added to in the larger project of building an Islamic psychology and psychotherapy.

References

Abdullah, C. H. B., Abidin, Z. B. Z., Hissan, W. S. M., Kechil, R., Razali, W. N., & Zin, M. Z. M. (2013). The effectiveness of generalized anxiety disorder intervention through Islamic psychotherapy: The preliminary study. *Asian Social Science, 9*(13), 157.

Abu-Raiya, H. (2012). Towards a systematic Qura'nic theory of personality. *Mental Health, Religion & Culture, 15*(3), 217–233. https://doi.org/10.1080/13674676.2011.640622

Ahmed, S. (2015). *What is Islam?: The importance of being Islamic.* Princeton University Press.

Al-Attas, S. M. N. (2001). The nature of man and the psychology of the human soul. In *Prolegomena to the metaphysics of Islam: An exposition of the fundamental elements of the worldview of Islam* (pp. 143–176). International Institute of Islamic Thought and Civilization.

Al-Ghazali, A. H. (2014). *Imam Al-Ghazali Mukhtasar Ihya Ulum Ad-din* (2nd ed.). Spohr Publishers.

Al-Jawziyah, I. Q. (2001). *Ar-Ruh-the soul's journey after death Ibn al-Qayyim al-Jawziyya* (D. Fatoohi & F. Fatoohi, Trans.). Islamic Book Service.

Al-Karam, C. Y. (Ed.). (2018). *Islamically integrated psychotherapy: Uniting faith and professional practice*. Templeton Press.

Appiah, K. a. (2012). Misunderstanding cultures: Islam and the West. *Philosophy and Social Criticism, 38*(4–5), 425–433. https://doi.org/10.1177/0191453712441153

Awaad, R., & Ali, S. (2015). Obsessional disorders in al-Balkhi's 9th century treatise: Sustenance of the body and soul. *Journal of Affective Disorders, 180*, 185–189. https://doi.org/10.1016/j.jad.2015.03

Badri, M. (1979). *The dilemma of Muslim psychologists*. MWH London.

Badri, M. (2013). *Abu Zayd al-Balkhi's sustenance of the soul: The cognitive behavior therapy of a ninth century physician*. International Institute of Islamic Thought.

Beshai, S., Clark, C. M., & Dobson, K. S. (2013). Conceptual and pragmatic considerations in the use of cognitive-behavioral therapy with Muslim clients. *Cognitive Therapy and Research, 37*(1), 197–206. https://doi.org/10.1007/s10608-012-9450-y

Bizina, M., & Gray, D. H. (2014). Radicalization of youth as a growing concern for counter-terrorism policy. *Global Security Studies, 5*(1), 72–79.

Bowker, J. (1975). *Problems of suffering in religions of the world*. Cambridge University Press.

Calhoun, L. G., & Tedeschi, R. G. (2014). *Handbook of posttraumatic growth: Research and practice*. Routledge.

Castella, R. de, & Simmonds, J. G. (2013). "There's a deeper level of meaning as to what suffering's all about": Experiences of religious and spiritual growth following trauma. *Mental Health, Religion & Culture, 16*(5), 536–556. https://doi.org/10.1080/13674676.2012.702738

Charmaz, K. (2014). *Constructing grounded theory: A practical guide through qualitative analysis*. Sage Publications.

Cuijpers, P., Sijbrandij, M., Koole, S., Huibers, M., Berking, M., & Andersson, G. (2014). Psychological treatment of generalized anxiety disorder: A meta-analysis. *Clinical Psychology Review, 34*(2), 130–140. https://doi.org/10.1016/j.cpr.2014.01.002

Elliott, R., Fischer, C. T., & Rennie, D. L. (1999). Evolving guidelines for publication of qualitative research studies in psychology and related fields. *British Journal of Clinical Psychology, 38*(3), 215–229. https://doi.org/10.1348/014466599162782

Ernst, C. W. (2017). *Sufism: An introduction to the mystical tradition of Islam*. Shambhala.

Friedman, H. L., & Hartelius, G. (2015). *The Wiley-Blackwell handbook of transpersonal psychology*. John Wiley & Sons.

Germer, C., Siegel, R. D., & Fulton, P. R. (2016). *Mindfulness and psychotherapy* (2nd ed.). Guilford Publications.

Glaser, B. G. (1978). *Theoretical sensitivity: Advances in the methodology of grounded theory* (1st ed.). The Sociology Press.

Glaser, B. G., & Strauss, A. L. (1967). *Discovery of grounded theory: Strategies for qualitative research*. Routledge. https://doi.org/10.4324/9780203793206

Hans, E., & Hiller, W. (2013). A meta-analysis of nonrandomized effectiveness studies on outpatient cognitive behavioral therapy for adult anxiety disorders. *Clinical Psychology Review, 33*(8), 954–964. https://doi.org/10.1016/j.cpr.2013.07.003

Haque, A. (2004). Religion and mental health: The case of American Muslims. *Journal of Religion & Health, 43*(1), 45–58.

Hatfield, G. (1995). Remaking the science of mind: Psychology as a natural science. In C. Fox, R. Porter, & R. Wokler (Eds.), *Inventing human science: Eighteenth century domains* (pp. 184–231). University of California Press.

Hathaway, W. L. (2009). Clinical use of explicit religious approaches: Christian role integration Issues. *Part of a Special Issue: Theophostic Prayer Ministry, 28*(2), 105–112.

Hefner, R. W., & Zaman, M. Q. (2010). *Schooling Islam: The culture and politics of modern Muslim education.* Princeton University Press.

Jackendoff, R. (1987). *Consciousness and the computational mind.* The MIT Press.

Kaplick, P. M., Chaudhary, Y., Hasan, A., Yusuf, A., & Keshavarzi, H. (2019). An interdisciplinary framework for Islamic cognitive theories. *Zygon®, 54*(1), 66–85. https://doi.org/10.1111/zygo.12500

Keshavarzi, H., & Haque, A. (2013). Outlining a psychotherapy model for enhancing Muslim mental health within an Islamic context. *International Journal for the Psychology of Religion, 23*(3), 230–249. https://doi.org/10.1080/10508619.2012.712000

Keshavarzi, H., & Khan, F. (2018). Outlining a case illustration of traditional Islamically integrated psychotherapy. In C. Y. Al-Karam (Ed.), *Islamically integrated psychotherapy: Uniting faith and professional practice* (pp. 175–207). Templeton Press.

Lynch, O. (2013). British Muslim youth: Radicalisation, terrorism and the construction of the "other." *Critical Studies on Terrorism, 6*(2), 241–261. https://doi.org/10.1080/17539153.2013.7

Mandaville, P. (1999). Digital Islam: Changing the boundaries of religious knowledge? *ISIM Newsletter Leiden University, 2,* 172–191.

Mandaville, Peter. (2007). Globalization and the politics of religious knowledge: Pluralizing authority in the Muslim world. *Theory, Culture & Society, 24*(2), 101–115. https://doi.org/10.1177/0263276407074998

McLemore, C. W., & Court, J. H. (1977). Religion and psychotherapy: Ethics, civil liberties, and clinical savvy: A critique. *Journal of Consulting and Clinical Psychology, 45*(6), 1172–1175. https://doi.org/10.1037/0022-006X.45.6.1172

McWilliams, N. (2004). *Psychoanalytic psychotherapy: A practitioner's guide.* Guilford Press.

Moghissi, H. (2007). *Muslim diaspora: Gender, culture and identity.* Routledge.

Mujiburrahman. (2001). The phenomenological approach in Islamic studies: An overview of a Western attempt to understand Islam. *Muslim World, 91*(3/4), 425–450. https://doi.org/10.1111/j.1478-1913.2001.tb03725.x

Naeem, F., Gobbi, M., Ayub, M., & Kingdon, D. (2009). University students' views about compatibility of cognitive behaviour therapy (CBT) with their personal, social and religious values (a study from Pakistan). *Mental Health, Religion & Culture, 12*(8), 847–855. https://doi.org/10.1080/13674670903115226

Niebuhr, R. (2004). *The nature and destiny of man: A Christian interpretation. Volume 1: Human nature.* Westminster John Knox Press.

Orlinsky, D. E., & Rønnestad, M. H. (2005). *How psychotherapists develop: A study of therapeutic work and professional growth.* American Psychological Association. https://doi.org/10.1037/11157-000

Penfield, W. (2015). *Mystery of the mind: A critical study of consciousness and the human brain.* Princeton University Press.

Plante, T. G. (2007). Integrating spirituality and psychotherapy: Ethical issues and principles to consider. *Journal of Clinical Psychology, 63*(9), 891–902. https://doi.org/10.1002/jclp.20383

Ragab, A. (2015). *The medieval Islamic hospital: Medicine, religion, and charity.* Cambridge University Press.

Reynolds, P. D. (2015). *Primer in theory construction: An A&B classics edition.* Routledge.

Rowan, J. (2014). Existential, humanistic, and transpersonal therapies and the relational approach. In D. Charura (Ed.), *The therapeutic relationship handbook: Theory and practice* (pp. 40–50). McGraw-Hill Education (UK).

Rubin, J. B. (2013). *Psychotherapy and Buddhism: Toward an integration.* Springer Science & Business Media.

Sadek, N. (2017). Islamophobia, shame, and the collapse of Muslim identities. *International Journal of Applied Psychoanalytic Studies, 14*(3), 200–221. https://doi.org/10.1002/aps.1534

Sanders, J. A. (2017). *Suffering as divine discipline in the old testament and post-biblical Judaism.* Wipf and Stock Publishers.

Sedgwick, M. (2016). *Western Sufism: From the Abbasids to the new age.* Oxford University Press.

Shaw, A., Joseph, S., & Linley, P. A. (2005). Religion, spirituality, and posttraumatic growth: A systematic review. *Mental Health, Religion & Culture, 8*(1), 1–11. https://doi.org/10.1080/1367467032000157981

Skinner R. (2010). An Islamic approach to psychology and mental health. *Mental Health, Religion & Culture, 13*(6), 547–551. https://doi.org/10.1080/13674676.2010.488441

Stewart, R. E., & Chambless, D. L. (2009). Cognitive–behavioral therapy for adult anxiety disorders in clinical practice: A meta-analysis of effectiveness studies. *Journal of Consulting and Clinical Psychology, 77*(4), 595–606. https://doi.org/10.1037/a0016032

Strunk, O. (1993). A prolegomenon to a history of pastoral counseling. In R. J. Wicks, R. D. Parsons, & D. Capps (Eds.), *Clinical handbook of pastoral counseling* (pp. 14–25). Paulist Press.

Tabah Foundation. (2017). Muslim Millennial Attitudes on Religion and Religious Leadership (No. 2). Tabah Foundation. https://mmasurvey.tabahfoundation.org/downloads/mmasurvey2_en_web-key-findings.pdf

Tan, S.-Y. (2011). *Counseling and psychotherapy: A Christian perspective.* Baker Academic.

Taylor, E. (1999). An intellectual renaissance of humanistic psychology? *Journal of Humanistic Psychology, 39*(2), 7–25. https://doi.org/10.1177/0022167899392002

Taylor, P. (2007). *Modernity and re-enchantment: Religion in post-revolutionary Vietnam.* Institute of Southeast Asian Studies.

Tedeschi, R. G., & Calhoun, L. G. (1995). *Trauma and transformation.* SAGE.

Tedeschi, R. G., & Calhoun, L. G. (1996). The posttraumatic growth inventory: Measuring the positive legacy of trauma. *Journal of Traumatic Stress, 9*(3), 455–471. https://doi.org/10.1007/BF02103658

Tedeschi, R. G., & Calhoun, L. G. (2004). Posttraumatic growth: Conceptual foundations and empirical evidence. *Psychological Inquiry, 15*(1), 1–18. https://doi.org/10.1207/s15327965pli1501_01

Tisdale, T. C. (2003). Listening and responding to spiritual issues in psychotherapy: An interdisciplinary perspective. *Journal of Psychology and Christianity*, *22*(3), 262–272.

Vasegh, S. (2009). Psychiatric treatments involving religion: Psychotherapy from an Islamic perspective. In P. Huguelet & H. G. Koenig (Eds.), *Religion and spirituality in psychiatry* (pp. 301–316). Cambridge University Press.

Vasegh, S. (2014). *Religious cognitive behavioral therapy: Muslim version*. http://www. spiritualityandhealth.duke.edu/images/pdfs/RCBT%20Manual%20Final%20Muslim %20Version%203-14-14.pdf

Watters, C. (2001). Emerging paradigms in the mental health care of refugees. *Social Science & Medicine*, *52*(11), 1709–1718. https://doi.org/10.1016/S0277-9536(00) 00284-7

Weed, M. (2017). Capturing the essence of grounded theory: The importance of understanding commonalities and variants. *Qualitative Research in Sport, Exercise and Health*, *9*(1), 149–156. https://doi.org/10.1080/2159676X.2016.1251701

Welwood, J. (1984). *Toward a psychology of awakening: Buddhism, psychotherapy, and the path of personal and spiritual transformation*. Boston: Shambhala Publications.

Whitman, S. M. (2007). Pain and suffering as viewed by the Hindu religion. *The Journal of Pain*, *8*(8), 607–613. https://doi.org/10.1016/j.jpain.2007.02.430

Worthington, E. L., Dupont, P. D., Berry, J. T., & Duncan, L. A. (1988). Christian therapists' and clients' perceptions of religious psychotherapy in private and agency settings. *Journal of Psychology and Theology*, *16*(3), 282–293. https://doi.org/10.1177/ 009164718801600307

Yardley, L. (2000). Dilemmas in qualitative health research. *Psychology & Health*, *15*(2), 215–228. https://doi.org/10.1080/08870440008400302

Young-Eisendrath, P., & Muramoto, S. (2003). *Awakening and Insight: Zen Buddhism and Psychotherapy*. Routledge.

Reflection 5: An Unwitting Academic in a New World of Theoretical Possibility

I started out this journey as a clinician looking to develop and formalize an approach to psychotherapy that I and my colleagues had been doing informally with clients in private practice. Even though when I started this research I already had a career in psychology for ten years, I did not consider myself an 'academic'. I wasn't exactly unknown in the small international community of Islamic psychology but I was known only as a practising psychotherapist. I did not set out to become nor did I imagine that I would ever be known as an academic, much less a spokesperson for the developing field of Islamic psychology.

My intention with this research from the start was just to fill the gap that was so apparent in the relatively young field of Islamic psychology. For almost 40 years, clinicians and academics had been recognizing the need for a theoretical framework from which to truly do the work of developing the field, but no one had ever invested any significant effort in this endeavour. That was partly due to the fact that in order to do it properly it would take people who understood both psychology from a practical standpoint and Islamic studies from a theoretical standpoint. Most of the people concerned with this effort were either academics who did not have the clinical experience and knowledge necessary to develop it in this way, or they were practising psychotherapists who either felt the Islamic studies aspect was out of their lane or were just too busy doing the work on the ground in clinical practice to take the time out to do the research required. I certainly did not see myself as having what it would take in the area of Islamic studies knowledge but what I did have was the sheer audacity to think that I might be able to con-tribute something useful. Really, the driving motivator for me in taking on such a huge project that was beyond my own capacity was simply the notion that someone needed to do it. So I felt as if I was sort of "putting my money where my mouth is" and "taking one for the team".

I realized from the beginning that what I was proposing to do was completely beyond the scope of what is normally taken on in one research project. I therefore started out with a more narrow focus of a comparative study of classical CBT with an Islamically oriented CBT model using Randomized Control Trials (RCT). However, once I began the work of following that plan, it became clear as a result of the initial phase of doing the research that in order to truly establish Islamic approaches to psychotherapy, there first needed to be a theoretical framework from within which to ground and define what an Islamic approach would even be.

Of course, how to actually go about establishing such a foundational project as to attempt to create new theory was the big question. I certainly did not have the slightest clue as to how something like this could be done. I started to research the development of theories of psychology and came up with nothing, as it's not generally something that people do very often, given that most of the major theories have been established early on. As a result of my investigation, I discovered grounded theory and found that if I really wanted to generate new theory, this was the way to do it. Through this methodology I devised a way to incorporate the Islamic studies knowledge that I was lacking, which seemed to be the missing link in developing a theory of Islamic psychology. Designing the first phase of the study around the construction of a theoretical framework, before developing the framework for practical application, allowed for just the type of foundational work that needed to be done while presenting the perfect way to bring in the relevant Islamic knowledge that was crucial in having it be grounded in the Islamic sources.

Not too long into the process of the first phase it became clear that what was unfolding and what I had the opportunity to create from the input of these 18 scholars was potentially ground breaking. When I had completed the fieldwork of phase one and was in the thick of the analytic process, seeing how I could construct all of this vast information into a coherent model, it suddenly all came together for me. I literally saw the model before my eyes as if in a dream and rushed to grab a pen and paper to sketch it out, to record it and get it out into reality before the vision was gone. Looking at the model that I had drawn out I questioned whether this could possibly be unique. I thought surely someone must have designed a similar model before as it seemed so obvious to me now. I searched far and wide trying to find it, convinced that something similar had to be out there, but came up with nothing. I asked around to some colleagues and then showed the model to my research participants to verify the accuracy and to see if they knew of anything like it. It seemed that indeed this diagram was a new contribution that hadn't existed before, even if the concepts and general framework had long been understood and utilized by a select group of learned people. I published the results from this first phase, along with the diagram, and it immediately found a large audience of interested readers. Within four months of publishing the article in the *Journal of Religion and Health* it was downloaded over 5,000 times, with almost a thousand more per month thereafter. This incredible response led to me being invited to multiple conferences, being presented with awards, teaching seminars and short courses on the model, and finding that PhD students, clinicians and professors all over the world have read my work.

Over the course of completing this research a flood of other developments happened, positioning me as an "expert" in the field: co-founding the International Association of Islamic Psychology with the father of the movement, Dr. Malik Badri; authoring several publications and being invited to use my research as the foundation for the development of a higher degree in Islamic psychology. Now people all over the world seem to know me for my research and academic work and don't even know me as a psychotherapist. I previously had identified only as a practitioner who was just doing this research to produce something that was needed for my clinical work and I would then go back to clinical practice. What I have found at this point in my journey is that while my heart is still in it for the purpose of helping people heal and the on-the-ground application of doing clinical work, I have discovered that there is a great deal more work that needs to be done to continue producing research to support the continuing development of the field of Islamic Psychology. While I still identify more as a clinician than a scholar, I feel compelled to develop this research further and to continue making contributions towards a more robust academic field of Islamic psychology.

Index